A Pictorial Guide to
THE MOUNTAINS OF SNOWDONIA

2. The Western Peaks

A Pictorial Guide to

THE MOUNTAINS OF SNOWDONIA

2. The Western Peaks

Yr Wyddfa

JOHN GILLHAM

F

FRANCES LINCOLN LIMITED

PUBLISHERS

For Albert and Betty

The author intends to keep this book as up-to-date as possible,
and will offer information updates on his website:
www.johngillham.com

Frances Lincoln Limited
4 Torriano Mews
Torriano Avenue
London NW5 2RZ

*A Pictorial Guide to the Mountains of Snowdonia
Volume 2. The Western Peaks*
Copyright © 2010 Frances Lincoln Limited

Text, photographs and 3D sketch maps
copyright © 2010 John Gillham
Edited by Roly Smith
Designed by Jane Havell Associates
First Frances Lincoln edition 2010

John Gillham has asserted his moral right to be
identified as Author of this Work in accordance
with the Copyright, Designs and Patents Act 1988

Mapping data licensed from Ordnance Survey®
with permission of HMSO.
© Crown copyright 2009. All rights reserved.
Ordnance Survey Licence number 100043293

British Library cataloguing-in-publication data
A catalogue record for this book is available from
the British Library
ISBN 978-0-7112-3062-0
Printed and bound in China
9 8 7 6 5 4 3 2 1

*Frontispiece: Snowdon from Llynnau Mymbyr
Title page map: Yr Wyddfa*

Contents

CONTENTS

CONTENTS

CONTENTS

CONTENTS

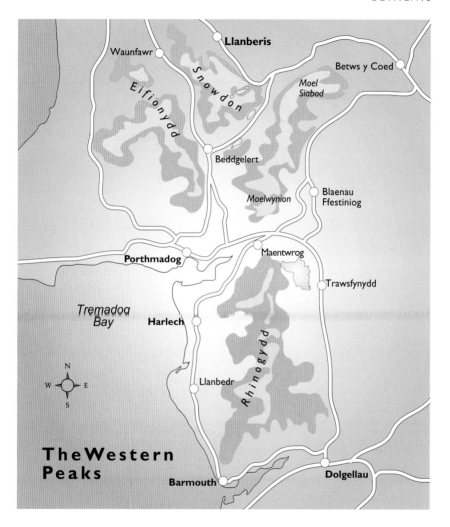

Who when he thinks of Snowdon does not associate it with the heroes of romance, Arthur and his knights? Whose fictitious adventures, the splendid dreams of Welsh and Breton minstrels, many of the scenes of which are the valleys and passes of Snowdon, are the origin of romance, before which what is classic has for more than half a century been waning, and is perhaps eventually destined to disappear. Yes, to romance Snowdon is indebted for its interest and consequently for its celebrity; but for romance Snowdon would assuredly not be what it at present is, one of the very celebrated hills of the world, and to the poets of modern Europe almost what Parnassus was to those of old.
GEORGE BORROW, WILD WALES (1862)

The boy of eight stood on Snowdon's summit, filled with wonder as he spied a hundred peaks fading into the misty horizons of Central Wales. He didn't know the mountains' names; he didn't know the places whose rooftops were tucked into the valleys below, but he was spellbound as he looked into this cavernous cliff-shaded hollow and its glimmering blue lakes.

Earlier he had seen the little steam trains with their 'plums and custard' carriages puff and chug up the mountain; he'd had home-made lemonade given to him by the nice lady at the Halfway House, and he'd stared down some precipice to a tiny village his dad had called Nant Peris. This was a good day.

'John. Do you want a drink?'

'I'll have a Coca Cola, Dad,' I said as I left my perch on the top of the world for a lunchtime seat in the summit café.

By evening this little boy, his eyes half-closed in sleep with the efforts of the day, vowed to climb every mountain in Britain. 'Is Snowdon the highest, Dad?'

Since then, year after year I've come back to Wales: at first with my parents, then with friends and family. Strangely, however, it was nearly twenty years before I set

Opposite: On the summit of Gallt y Wenallt, looking to Moel Siabod bathed in sunlight.

foot on another high mountain summit. My nephew Roy Clayton had started fell-walking on school trips and persuaded me to go with him. Since then I've come to think of the mountains of Snowdonia as my friends, and have climbed almost all of them, some many times.

This is the second book of four and covers Western Snowdonia – Snowdon, the Eifionydd and the Rhinogydd ranges.

Snowdon is a little messed about by its fancy new Hafod Eryri summit café of glass and steel, and by the excavations of quarries and old copper mines, but it has perfect mountain form, with textbook glacial corries and knife-edged arêtes. The summit massif, Yr Wyddfa, appears from Cwm Dyli as a pristine pyramid, craggy and proud. Snowdon has big paths, which are often overcrowded, but when you turn your back on the café and look across the horizon of a hundred hills you'll know why you came.

Below: Descending the rocky Rhinogydd slopes of Moel Ysgafarnogod near Llyn Du.

Above: Moel Eilio and the Snowdon train.

As I ran out of the big Eryri peaks to climb I shifted my attention further afield. Helped by the works of W. A. Poucher, I discovered the Rhinogydd, a group of rugged mountains stretching from the Ffestiniog Valley to Barmouth. They were unlike anything I had walked before: gnarled, unkempt, heather-clad, almost pathless by comparison to Snowdon, and traversed by old drovers' trails through craggy canyons. The Rhinogydd quickly became a favoured tramping ground for both backpacking and day walks. I loved the fact that walkers could pioneer their own routes, wander almost at will and stumble upon some half-hidden secret tarn or crag to clamber upon.

The Eifionydd waited for me for many more years. I had heard stories of a local farmer who used to fire a shotgun over walkers' heads if they strayed off the low-level rights of way. Access agreements eased the situation and many walkers climbed to the Nantlle and Moel Hebog ridges. The CROW Act improved things further and there are now many possibilities, although the situation could have been better in the

Nantlle Valley, where rights of way across farming pastures never seem to reach the mountains. The mountains of the Eifionydd are as shapely as any in Snowdonia, something George Borrow acknowledged when he referred to Carn Drws-y-coed (which we know as Y Garn) as a 'beautiful hill' and a 'couchant elephant'.

The Nantlle Valley has been disfigured by quarrying but it still manages a certain grandeur, with its twin lakes made famous by the painter Richard Wilson and the dusky corries forming the north faces of the mountains. For a truly beautiful valley, Cwm Pennant, which furrows into the mountains from the south, is unbeatable. No major highway makes inroads to Cwm Pennant, a place that brings back memories of the 1950s, when country lanes were narrow, peaceful and bound by hedgerows.

So there you have it. The most popular mountain range in Wales combined with the two that will never cease to surprise and delight you. All three are so wonderfully different: made out of different rock, in different ions of pre-history.

Volume One of the series covers Northern Snowdonia. Here, the 3000ft Carneddau whaleback ridges vie for attention with those of the Glyderau, Wales's most rocky peaks, and Moel Siabod and the Nantgwynant Mountains, perhaps the least walked but the prettiest peaks in Snowdonia.

Volume Three will cover Eastern Snowdonia. The Migneint is wilderness, more than any other area of the National Park – it's for lovers of solitude and wet feet. Only slightly less remote are the larger and rockier Arenig Mountains. The Moelwynion and Ffestiniog peaks have been ravaged but not tamed by the quarrymen and the miners. The sense of history is heightened as you pass long-abandoned barracks and the remains of old tramway bogies and pulleys. Finally, there are the long ridges and glacial rocky cwms of the Berwyns. Most of the peaks of the range are outside the National Park but they're too near, too big and too beautiful to be ignored.

Volume Four includes Cadair Idris, the Dyfi Hills, the Aran range and the Tarren Hills – here you will be able to walk some of the longest ridges in Wales.

In the books I will try to cover all the hills and mountains that are of interest to the walker. Some will be famous; others will not.

Let's hope that Snowdonia and its mountains bring to you, the reader, as much joy as they have done to me.

I've divided the book up into three sections, one for each mountain range. For each mountain I've given various routes to the top, followed by ridge routes to the next peak. This allows readers to devise their own combinations of routes. The routes are numbered within each section, and the corresponding numbers are marked in yellow circles on the location maps at the beginning of each section. At the end of the section for each mountain range I've added a couple of big day-walks – usually, but not always, circular routes. These will take in the best of the mountains and also add some low-level link routes. If there's anything special to watch out for, I've added notes on route-finding in descent.

The panoramic drawings are not to scale and are no substitute for the recommended use of OS Explorer or Harvey maps. In the interests of clarity, I've often raised or lowered a ridge and pulled 'out of sight' detail to the right or left a tad. Artistic licence is my advantage over modern digital imaging: I can see around a bend.

All the routes are safe for experienced walkers in clement conditions, but in wintry conditions even some of the most innocuous routes become dangerous and may be impassable. If these conditions are possible, take an ice axe and crampons, but first make sure you know how to use them. Be ready to turn around where necessary. A few routes, such as Crib Goch and the Snowdon Horseshoe, are Grade 1 scrambles and shouldn't be attempted by the inexperienced or by those without a good head for heights or sense of balance. Anything above Grade 1 I've left for more specialist books.

Remember, too, even the mountains change. A storm could have brought down a path across loose mountain scree or friable terrain; a bridge could have been washed away by those storms, or operations of some sort or another could have necessitated a diversion or closure of a path. River crossings can become difficult or even impossible after periods of snow or heavy rainfall and conifer plantations are forever changing. Trees reach maturity and whole blocks are felled leaving behind hard-to-follow or diverted footpaths. Always be prepared to adjust your itinerary.

Overleaf: Looking across the slopes of Moel Cynghorion to Carnedd Ugain and Yr Wyddfa, with the cliffs of Clogwyn Du'r Arddu prominent in the mid-distance.

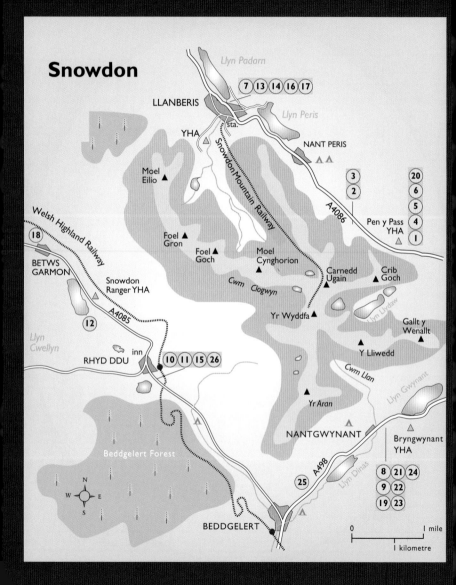

The mountainous land of Wales reaches its summit on Snowdon, known in Welsh as Creigiau Eryri, the crags of the eagles. Although the name Snowdon is English, it has been in use for many centuries. Llewelyn the Great used to call himself Dominius Snaudoniae, Lord of Snowdon, while the Norman king, William Rufus, is reported to have brought an army to Snowdon in 1095. One suggestion is that the name refers to the fact that the peak had snow on it for much of the year and was used as a landmark by sailors on the Irish Sea.

THE PEAKS

Main Tops	height	
Yr Wyddfa	3560ft	1085m
Carnedd Ugain	3493ft	1065m
Crib Goch	3027ft	923m
Y Lliwedd (West Peak)	2946ft	898m
Yr Aran	2450ft	747m
Moel Eilio	2381ft	726m
Moel Cynghorion	2210ft	674m
Gallt y Wenallt	2030ft	619m
Foel Goch	1984ft	605m

The name Snowdon refers to the range and not the highest peak in that range, which is Yr Wyddfa, the tomb. Yr Wyddfa (3560ft/1085m) and Carnedd Ugain (3493ft/1065m), linked by a half-mile ridge, together form the nucleus of a complex of ridges, which in plan resemble the fluid outlines of a swimming starfish.

Two of the ridges encircle Cwm Dyli, a cavernous hanging valley with two levels. In the upper regions of the cwm, Glaslyn, a curiously green, circular lake, is tightly enclosed by Yr Wyddfa's dark summit crags and Y Gribin, a solid-rock spur which is ideal for scrambling. The lower cwm and its elongated lake, Llyn Llydaw, form the larger part in a scene, enlivened by the 1000ft/300m cliffs of Y Lliwedd and the knife-edged and pinnacled arête of Crib Goch.

The view from the summit shows the difference between the north and south faces of the range. Y Lliwedd's north face is hung with cliffs and gullies, but in contrast the south faces of Carnedd Ugain and Crib Goch are pallid and barren, consisting of dusty pink screes and broken rock.

These peaks and the ridges are the basis of the range's finest expedition, the Snowdon Horseshoe. This 8-mile/13km walk, with Grade 1 scrambling thrown in, takes around six or seven hours in good conditions.

Snowdon is at its most rugged as its flanks coincide with the top of the Llanberis Pass. Here, huge glaciers, which were slow to melt on the shady side of the mountain, scoured out the gorge, leaving a devastation of boulders and severe precipices which must have struck fear into the early traveller. Cwm Glas, beneath the Crib Goch and Crib y Ddysgl ridges and high above the pass, is a brooding and inhospitable hollow dominated by the great climbers' crag of Dinas Mot, a scattering of huge erratic boulders, and the broken cliffs of Gyrn Las. Several spouting waterfalls tumble down narrow gullies, their white waters exaggerating the darkness of the rock. Still higher up the cwm, the green-black waters of Llyn Glas cower beneath the domed temple of Clogwyn y Person.

Below: Yr Wyddfa's summit massif from Cwm Dyli.

Above: In the sullen corrie of Cwm Glas.

The sombre but spectacular scene has for many years inspired serious walkers, scramblers and climbers keen to dodge the masses and make their own ways to the summit. Patrick Monkhouse wrote in his 1934 book, *On Foot in North Wales*: 'Cwm Glas is high enough to cut you off from your fellow man but not so high that you can feel you've bettered your mountain. Until you have been there you have not been to the heart of Snowdon.'

Seen from the west, Snowdon doesn't have the same presence, displaying shaley slopes running down to the pastoral Gwyrfai Valley, but all isn't as it seems. Two of the seemingly sketchy ridges, Llechog and Clogwyn Du'r Arddu, face inwards, hiding spectacular cliffs which overlook wild stony cwms with a scattering of small lakes. Clogwyn Du'r Arddu (the black cliff) is particularly severe.

In a 1920s Climbers' Club guide, Herbert Carr wrote: 'No breach seems either possible or desirable along the whole extent of the West Buttress, though there is the faintest of faint hopes for a human fly rather on its left side.' In 1928, Jack Longland's party conquered the face. The fact that one of the party, A. S. Piggott, drove in a piton to achieve the feat aroused the wrath of the Alpine Club, whose president declared: 'The hand that could drive a piton into English rock could shoot a fox.'

Looking across the valley of the Arddu, the Moel Eilio–Moel Cynghorion mountains are amiable grassy ridges, rounded in profile with crags and screes ringing their cwms. In a way these mountains are more intimate with Llanberis than Yr Wyddfa, and appear in almost every postcard view across Llyn Padarn. Eilio's north-east ridge declines right down to the churchyard. The complete traverse along these ridges, over Snowdon and down to either Beddgelert or Pen y Pass, is one of the classic routes and is recommended to strong walkers.

Although legends have it that King Arthur, his knights and the giant, Rhudda Gawr, all spent time on Yr Wyddfa, the first recorded summiteer was botanist Thomas Johnson in 1639. There were also those hardy souls who had to make their way on to the mountains on a regular basis – for work.

Snowdon was rich in copper and slate. The relics and spoil heaps of the slate quarries are dotted all over the mountain – in Cwm Llan, above Rhyd Ddu and at Nant Peris. The Brittania Copper Mines were founded in the 18th century. Originally, the ore had to be hauled up the mountainside to Bwlch Glas, then taken down the other side on horse-drawn sledges to Rhyd Ddu, where it was transported by horse and cart to Caernarfon. However, the building of the Miners' Track and the causeway across Llyn Llydaw in 1853 made it possible for the ore carts to be taken the shorter distance to Pen y Pass. Many of the miners lived in Bethesda and had to take the Miners' Track over the shoulders of Tryfan and Glyder Fach before starting work. The copper mines closed in 1926.

Snowdon's popularity increased in the early 19th century with the building of good roads. Around 1850, when George Borrow came here, he observed that people were going up or descending the mountain as far as the eye could see. By 1847 the stone-built summit café of 1820 had been replaced by the larger Roberts Hotel and Owens Bazaar. The railways of the Victorian era brought further tourists to Wales, and the attention of their engineers was naturally drawn to the principality's highest peak, Snowdon, and Llanberis, the village at its foot. After the engineering of a 5-mile/8km route on the mountainside above the Arddu Valley, the Snowdon Mountain

Railway opened on Easter Monday, 1896. Triumph turned to tragedy on that first day when an out-of-control descending train derailed itself, before hurtling down the mountainside. One passenger, Ellis Roberts, who had jumped from a falling carriage, was fatally injured. Thankfully, since that day the 2ft 7in-gauge rack-and-pinion steam engines with their red-and-cream carriages have chugged and whistled their way up the mountain without serious incident.

The latest chapter in Snowdon's history is the demolition of the old summit 'hotel' and the building of a new one. Finally completed in 2009, the new building, Hafod Eryri, features non-reflective panoramic windows and sympathetic stone walls, and should appeal to more visitors. But I feel this was a lost opportunity to free the summit and build a new 'Alpine style' hotel with dormitory accommodation and a new top railway station further down the mountain – say, by the current Clogwyn station.

Below: Snowdon from the west.

CRIB GOCH

Although it is the second lowest 3000ft peak and is dwarfed by nearby Yr Wyddfa, Crib Goch, the red ridge, is still a mountaineers' mountain. There are no easy routes here, all include exposed situations and some scrambling and all require a head for heights and a good sense of balance.

The mountain has three ridges: the short but steep East Ridge, with its blunt nose of crag dipping down to Bwlch y Moch (pass of the pig); the knife-edged, scree-covered North Ridge and, last but definitely not least, the pinnacled arête, which leads scramblers across another knife-edge to the sanctuary of Bwlch Coch's wide grass saddle. Seen in retrospect, those pinnacles rise to the sky like great spires, temples to treat with reverence and respect.

Seen from Cwm Dyli, the mountain is unremarkable. Its slopes are of loose rock and scree with no nooks or crannies to create light, shadow and form or give an impression of scale. It's all so different from the Llanberis Pass. From the top, the pointed summit, the red hues of the rock and the gently angled North Ridge give the mountain real presence. Crib Goch's real magic lies a little further

Opposite: Crib Goch seen from across the Pass of Llanberis.

west down the pass above Blaen-y-nant. Here a little path climbs into Cwm Glas (the blue-green corrie), past the great climbers' crag of Dinas Mot and the dripping Craig Rhaeadr (waterfall crag). The dark cliffs of Gyrn Las seem to block the way to the ridge, but several waterfalls pouring down breaks in the rock-faces to the left offer hope of further progress into Cwm Uchaf, an inhospitable but romantically wild hollow, where Llyn Glas rests beneath the cliffs of Clogwyn y Person. The terrain is of squat terraced crags, hardy mosses and heather, all overlooked by Crib Goch's great pinnacled arête and the reddish screes of the North Ridge. The mountain beckons …

Route S1
Pen y Pass

A rugged scramble from the pass to the summit

Start: Pen y Pass car park (toll)
 (GR: SH 648557)
Distance: 1½ miles/2.5km
Height gain: 1870ft/570m
Time: 1–1½ hours

For the first part, this route follows the Pig Track to Snowdon, which begins from the top (Llanberis) end of the car park. A wide, engineered track weaves through bluffs and boulders high above and parallel to the Llanberis Pass. In these early stages, your attention will be drawn to the fierce crags and screes of Esgair Felen, but soon the conical-shaped Crib Goch and the reddish rocks of its North Ridge tower above the rugged valley below.

The Pig Track comes to Bwlch Moch where you look down on Cwm Dyli, and the expansive blue-green waters of Llyn Llydaw, flanked by the near 1000ft cliffs of Y Lliwedd. As the track descends towards the cwm, the path up to Crib Goch climbs right on a bold course up the broad East Ridge. The bootmarks of generations of walkers make routefinding easy. In the middle section, the path comes head to head with a steep crag. Although intimidating at first glance, the rock is good with plenty of handholds. Beyond this the path scrambles on a straightforward if slightly exposed route across broken reddish rock to the summit.

Above: Clambering up the steep, broken rock high on Crib Goch's East Ridge.
Right: The path from Bwlch Moch suddenly comes to the steep crag, which fortunately has plenty of hand-holds.

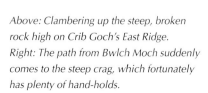

Route S2
Blaen-y-nant and Llyn Glas

*A rugged route all the way from the pass
   to the summit*

Start: Blaen-y-nant (toll) (GR: SH 622571)
Distance: 1½ miles/2.5km
Height gain: 2460ft/750m
Time: 1½ hours

---

*Note: This route is unsuitable for novices or
in bad weather*

The path begins at Blaen y Nant, where there
is a small charge for parking in a field just
beyond the roadside bridge. Follow the
streamside path over a stile and turn right to
cross the footbridge over the stream. Continue the climb alongside the west bank of
the stream. The faint path becomes clearer
and stony as it zigzags up steep grassy slopes.

It levels out as it enters Cwm Glas Mawr,
with scattered erratic boulders dotted about
its grassy basin. The path crosses to the east
bank by a particularly large rock outcrop.
Although there's a path ahead aiming
upstream towards the waterfall tumbling
down the Gyrn Las crags, ignore it and aim
half-left in the direction of Crib Goch's Pinnacles and another waterfall which tumbles
down to the right of a huge dark crag, appro-
priately known as Craig Rhaeadr – the waterfall crag.

After crossing another stream by a huge
rounded boulder, a path develops up stony
ground to the right of the waterfall and
beneath unnamed crags further to the right.
Where the last-mentioned crag ends, climb
right to reach the shores of Llyn Glas. If you
miss this, you'll find yourself scrambling up
the series of squat rock terraces used in Route
S3 and you'll suddenly see Llyn Glas in a
rocky hollow way below.

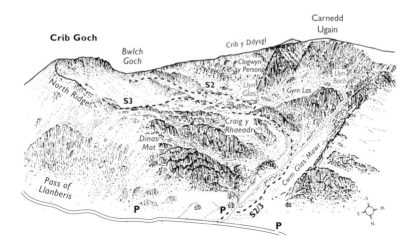

From Llyn Glas, follow the lake's eastern shoreline before climbing along the hollow of its feeder stream before taking an extremely steep scree path to the grassy col of Bwlch Goch.

Turn left here, heading for the great pinnacles of Crib Goch. These are usually bypassed on the right (Cwm Dyli) side before joining the crest. If the coast is clear, scramble either on the crest or on the Cwm Dyli side where a polished rock course allows the use of a steady hand on the rocks to the left.

Route S3

Blaen-y-nant and the North Ridge

A rough route with some nice little scrambles and an exhilarating knife-edged ridge to finish

Start: Blaen-y-nant (toll) (GR: SH 622571

Distance: 2 miles/3km

Height gain: 2460ft/750m

Time: 1½ hours

Note: As with Route S2, this route is unsuitable for novices or in foul weather

Below: In Cwm Glas Mawr, with Gyrn Las ahead and Crib Goch on the skyline.

As in Route S2 from Blaen-y-nant, follow the streamside path, go over a stile and footbridge to the right before continuing along the west bank of the stream, crossing it on the level section among gigantic boulders. Follow the same line as Route S2 to the left of Craig Rhaeadr and the falls, but where that route turns left, this one maintains direction with occasional scrambles up rock terraces. On reaching a craggy shelf, Crib Goch's North Ridge is paraded before you, as is the red scree path on the left which climbs to the ridge. Continue across trackless rocky ground to the bottom of the path. After slogging up those screes, climb the narrow North Ridge taking care on the upper section – the rock isn't quite as stable here.

Other route options

It is possible to access the North Ridge by crossing the Afon Cwm Glas Mawr at GR 620566 and heading south to scramble up crags by the falls at GR 622562. Further climbing brings you to a heathery hollow above the crags of Dinas Mot, where a scree path climbs to the North Ridge.

Below: View from Crib Goch's north summit across the serrated arête to the Pinnacles and Carnedd Ugain. Yr Wyddfa lies to the left, above Llyn Llydaw.

RIDGE ROUTES

Carnedd Ugain

Distance: ⅔ mile/1km
Height gain: 720ft/220m
Time: ½ hour

Note: This is a Grade 1 scramble with big drops either side of the knife-edged crest

Those with good balance stride over the crest; others take the path on the left using the crest for handholds. The path rounds the pinnacles on the Cwm Dyli side before descending scree to the grassy saddle of Bwlch Coch. Another scramble follows along the Crib y Ddysgl ridge. There is still some easy scrambling along narrow splintery rock sections of this arête. Stay close to the crest rather than wandering off to the left. The ridge broadens as it approaches the summit of Carnedd Ugain and the difficulties are over.

Below: Climbing in Cwm Glass Mawr with Craig Rhaeadr on the left.

CARNEDD UGAIN

Carnedd Ugain, the cairn of twenty, may be the second highest peak in Wales, but it's not even in the top ten for numbers of visitors, even though it's on the famous Snowdon Horseshoe. It's just too close to Yr Wyddfa for its own good. The cog railway and many of the walkers' routes to the top of Snowdon pass within minutes of the summit, but they all turn away at the last moment.

Seen from Cwm Dyli you can understand this, for the featureless loose scree slopes look uninviting. However, there's so much more to Carnedd Ugain than meets the eye.

The followers of the Welsh Three Thou sands route will know that Crib y Ddysgl (the ridge of the dish), is an exciting arête with its own knife-edged sections. Forming Carnedd Ugain's east ridge, it's not quite as spectacular as Crib Goch's pinnacled arête, but offers some nice scrambling none the less.

Seen from Llanberis and its pass, the mountain really shows its pedigree. From the Llanberis Pass, Yr Wyddfa is all but hidden and, contrary to popular belief, the spectacular cliffs of 'Cloggy' belong to Ugain, and the fine craggy ridge above Nant Peris is Ugain's west ridge. From Cwm Glas above the Llan-

Left: Crib Goch and the Pass of Llanberis from the Llanberis Ridge.

beris Pass, this noble mountain looks even more spectacular than Crib Goch. It's fronted by the bold dark crags of Clogwyn y Person and Gyrn Las, and throws out one tremendous ridge down to Clogwyn Mawr at the valley bottom. Known well to climbers and bold scramblers, this side of the mountain offers some very stiff challenges.

Route S4
Llanberis

A tough climb on to the first peak, Tryfan,
followed by a fine ridge with great views

Start: Pen y Pass car park (toll)
  (GR: SH 648557)
Distance: 4 miles/6.5.km
Height gain: 3350ft/1020m
Time: 3 hours

From the lakeside car park in Llanberis turn left along the main road. Opposite the Royal Victoria Hotel (until recently known as the Quality Hotel Snowdonia), turn right along a tarred lane, Victoria Terrace, climbing into the cwm of the Afon Arddu. Leave the lane for a signed path on the left. As the path draws level to Hebron station leave it and climb

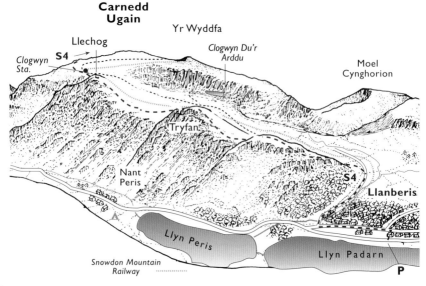

eastward on a trackless course over grass to the Llanberis ridge, keeping a spur of rocks well to the left. You should reach the ridge a short way south of the top of Derlwyn. An extremely steep climb follows to the first of three craggy knolls known collectively as Tryfan, not to be confused with the famous Glyderau peak of the same name.

There are splendid views down to Nant Peris from here, as there will be for much of the time on this route. The devastation rendered to Elidir Fawr by the slate quarries and the Llyn Padarn Electric Mountain scheme can be seen in all of its gory horror.

A ridge fence guides the route over the other two knolls of Tryfan before confronting Llechog, one of many peaks with that name – confusing, isn't it? Llechog is the pride of the ridge, its craggy diadem being the culmination of a great rocky rib descending all the way down to the valley below. A boulder scramble on the other side leads down to the Snowdon Railway, which squeezes the route close to the edge. When wintry conditions prevail, cross the railway with extreme care and follow grassy slopes on the other side, but do not use the railway's trackbed in any circumstances.

After passing Clogwyn station, the route is joined by the wide Llanberis path, but leave this after a couple of hundred yards for a trackless course up Carnedd Ugain's grassy north ridge, where there are spectacular views across the shady Cwm Glas to Crib Goch. It's a wonderful finale to the summit trig point on Carnedd Ugain.

Below: A crocodile-like rock on the Llanberis Ridge, with Moel Cynghorion behind.

Other route options

The route over Crib Goch is the obvious one – it's half the Horseshoe route. There are various routes from the Llanberis Pass, but most involve a good deal of scrambling above Grade 1 and a head for heights. There's a route up Cwm Glas Bach and Cwm Hetiau, but there is currently a dispute over access to the footbridge by the road.

Below: Carnedd Ugain across Gwastadnant from Dinas.

RIDGE ROUTES

Crib Goch

Distance: ⅔ mile/1km
Height gain: 260ft/80m
Time: ¾ hour

Note: this is a Grade 1 scramble and not recommended in inclement or wintry conditions

The grass ridge narrows on to a rocky arête that leads down to the grassy col of Bwlch Coch. A scree gully leads up to the Crib Goch Pinnacles, which are generally traversed on the Cwm Dyli side – but don't go too far down to the right. Beyond the pinnacles either stay on the crest – for those with good balance – or take the little track on the Cwm Dyli side, using the crest for hand-holds.

Yr Wyddfa

Distance: ⅔ mile/1km
Height gain: 295ft/90m
Time: ½ hour

Descend the easy grass slopes and turn left on the Llanberis Path, which takes the route to the obelisk at Bwlch Glas. An engineered path climbs between the railway and the rim of Cwm Dyli to Yr Wyddfa's summit rock-pile.

Opposite: Yr Wyddfa (right) and Y Lliwedd (left) across Llyn Llydaw.

At 3560ft/1085m Yr Wyddfa, whose name means the tomb, is not only Snowdon's highest summit, it's the highest south of Scotland's Highland Line. Legend has it that this is the burial place of Rhudda Gawr, a giant said to have had a penchant for cutting off the beards of passers-by. One day Rhudda tried to cut off King Arthur's beard. In revenge Arthur drew his sword and with one blow cut off the giant's head. Another legend has it that Arthur himself was killed in his final battle against his nephew Mordred on Bwlch y Saethau, the pass of the arrows.

Yr Wyddfa commands four cwms: Tregalan, Clogwyn, Caregog and Dyli, which are divided by four fine ridges. All the cwms have lakes and a unique presence. Tregalan is deep and rugged, with the stony sides of Y Lliwedd contrasting with the dark cliffs of Clogwyn Du on the South Ridge. Clogwyn is wild and stony with Snowdon's scree-scarred west face crowding a semi-circular hollow where three small tarns vie for space. Caregog is barren and little frequented since being abandoned by the quarrymen.

The pride of Yr Wyddfa, however, is Cwm Dyli, a vast hollow flanked by mountains, cliffs and scree slopes. The top lake, Glaslyn, is tightly cupped by Carnedd Ugain's lower slopes and Y Gribin, a delightful stairway of

rock rising to Bwlch y Saethau. Glaslyn is dwarfed by the blue waters of Llyn Llydaw, which was enlarged to form a reservoir to supply a head of water to the little Nant-gwynant Hydro-electric Power Station.

The complexity of cwm and ridge allows many routes to the top and, although some are over-used, there's always a devious route to a quiet corner for those who want to time their ascent.

Snowdon's popular summit (an estimated 355,000 people reach it every year) was once famously described by the Prince of Wales as 'the highest slum in Europe'. And there's no doubt that the run-down café just below the summit, built as Robert's Hotel in 1850, had certainly seen better days. The National Park Authority, the Welsh Assembly, the Wales Tourist Board and the Snowdon Mountain Railway pooled resources for the building of a new £8-million café and visitor centre. The futuristic glass-and-granite-walled building, named Hafod Eryri – the summer residence of Eryri – was completed in 2009.

Route S5
The Miners' Track

An easy route with a sting in the tail
Start: Pen y Pass (GR: SH 648557)
Distance: 3½ miles/6km
Height gain: 2500ft/760m
Time: 2½ hours

The Miners' Track begins from the south-east side of the lower car park. A wide, surfaced track eases around the head of the Afon Trawsnant's grassy cwm before circling right to emerge high above Llyn Teyrn, the monarch's lake, where you get a sneak pre-view of Y Lliwedd and the pipeline that conveys a head of water down to the small hydro-electric station in Nantgwynant.

After passing the remains of copper mines, the path comes close to the huge pipeline before turning right by the pumphouse to reach the south shore of Llyn Llydaw. This enlarged lake occupies almost the whole of Cwm Dyli. The views from here are magnificent, with 1000ft cliffs, usually in shadow, rising almost vertically to the twin summits of Y Lliwedd, with Yr Wyddfa's summit massif appearing as a dark pyramid of rock.

A raised causeway takes the Miners' Track across to the far shores. Very occasionally this is submerged by high water levels, necessitating a shoreline detour to the right to regain the track. After closely following Llydaw's north shore past the barracks of the Britannia Copper Mines, the track starts its climb by the lively Afon Glaslyn to reach the lake of the same name. The deep waters of the blue-green lake are tightly enclosed by Yr Wyddfa's summit cliffs, the rocky arm of Y Gribin, a splendid spur rising to Bwlch y Saethau and the more broken crags and screes of Carnedd Ugain.

Now the path makes its way up the loose scree slopes of Carnedd Ugain to join the Pig Track. After traversing more loose screes, the path, now heavily engineered to avoid being washed away (as it regularly used to be) by storms, zigzags to Bwlch Glas, the col between Carnedd Ugain and Yr Wyddfa. The spot on the col is marked by a huge monolith. Now a wide path climbs left above the Snowdon Railway to reach the summit hotel. The pile of boulders that marks the very top lies to the left of the hotel and railway station.

Yr Wyddfa
Carnedd Ugain
Crib Goch
Glaslyn
S6
Llyn Llydaw
S6
cafe
P
S5
YH
Llyn Teyrn
Pen y Pass

Route S6
The Pig Track

A classic mountain path

Start: Pen y Pass (GR: SH 648557)
Distance: 3 miles/5km
Height gain: 2400ft/740m
Time: 2½ hours

The Pig Track begins from the top (western) end of the car park. A wide, flagged path emblazons its way through bluffs and boulders high above the Llanberis Pass. The scene is dominated by the cone of Crib Goch directly ahead, and the fierce and rugged face of Esgair Felen on the far side of the pass.

The path veers left to climb to the col of Bwlch Moch. Here it rounds the foot of Crib Goch and descends slightly into Cwm Dyli where Llyn Llydaw comes into view beneath the shadowy cliffs of Y Lliwedd. The path traverses the shaley lower slopes of Carnedd Ugain, to pass high above Glaslyn where it is joined by the Miners' Track. Now it climbs an area of loose rock and scree before climbing the engineered zigzags to the skyline at the Bwlch Glas obelisk. From here a good path threads between the edge and the Snowdon Railway to reach the summit.

Overleaf: The Y Wyddfa massif from the Miners' Track.

Route S7
The Llanberis Path

A long steady walk – easy in summer
Start: Llanberis lakeside car park
  (GR: SH 578605)
Distance: 5 miles/8km
Height gain: 3200ft/980m
Time: 3 hours

From the lakeside car park in Llanberis turn left along the main road. Opposite the Royal Victoria Hotel, turn right along a tarred lane, Victoria Terrace, climbing into the cwm of the Afon Arddu. Leave the lane for a signed path on the left. The wide track climbs gently up the hillside to cross the railway just short of Halfway station. The yawning grassy valley of the Arddu leads the eye to a long, slightly curved line of cliffs known as Clogwyn Coch and Clogwyn Du'r Arddu.

After passing Halfway House where, after a long gap, they once again serve refreshments,

the path climbs towards Clogwyn station. Llyn Du'r Arddu comes into view and you'll probably see climbers on the cliffs above it.

The track passes under a railway bridge to reach the edge of cliffs high above Nant Peris. The views down into the Llanberis Pass are stunning and really do exaggerate the impression of height. The craggy hollow you'll be looking down is Cwm Hetiau, the pass of hats, apparently so-called because so many Victorian tourists had their hats blown off here.

The track swings right by the railway at first, then way above it, to traverse Carnedd Ugain's stony sides. Just before the monolith at Bwlch Glas it is joined by the Snowdon Ranger route, then at the monolith by the Miners' and Pig tracks. The new views down Cwm Dyli, its lakes and the horseshoe ridges are captivating and will be all the way to Yr Wyddfa's summit, because the wide path follows the very edge.

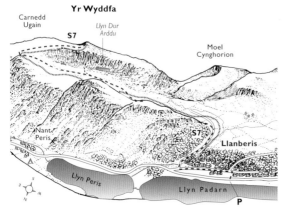

Opposite: Climbing on the Llanberis Path with the cliffs of Clogwyn Du'r Arddu ahead and the summit of Carnedd Ugain on the left.

Route S8
The Watkin Path

A pleasant if unspectacular route
Start: Nantgwynant (GR: SH 628506)
Distance: 4 miles/6.4km
Height gain: 3400ft/1045m
Time: 3½ hours

---

*Note: The final section from Bwlch y
Saethau is serious in wintry conditions,
when crampons, ice axes and good winter
experience are needed*

The path was named after Sir Edward Watkin,
a wealthy Victorian railway industrialist and
Liberal MP, who originally built it as a donkey
track and gifted it to the nation when he
retired. It was opened by Prime Minister
William Ewart Gladstone in 1892, a fact
commemorated by the plaque fixed on to
what is known as the Gladstone Rock.

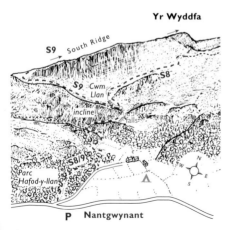

From the car park at Nantgwynant, cross
the road and follow the narrow lane opposite. A delightful path through the woods of
Parc Hafod-y-llan begins a few paces along
the lane and to the left. It emerges on to a
stony track, which leads out of the woods to
pass to the left of some impressive waterfalls,
before cutting across an old quarry tramway
and climbing by the river into Cwm Llan.

The Watkin Path leaves the old quarry track
and crosses a river bridge to the ruins of Plas
Cwm y Llan, once the residence of the quarry
manager but later laid to ruin after being used
for target practice by World War II soldiers.

Beyond the Gladstone Rock, the path
swings left to round the precipices of Craig
Ddu and some old mine workings to enter
the wild stony hollow of Cwm Tregalan,
which is encircled by the crags of Yr Wyddfa's
South Ridge and the seemingly endless
boulder flanks of Y Lliwedd.

The path now swings right on the lower
slopes of Y Lliwedd and eventually zigzags
up to the ridge at Bwlch Ciliau, from where
you can look across the huge lake-filled
chasm of Cwm Dyli. Turn left along an almost
level path to Bwlch y Saethau. Beyond this
second pass the paths divide. The right fork
follows the edge and is looser, more exposed
and can be quite dangerous. The preferable
left fork rakes across loose rocky slopes to
join the South Ridge halfway between Bwlch
Main and the summit – the spot is marked
by a finger of rock, an invaluable marker if
you're doing the route in reverse. A short
climb to the right leads to the summit.

Route S9
Cwm Llan and the South Ridge

One of the best of Snowdon's ridges
Start: Nantgwynant (GR: SH 628506)
Distance: 4 miles/6.4km
Height gain: 3400ft/1045m
Time: 3½ hours

As in Route S8, follow the woodland path through Parc Hafod-y-llan and out on to the stony track, passing the waterfalls, into Cwm Llan. For this route do not cross the stream. Where the path levels out at GR 622520, climb left to an old quarry tramway. At GR 617521 a path leads left off this into a grassy hollow beneath Yr Aran's East Ridge before climbing to Bwlch Cwm Llan, the pass be-

tween Yr Aran and Yr Wyddfa's South Ridge. There's a small tarn and quarry across which you can see to Rhyd Ddu, Llyn Cwellyn and Mynydd Mawr, the mountain beyond.

The route now gets straight to grips with the South Ridge. In some places it uses little ledge paths and in others the natural slabs of the ridge. It's always an entertaining climb, with wonderful views over the cliffs of Clogwyn Du on the right side of the ridge towards Y Lliwedd, whose stony flanks rise from the far side of Cwm Tregalan. After going over a little peak known as the Saddle, the path is joined by the Rhyd Ddu Path. It flirts with both sides of the ridge before taking a bouldery final course up to the summit where it passes to the left of the hotel.

Below: Yr Wyddfa's South Ridge.

Route S10
Rhyd Ddu Path

A dull start, but a fine finish on Llechog and Bwlch Main

Start: Rhyd Ddu (GR: SH 571526)
Distance: 3¾ miles/6km
Height gain: 2950ft/910m
Time: 3 hours

A track from the north of the car park passes the Welsh Highland Line railway station and leads to the start of the Rhyd Ddu Path. Here you turn right to cross the railway (with care) and continue along an old quarry track that winds among rock outcrops. On one of these to the right are the remains of a 16th-century smallholding. Snowdon is always in view but its shaley flanks hide its inner western cwms until much later.

Leave the quarry track for a signed footpath which begins beyond a kissing gate on the left. This heads north-east towards the Llechog Ridge. The path climbs more steeply as it reaches the squat crags of the ridge's southern flank. Beyond an iron kissing gate in a tall wall, the path begins to get more entertaining as it nears the cliff edges. It takes a winding course up the ridge before following the edge, with further views down the cliffs to the three lakes of Cwm Clogwyn. A zigzagging course brings the path to the South Ridge at Bwlch Main, where a slightly undulating course leads to Yr Wyddfa's summit.

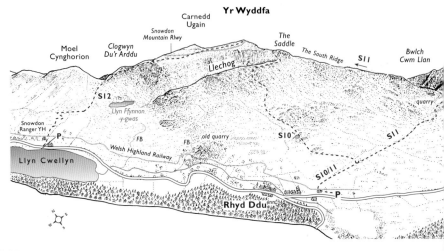

Route S11
Rhyd Ddu and the South Ridge

*After another dull start this relatively
easy route improves on reaching the
Llechog Ridge*

Start: Rhyd Ddu (GR: SH 571526)
Distance: 4 miles/6.4km
Height gain: 3050ft/930m
Time: 3½ hours

Start as in Route S10 by taking the track by
the railway station and turning right across
the railway on to the Rhyd Ddu Path. This
time stay with the quarry track as it heads
straight for the gap between Yr Wyddfa's
South Ridge and Yr Aran. The track passes tiny
pools and quarry tips before passing the main
quarry and its two reservoirs.

At Bwlch Cwm Llan, there's a sudden view
into Cwm Llan and across to Y Lliwedd.
Climb left here, following the South Ridge as
in Route S9 all the way over the Saddle and
onwards to Yr Wyddfa.

*Above: 16th-century ruins by Rhyd Ddu
Path.*
*Overleaf: The cliffs of Lechog from Bwlch
Main.*

Route S12
Snowdon Ranger Path

*Another dull start improves on the spur
above Clogwyn Du'r Arddu*

Start: Car park opposite Snowdon Ranger
Youth Hostel (GR: SH 565551)
Distance: 3½ miles/6km
Height gain: 3000ft/930m
Time: 2½ hours

The path starts from the left of the youth hostel and rakes across pastureland, past Llwyn
Onn before zigzagging up the steep flanks of
Foel Goch. There are lovely views across Llyn
Cwellyn to Mynydd Mawr and the Eifionydd
Mountains, and across an extensive marshy
hollow to the right are the cliffs of Llechog.
Beyond a ladder stile the path enters open
country and steers a course beneath grassy
hillsides on the left towards the pass of Bwlch
Cwm Brwynog. As the lake of Llyn Ffynnon-
y-gwas comes into view, the path swings right
to pass beneath the col and on to the stony
ridge of Clogwyn Du'r Arddu where the
zigzag course of an eroded stony path begins.

It is well worth straying from the path to
look at the climbing crags of 'Cloggy', as the
crag is universally known to climbers. By
now the three lakes of Cwm Clogwyn will
have come into view. It's an especially pleasant scene in soft evening light.

The path eventually crosses the Snowdon
Railway to join the Llanberis Path near
the Bwlch Glas monolith. Follow the edge
path around Cwm Dyli to the summit of Yr
Wyddfa.

Other route options

Any one of the routes up Crib Goch, Y Lli-wedd, Yr Aran or Carnedd Ugain could be continued to Snowdon. There's also the Snowdon Horseshoe (see Days Out on Snowdon) and by way of the Moel Eilio Ridge, either from Llanberis, Waunfawr or Betws Garmon.

The rocky ridge of Y Gribin above Glaslyn is a good way for competent scramblers to reach Bwlch y Saethau, high up on the Watkin Path. Although steep and exposed, the rock is good with plenty of hand-holds. Climbers have even more choice using the crags of Clogwyn Du'r Arddu or Gyrn Las.

RIDGE ROUTES

Carnedd Ugain

Distance: ⅔ miles/1km
Height gain: 280ft/85m
Time: 20 minutes

This very easy route descends by the edge path to the right of the railway, passing the monolith at Bwlch Glas. Where the Llanberis Path descends north away from the edge, leave it for the path arcing right up easy grass slopes to Carnedd Ugain's summit.

Below: Looking back down Yr Wyddfa's South Ridge.

Y Lliwedd (West Peak)
Distance: 1¼ miles/2km
Height gain: 525ft/160m
Time: 1 hour

Yr Aran
Distance: 2 miles/3km
Height gain: 720ft/220m
Time: 1 hour

From the summit hotel descend south-westwards towards Bwlch Main. Turn off left on the Watkin Path, a spot marked by a finger of rock. Take care on the loose, shaley surface as the path descends to Bwlch y Saethau. A fairly level stretch brings the route to Bwlch Ciliau where the bouldery climb to Y Lliwedd begins. By keeping to the edge you'll have to do some scrambling to get to the West Peak, but there's an obvious and easier path keeping to the right of the crest until the last steps.

From the summit hotel descend south-westwards to Bwlch Main. The path makes a slight climb to a subsidiary top known as the Saddle, before descending over the slabbed South Ridge to Bwlch Cwm Llan (GR 605 523). The path to Yr Aran follows the drystone wall ahead and turns sharp left halfway up to rake across the north face. This brings the route to the easier gradients of the East Ridge. Go over the ladder stile straddling an electric fence before climbing right to the summit.

Below: Llechog Ridge from the Snowdon Ranger Path.

Seen from across the great scoop of the Arddu Valley, Moel Cynghorion is an imposing mountain, rugged with rock faces and with an interesting knobbly spur dividing two cwms. The name translated means 'the hill of the counsellor or councillors', a meaning lost in time but conjuring up images of ancient Celtic lords deliberating on the fate of their nation from on high.

They would have had a marvellous view of their land and their people from the grassy summit, which ends abruptly with the cliffs and crags of Clogwyn Llechwedd Llo. Across Arddu is Snowdon, fronted by the great climbers' cliff of Clogwyn Du'r Arddu, which always seem to be in shadow. Over Snowdon's shoulder, Llyn Padarn and the village of Llanberis lead the eye out to the coast. In the opposite direction lie Rhyd Ddu and Llyn Cwellyn, with the shapely ridges of the Eifionydd stretching across the skyline.

Moel Cynghorion is usually tackled as part of a ridge walk, taking in Moel Eilio, Foel Goch, Foel Fron and Snowdon. The ridges are delightfully grassy but the walk has been described as a 'big dipper', with quite steep drops to the mountain passes, and climbs out of them. Cynghorion's ridges are probably the steepest, reinforcing the theory that it is very hard to see a councillor when you want one.

Route S13
Llanberis and Bwlch Maesgwm
A pleasant if unspectacular walk on good paths and tracks
Start: Lakeside car park near Electric Mountain Centre, Llanberis (GR: SH 578605)
Distance: 4½ miles/7km
Height gain: 1900ft/580m
Time: 2½–3 hours

A narrow lane across the main road opposite the car park leads past the public toilets to the High Street. Turn left here before turning right up Capel Coch Road. Go straight ahead at a junction, where the road changes its name to Stryd Ceunant, and climbs past the youth hostel on to rough-pastured hillsides.

Where the tarmac ends at the foot of Moel Eilio, turn left along the track heading into the expansive, wild valley of the Afon Arddu. On the grassy hillsides on the far side of the valley you'll see the trains of the Snowdon Mountain Railway, puffing up and down the line, their plumes of smoke billowing into the sky.

After skirting the base of Foel Goch's northern spur, Cefn Drum, the track swings right into the side valley of Maesgwm and climbs to the craggy head of the cwm to reach a narrow pass, Bwlch Maesgwm, between Foel Goch and Moel Cynghorion. Go through the

Opposite: Moel Cynghorion from the Llanberis path.

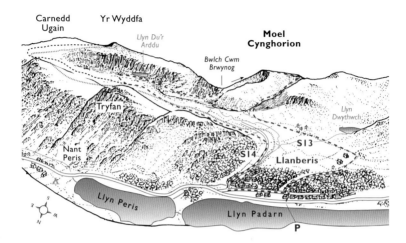

gate here before turning left on a steep climb up Moel Cynghorion's grassy west ridge – a fence guides the route all the way to the summit.

Below: Bwlch Cwm Brwynog.

Route S14
Llanberis and Llyn Du'r Arddu

A devious route taking in the spectacular climbers' cliffs of 'Cloggy'

Start: Lakeside car park near Electric Mountain Centre, Llanberis (GR: SH 578605)

Distance: 5 miles/8km

Height gain: 2360ft/720m

Time: 3 hours

From the lakeside car park in Llanberis turn left along the main road to pass the Snowdon Mountain Railway Station. Opposite the Royal Victoria Hotel, turn right along Victoria Terrace, climbing into the cwm of the Afon Arddu. Leave the lane for the signed Llanberis Path on the left. The wide track climbs gently up the hillside and crosses the railway track just short of Halfway station before continuing up the valley.

Leave the Llanberis Path as it steepens and veers left to climb the hillside towards Clogwyn station. The new path follows the course of an old tramway heading straight on towards the cliffs of Clogwyn Coch.

When the lake of Llyn Du'r Arddu comes into view below the cliffs, leave the tramway, which heads for the base of the cliffs, and go right over a low rock-crested grassy ridge overlooking the lake. Keep the bouldery sections to the left – that way you'll still get intimate views of the lake and the dark precipices of Clogwyn Du'r Arddu. Gazing at those cliffs it's not hard to understand why early climbers thought they were unclimbable – but they were climbed, of course, in 1928, by a party led by Jack Longland.

Soon you find yourself at the far end of the ridge looking across to the head of the Arddu Valley and down to a pass, Bwlch Cwm Brwynog, which lies between the Clogwyn Du'r Arddu ridge and Moel Cynghorion. To avoid losing too much height you need to keep as far left as you can – look out for a narrow path beginning on the other side of the lake's outflow stream.

After descending to cross the stream the path skirts the foot of some low cliffs before climbing to the col. The Snowdon Ranger Path, which has come down the 'Cloggy' ridge, can be seen below, but your route tackles Moel Cynghorion's steep southern ridge overlooking the crags of Clogwyn Llechwedd Llo. It's a short, steep course to the summit.

Below: Clogwyn Du'r Arddu, its lake, and Bwlch Cwm Brwynog from Route S14.

Route S15
Rhyd Ddu

*An intricate route once used by quarrymen
and miners*

Start: Rhyd Ddu (GR: SH 571526)
Distance: 3¼ miles/6km
Height gain: 1740ft/530m
Time: 2¼ hours

From the car park head past the toilet block
and past the railway station before following
a stony lane which runs along the back of
some houses. Near the end a kissing gate
marks the start of a well waymarked path,
which is soon joined by another path from
the village's Cwellyn Arms.

The path traverses rough pastures before
crossing the Welsh Highland Railway line
using two kissing gates. It then climbs
through a pleasant hollow between craggy
knolls before coming to the spoil tips of some
extensive old slate quarries. After scaling one
of the mounds, the path drops into a grassy

corridor through the slate heaps. Turn left
here to pass the old barracks.

More waymarks guide you to the right to
skirt the northern perimeter of the quarries
before dropping down to cross a metal footbridge spanning the Afon Treweunydd. There
are very pleasing views downstream across
pastoral countryside towards Llyn Cwellyn
and the majestic cliffs of Craig y Bera.

After climbing the far banks the path continues through a marshy area, heading generally northwards towards the grassy ridges
ahead. Fingerposts now direct the route,
which is becoming very much clearer.

The path meets the Snowdon Ranger path
beyond a ladder stile. Turn right to climb
along the Snowdon path, which traverses a
wide cwm beneath Moel Cynghorion's grassy
southern flanks. Llyn Ffynnon-y-gwas comes
into view beneath the ridge of Clogwyn Du'r
Arddu.

The path now heads for the foot of the
Clogwyn Du'r Arddu ridge, but leave it for a
short trackless course up grass slopes to the
col, Bwlch Cwm Brwynog. Here you'll be
able to look across to the cliffs of Clogwyn
Du'r Arddu. As in Route S14, climb Moel
Cynghorion's steep southern ridge to the
summit.

Other route options
The obvious one here is to climb the Snow-
don Ranger Path (Route S12) to Bwlch Cwm
Brwynog before taking the East Ridge route
(Route S14/S15).

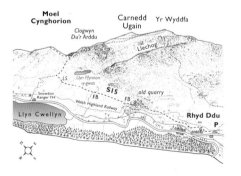

RIDGE ROUTES

Carnedd Ugain
Distance: 2 miles/3km
Height gain: 1800ft/550m
Time: 1 hour

Descend eastwards by a fence down a steep grass ridge to Bwlch Cwm Brwynog. It is possible to veer right to join the Snowdon Ranger Path, but while you're on the edge it's best to stay that way and follow the bouldery rim above Clogwyn Du'r Arddu, with its tremendous views down the crags. The ridge broadens out near the top and the cliff-edge swings left around the head of Cwm Arddu. To reach Carnedd Ugain maintain your direction (ESE) up grassy terrain all the way to the summit.

Foel Goch
Distance: 1¼ miles/2km
Height gain: 460ft/140m
Time: ¾ hour

A steep grassy ridge leads WSW to the narrow pass of Bwlch Maesgwm and an equally steep but shorter grassy ridge climbs by a fence all the way back up to Foel Goch.

Above: Moel Eilio, Foel Gron and Foel Goch.

MOEL EILIO

'I was drawing nigh to the mountainous district of the Eryri – a noble hill called Mount Eilio appeared before me to the north; an immense mountain called Pen Drws Coed lay over against it to the south . . . I never was in such a lovely spot.' Thus 19th-century author George Borrow enthused about the view from Betws Garmon in his classic book *Wild Wales*.

Moel Eilio, Snowdon's northern outlier and highest summit in a long grassy ridge between Bwlch Cwm Brwynog beneath Clogwyn Du'r Arddu and Llanberis, is indeed a noble mountain. Borrow's view is very pastoral and green, a gentle mountainscape from the banks of the Afon Gwyrfai. From here Eilio is a rounded grassy peak grazed with patches of scree and a little dusky splintered crag on its steep lower slopes.

Seen from the other side at Llanberis, Eilio has a fine domed shape with its scarp face etched with a symmetrical crescent of pinkish scree. Indeed it could be said that Eilio belonged to Llanberis, with its slopes rising from the back gardens of the cottages in the upper village.

Left: Looking back towards Betws Garmon and Mynydd Mawr from the Moel Eilio Route S18 path.

Along with three subsidiary summits, Foel Goch, Foel Fron and an unnamed top, Moel Eilio sends out two long spurs enclosing Cwm Dwythwch, a seldom-trod, marshy hollow where Llyn Dwythwch reposes beneath stern crags and scree.

Although it suffers from unfavourable comparisons with neighbouring Snowdon, Eilio is a worthwhile peak in its own right. Try a late sojourn to view the sunset over Llanberis and Llyn Padarn to see what I mean.

Route S16
North Ridge

The easiest but the longest route up

Start: Lakeside car park near Electric Mountain Centre, Llanberis (GR: SH 578605)

Distance: 3½ miles/5.5km

Height gain: 2030ft/620m

Time: 2 hours

A narrow lane opposite the lakeside car park passes the public toilets to reach the High Street. Turn left here before turning right up Capel Coch Road, which climbs past the huge chapel and changes its name to Stryd Ceunant. At the road-end, turn right over the

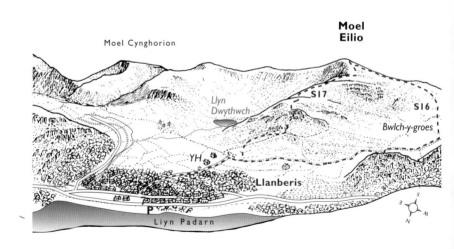

ladder stile following a stony track to pass the sad ruins of Main-llwyd-isaf. Turn left along a lane that is tarred until the first right-hand bend. Continue on the unsurfaced lane above the slate heaps of disused quarries. There are fine views into the wild cwm of Arddu, where the Llanberis Path and the Snowdon Mountain Railway lead the eye to the great cliffs of Clogwyn Du'r Arddu.

The pleasant green lane reaches its summit at Bwlch-y-groes. Here you turn left, following tractor tracks up rough grass slopes. Soon a fence-side path develops, climbing the steady grass spur to Bryn Mawr. Over a ladder stile at a fence corner turn right to climb to Moel Eilio's summit.

Below: Llyn Dwythwch

Route S17
North-east Ridge
A tough route but the most interesting, with good views to Snowdon
Start: Lakeside car park near Electric Mountain Centre, Llanberis (GR: SH 578605)
Distance: 2½ miles/4km
Height gain: 2030ft/620m
Time: 1½ hours

___

As in Route S16 follow the narrow lane across the main road opposite the car park and turn left along the High Street. Again climb right along Capel Coch Road. Go straight ahead at a junction where the road changes its name to Stryd Ceunant and climbs past the youth hostel into the country-side.

At the road-end, turn right over the ladder stile and follow the track for a few paces to locate the ladder stile in the wall on the hill slopes to the left. This marks the start of the North-east Ridge. The initial stages are path-less and very steep. Follow the wall and clamber up the rocky lower slopes of Braich y Foel. There's a glimpse of Llyn Dwythwch, set in a damp cwm to the left. A path develops on each side of the wall and you can choose either at the ladder stile straddling it. From here the gradient eases from steep to steady. The North Ridge path joins from the right high on the ridge and not far from the summit.

Route S18

Betws Garmon and the Iron Mines

An interesting if scrappy route with good retrospective views

Start: Betws Garmon (GR: SH 536577) (parking for two cars by Ystrad Uchaf and three by the church)

Distance: 3 miles/5km

Height gain: 1970ft/600m

Time: 2 hours

Walk up the road south-east past Ystrad Uchaf. Turn left through the kissing gate opposite Cae Hywel cottage, then turn right over a ladder stile to gain a waymarked path which threads a course between low craggy knolls. The path curves left over several ladder stiles to reach some crumbling mine buildings at GR 543578.

After rounding a large tree, join a well-defined track with a fence/wall on the left. Watch out for a grassy track on the right,

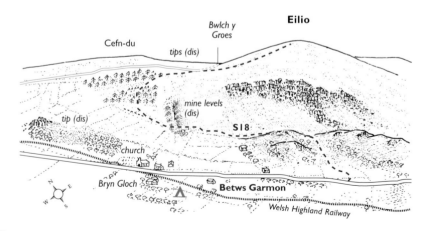

which rakes NNE uphill to reach a conifer plantation. The path follows the edge of the forest for a short way before following what was a very overgrown track through the trees. Occasional waymarks in the middle of the forest help guide the route to the kissing gate on the northern perimeter (GR 547587).

Now head NNE across rough pasture towards another plantation whose southern edge should be followed for about 400yds/m when you can climb east up the slopes of Bryn Mawr to join the North Ridge path to Moel Eilio's summit.

Other route options

A tarmac road climbs from Waunfawr up to the quarries near Bwlch-y-groes giving a quick way up to the summit. A path from Waunfawr could also be used. It begins at GR 539593 and climbs east through fields before entering open country. A path then keeps to the south of the woods at Donen Las to join Route S18 where trackless grass slopes lead to Bryn Mawr, Moel Eilio's north ridge.

RIDGE ROUTES

Foel Goch

Distance: 1¼ miles/2km
Height gain: 460ft/140m
Time: ¾ hour

A good path descends the broad grassy ridge to the south with good views across intervening ridges and spurs to Snowdon and the wide valley of the Arddu. The route straddles two intermediate tops – one unnamed, the other called Foel Gron – before making a short ascent, again on grass, to Foel Goch.

Right: The climb from Betws Garmon to Moel Eilio.

Above: Gallt y Wenallt across Nant Gwynant.

FOEL GOCH / FOEL GRON

GALLT Y WENALLT

Two of several tops on the Eilio ridge, Foel Goch (the red hill) and Foel Gron (the rounded hill) don't have quite enough about them to feature as separate mountains – they're really subsidiary tops of Moel Eilio.

Foel Gron is just a knoll in the ridge, and while Foel Goch has a pleasant northern ridge separating the cwms of Tan yr Allt and Maesgwm, and a rash of crags just beneath the grassy summit, it is in no way a destination in its own right.

Sometimes referred to as the last nail in the Snowdon Horseshoe, Gallt y Wenallt, the hill of the white slope, has often been trodden as a means to an end by the purists who want to walk the entire Cwm Dyli ridge.

Seen from across the Glaslyn valley, the mountain's south-east face dwarfs the little Cwm Dyli power station as it soars in one continuous slope of steep grass, fractured crag and scree. Tempered by oak woods and scattered patches of twisted hawthorn, this is an extremely impressive mountain view.

Gallt y Wenallt's summit is a pleasant place of little rock knolls forming islands in the grass. Although Y Lliwedd acts as a barrier, the mountain top offers fine views in other directions including an exquisite one across Nantgwynant where Llyn Gwynant can often be seen as a shimmering jewel among the incredible maze of rocky heather knolls which make up the rugged Moel Meirch – in autumn the view is ablaze with colour.

Gallt y Wenallt's south-west spur guards Cwm Merch, along with the south slopes of Y Lliwedd. This presents walkers with the finest route, past waterfalls, ancient woodland and old mines – and here they can discover some of Snowdon's secrets on their way to one of its most underrated little peaks.

Route S19

Cwm Merch

A quiet route with fine views of Gwynant
Start: Nantgwynant (GR: SH 628506)
Distance: 3 miles/5km
Height gain: 1870ft/570m
Time: 1½–2 hours

From the car park at Nantgwynant, cross the road and the road bridge before turning on to the narrow Cwm Llan lane. After a few paces turn left on to a pleasant path through the woodland of Parc Hafod-y-llan. This joins a stony track which continues across open fell to pass some fine waterfalls.

Beyond these, take the path on the right, descending to a slab bridge across the river. Take the second (right) of two ladder stiles at the foot of more woodland, before climbing right on a good track traversing the mid flanks of Lliwedd. On reaching a fenced enclosure turn left through a gap in the intake wall and climb on a path which zigzags up grassy slopes before resuming its NE course. The path ends at some old mine workings.

Descend to cross a stream below a waterfall before climbing NW along rocky ribs to reach the col between Lliwedd Bach and Gallt y Wenallt. Turn right weaving through rocky outcrops to Gallt y Wenallt's summit.

Other route options

Galt y Wenallt is often used as the last peak in the Snowdon Horseshoe. The route generally used drops down to the little valley, and crosses the Glaslyn (difficult when in spate) and the pipeline before climbing between the craggy knolls to return to the Miners' Track to Pen y Pass. In ascent this would be a dull slog.

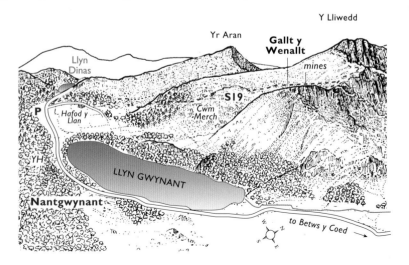

RIDGE ROUTES

Y Lliwedd

Distance: 1¼ miles/2km
Height gain: 820ft/250m
Time: ¾ hour

Descend the faint grass path to a shallow col before an undulating ridge reaches the place where the Llyn Llydaw path to Y Lliwedd joins the ridge, a spot marked by a cairn. After rounding the left side of Y Lliwedd Bach, the path climbs up the rocky crest to Lliwedd's East Peak before dropping down to a shallow col and climbing back up the slightly higher West Peak.

Below: Llyn Gwynant from Cwm Merch.
Overleaf: Storm over Nantgwynant.

Y Lliwedd has the highest inland cliff in Wales, rising some 1000ft/300m from the shores of Llyn Llydaw to the twin East and West Peaks. Often in shadow, the scene is transformed when the rays of early morning or late evening flicker across the faulted crags, highlighting all the nooks and crannies with columns of gold.

In the pioneering days of climbing, Y Lliwedd's cliffs were a major venue, attracting the likes of Geoffrey Winthrop Young and George Mallory. These days there are fewer climbers, partly due to the fact that there are crags nearer to the road, and partly due to the difficulties of many of the climbs, which are time-consuming and serious.

The East and West Peaks of the mountain are almost indistinguishable in height, but

Opposite: Climbing out of Cwm Dyli to Y Lliwedd.
Below: Y Lliwedd seen across Llyn Llydaw.

those men from the OS have measured them as 2946ft/898m to 2929ft/893m in favour of the West Peak. The magnificent clifftop view from the highest justifies the effort of straddling the col between the two.

Bwlch y Saethau, the pass of the arrows, was the legendary scene of a great battle between King Arthur and his Knights and the evil Sir Mordred, who had gathered together an army of Saxons. Sir Mordred dealt King Arthur a fatal blow but, before he fell, Arthur wielded Excalibur and, with one mighty blow to the head, killed his foe. While Arthur's body was taken down the mountainside, many of the Knights of the Round Table retreated to a cave in Y Lliwedd's cliffs to await the time when their king would return to lead them. It is said they are still there, waiting . . .

Route S20
The Miners' Track and Y Lliwedd Bach

Great views of the precipices from start to finish

Start: Pen y Pass (GR: SH 648557))

Distance: 2½ miles/4km

Height gain: 1800ft/550m

Time: 1½–2 hours

Take the wide Miners' Track, which begins from the south-east side of the lower car park. This takes the route easily around the head of Nantgwynant before circling right. Here Llyn Teyrn, the monarch's lake, comes into view, with the cliffs of Y Lliwedd peeping over lower grass slopes beyond the huge pipelines of the hydro-electric scheme.

The path continues its easy progress climbing by the pipeline to the pumphouse by the

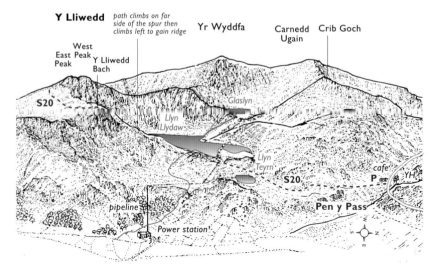

Y Lliwedd *path climbs on far side of the spur then climbs left to gain ridge*   **Yr Wyddfa**   **Carnedd Ugain**   **Crib Goch**

West East Peak Peak   Y Lliwedd Bach

S20   *Glaslyn*

Llyn Llydaw

Llyn Teyrn   *café*   **P**   YH

S20

pipeline   **Pen y Pass**

Power station

shores of Llyn Llydaw. This enlarged lake stretches out for almost the entire length of the cavernous Cwm Dyli. Now the full majesty of Y Lliwedd's cliffs can be appreciated. Often in shadow, they rise almost vertically for around 1000ft to the twin east and west summits.

Leave the Miners' Track at the pumphouse for a left fork path which follows Llydaw's south shores. After crossing a footbridge spanning the outflow of the lake, the footpath begins the climb on an engineered, stepped path. Where this ends the path begins to steepen as it scrambles over rocks. In the upper regions the route often involves a

winding scramble up rock steps to the left. It reaches the ridge at a cairn north west of Y Lliwedd Bach. New views of Nantgwynant Cnicht and the Moelwyns appear as the path eases up the south side of Y Lliwedd Bach to miss the summit by no more than 50ft. There are now tremendous views over the precipices and across Cwm Dyli.

The climb to Y Lliwedd's East Peak is laid out before you. Sometimes the path is stony and sometimes it can be recognised by the paler colour of the rock it clambers over. On reaching the top of the East Peak, there's a slight drop to negotiate before continuing over similar rocky ground to the West Peak.

Below: Climbing towards Y Lliwedd ridge.

Route S21
Watkin Path and Bwlch Ciliau

A long, slightly less spectacular route
Start: Nantgwynant (GR: SH 628506)
Distance: 3¾ miles/6km
Height gain: 2790ft/850m
Time: 2½ hours

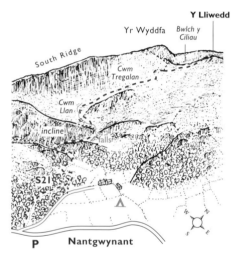

Cross the road from Nantgwynant's main car park and follow the lane opposite for a few paces before taking a woodland path through Parc Hafod-y-llan. The path joins a stony track leading past some fine waterfalls, then it cuts across an old quarry tramway to enter the mountainous Cwm Llan.

The Watkin Path leaves the old quarry track and crosses the river on a wide bridge close to the ruins of Plas Cwm y Llan. After passing the Gladstone Rock, the path swings left to round the precipices of Craig Ddu and some old mine workings. The scenery becomes more barren as the path climbs into Cwm Tregalan, a stony hollow encircled by the crags of Yr Wyddfa's South Ridge and Y Lliwedd's bouldery slopes.

The path zigzags up Y Lliwedd to attain the ridge at Bwlch Ciliau, the pass of the retreat – a reference to the final battle between King Arthur and Mordred. From here there are new views down the length of Cwm Dyli and its huge lake.

By keeping to the crest walkers commit themselves to some scrambling. An easier alternative follows a stony, later bouldery path that stays to the right (Cwm Tregalan) side of the crest to reach the West Peak.

Left: Waterfalls in the early stages of the Watkin Path, with Y Lliwedd on the skyline.

Route S22

Cwm Merch

A quiet route until the ridge; fine
   Nantgwynant views

Start: Nantgwynant (GR: SH 628506)

Distance: 3¾ miles/6km

Height gain: 2790ft/850m

Time: 2½ hours

This route follows the Watkin Path of Route S21 through the woodland of Parc Hafod-y-llan. Just beyond the waterfalls follow the path on the right descending to a slab bridge across the river. Take the second (right) of two ladder stiles at the foot of some more woodland, then climb right on a good track traversing the mid flanks of Lliwedd.

On reaching a fenced enclosure, turn left through a gap in the intake wall and climb on a path that zigzags up grassy slopes before resuming its NE course. The path ends at some old mine workings. Here you can climb steep pathless slopes past mine levels and spoil to meet the Pen y Pass route on the Lliwedd ridge. Turn left and follow the crest over Y Lliwedd Bach to reach the East Peak. A small col needs to be negotiated before continuing to the West Peak.

Other route options

It is feasible to follow Route S20 to the mines and continue to the col between Y Lliwedd Bach and Gallt y Wenallt (Route S22), before turning right along a grass ridge to rejoin S20 at the point where it is joined by the Pen y Pass route. Competent scramblers could climb the very steep rocky spur of Y Gribin. This is accessed from the Miners' Track near to the outflow of Glaslyn, but there could be a tricky river crossing after rain. The ridge climbs to Bwlch y Saethau, where a level track leads to Bwlch y Ciliau and Route S21.

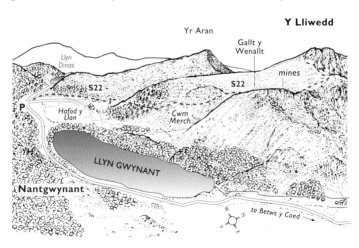

Y Lliwedd

Yr Aran

Gallt y Wenallt

mines

Llyn Dinas

S22

S22

P

Hafod y Llan

Cwm Merch

LLYN GWYNANT

Nantgwynant

to Betws y Coed

RIDGE ROUTES

Yr Wyddfa

Distance: 1½ miles/2.5km
Height gain: 1180ft/360m
Time: 1 hour

---

*Note: This rough ridge route can be very
serious in wintry conditions*

Descend from the west summit either by
scrambling down on the crest or taking the
bouldery path on the left (Cwm Tregalan) side
to reach Bwlch y Ciliau before a level path
leads to Bwlch y Saethau. Here take the left
fork path, which rakes across loose rock
slopes to join the South Ridge halfway
between Bwlch Main and the summit – the
spot is marked by a finger of rock. A short
climb to the right leads to the summit.

Gallt y Wenallt

Distance: 1¼ miles/2km
Height gain: 200ft/60m
Time: ¼ hour

Descend along the crest to the col between
the West and East Peaks, continue over the
latter, then down to Y Lliwedd Bach, beyond
which the ridge becomes wider and grassier.
After coming to a shallow col, weave through
rocky outcrops to Gallt y Wenallt's summit.

Opposite: On Y Lliwedd ridge.

YR ARAN

Seen in many a postcard view, Yr Aran rises from the sylvan shores of Llyn Gwynant with a gracefully arcing ridge and an angular rocky crown which reflect perfectly in the sheltered waters.

Forming the southern outlier of Yr Wyddfa, it's a bit out on a limb to be included in a big Snowdon day-walk, and not quite high enough at 2450ft/747m to attract many walkers to make it their sole destination, unless they include it on a linear walk.

But Yr Aran, which simply means the height, is a noble peak; with more attitude than altitude, granted – but its fine ridges, secretive cwms and crags make it a worthwhile excursion. The remoteness from the more celebrated Snowdon peaks means Yr Aran's summit is particularly airy with expansive views over the Glaslyn Estuary and Tremadog Bay, across Nantgwynant to Moel Siabod and the Moelwyn, and to Moel Hebog and the Eifionydd peaks.

Yr Aran's finest feature is its craggy northeast face, Clogwyn Brith, which towers above Bwlch Cwm Llan. Walkers coming from that direction get to make an exciting traverse of this face on their way to the easier east ridge.

In the lower regions by Llyn Dinas, land acquisition by the National Trust has opened up new paths around the grounds of the

Left: Yr Aran from Llyn Gwynant.

manor house of Craflwyn. Here is a land-scape of ancient oak woodland, defiant craggy knolls and rushing streams. The nearby hillside fort of Dinas Emrys has legends linking it with the Arthurian magician Merlin and the Saxon king Vortigern, who was left to organise Britain when the Romans left. The most likely scenario, however, is that it was one of many built on the orders of Llewelyn the Great, a 13th-century Prince of Wales.

Yr Aran

see map on page 86
for route beyond
Cwm Llan

Bwlch
Cwm Llan

S24

Cwm
Llan

incline

S23/24

Parc Hafod-y-llan

Nantgwynant   **P**

Route S23
Nantgwynant and Bwlch Cwm Llan

*An engaging route taking in two cwms and
   the craggy environs of the north-east face*

Start: Nantgwynant (GR: SH 628506)

Distance: 3 miles/5km

Height gain: 2300ft/700m

Time: 2 hours

From the car park at Nantgwynant cross the road and follow the narrow lane opposite. A delightful path through the woods of Parc Hafod-y-llan begins a few paces along the lane and to the left. It emerges on to a stony path that leads out of the woods to pass to the left of some impressive waterfalls. The track cuts across an old quarry tramway before climbing by the river into Cwm Llan. Where it levels out by the riverbank (GR 622520), leave it for a path on the left. This climbs to meet an old quarry tramway which leads the route a little further into Cwm Llan.

At GR 617521, a path leads left off this into a grassy hollow beneath Yr Aran's East Ridge before climbing to Bwlch Cwm Llan, the pass between Yr Aran and Yr Wyddfa. There's a small tarn and quarry across which you can see down to Rhyd Ddu, Llyn Cwellyn and Mynydd Mawr, the mountain beyond.

The path to Yr Aran climbs left beside a drystone wall and turns sharp left halfway up to rake beneath the screes and craggy outcrops of the north face to reach the easier gradients of the East Ridge. Go over the ladder stile straddling an electric fence before climbing right to the summit.

Above: Yr Aran rises above the quarried hill pastures of Cwm Llan.

Route S24
Nantgwynant and the East Ridge

A quarryman's route to the mountain
Start: Nantgwynant (GR: SH 628506)
Distance: 2½ miles/4km
Height gain: 2300ft/700m
Time: 1½ hours

Note: This route is especially pleasant in descent when the views down the ridge to Llyn Gwynant and Moel Siabod can be stunning in the right conditions

---

As in Route S22, follow the path through the woods of Parc Hafod-y-llan, passing the waterfalls into Cwm Llan where climbing left brings the route on to the previously mentioned quarry tramway. On this route you don't follow the tramway but climb further by a stream on an intermittent path passing quarry workings and spoil heaps to gain Yr Aran's East Ridge. A stone wall now leads the route to the ladder stile over an electric fence, where you join Route S23 on a simple stroll to the summit.

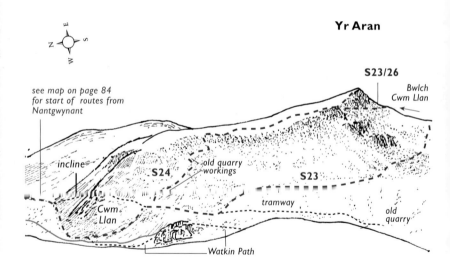

Yr Aran

S23/26

Bwlch
Cwm Llan

see map on page 84
for start of routes from
Nantgwynant

incline

old quarry
workings

S24

S23

Cwm
Llan

tramway

old
quarry

Watkin Path

Above: Yr Aran's East Ridge seen across Cwm Llan. The reddish scars of the miners' paths used on Route S24 show clearly on the left.

Route S25
Craflwyn and Cwm y Bleiddiaid
A tough but varied and very scenic route
Start: Craflwyn (GR: SH 599489)
Distance: 2¼ miles/3.5km
Height gain: 2330ft/710m
Time: 1½ hours

From the car park turn left along the drive and take the left fork, which passes between the hall and some outbuildings. Turn left shortly afterwards, following the yellow arrows on a narrow path that passes between woods. At a junction of paths, turn right on the one marked with a red arrow. This climbs the hillside, passing through a gap in an old stone wall. There are now wonderful views back to Nantgwynant and the rhododendron-covered slopes beyond the river and road. Just a few paces to the right of the path is a huge wooden throne where you can enjoy the view in comfort.

From the chair, the path curves left and goes over a stile in a fence before traversing more bracken. Leave the path for one on the right, marked by a black arrow. This traverses more thick bracken and winds ENE across rough hillside before descending to the first of two ladder stiles either side of the Afon y Cwm river, which should be forded.

Beyond the second of these stiles, turn left on an old mine track which follows the river to terminate just beyond a mine building. The path, still marked by black arrows, continues between the rocky heather knolls of Cwm y Bleiddiaid, the valley of wolves. Where the path starts to descend to a ladder stile in a tall stone wall – easily identified by the prairie-like grassy bowl beyond – leave it to climb over extremely rough terrain of heather, tufty grass and crag, parallel to the wall, which will eventually lead to Y Aran's East Ridge.

Just before coming to a tall cross-wall, step over the wall on the right at a point where it abuts a crag. Steep grassy slopes now lead further up the spur. Where the wall attains the East Ridge it turns left to guide the route to the ladder stile used in Route S22.

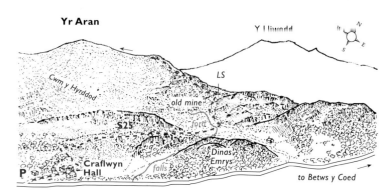

*Wild country (above)
and waterfalls (right)
above Craflwyn.*

Route S26
Rhyd Ddu

A traverse of wild and open country
Start: Rhyd Ddu (GR: SH 571526)
Distance: 2¾ miles/4.5km
Height gain: 18400ft/560m
Time: 1¾–2 hours

From the car park take the northbound track past the railway station before turning right with the Rhyd Ddu Snowdon Path across the railway. The route follows the Snowdon route until it veers off left through a kissing gate. Your route stays with the quarry track as it climbs across barren lands of grass thistles and rocky outcrops. It heads for the nick between Yr Wyddfa's South Ridge and Yr Aran. After passing tiny pools and quarry tips, the route comes to the main Bwlch Cwm Llan quarry and its two reservoirs. On the other side, views into Cwm Llan are dominated by the bare stony flanks of Y Lliwedd.

From the bwlch, the path to Yr Aran climbs beside a drystone wall and, like Route S25, turns sharp left halfway up to reach the easier gradients of the East Ridge. Go over the ladder stile straddling an electric fence before climbing right to the summit.

Other route options

It is possible to leave Route S25 before fording the Afon-y-cwm and climb through Cwm yr Hyrddod, but this involves cutting across rough vegetation of bracken and heather in the early stages with no path to help and no ladder stiles in the tall cross-walls.

RIDGE ROUTES

Yr Wyddfa

Distance: 2 miles/3km
Height gain: 1770ft/540m
Time: 1½ hours

Descend along Yr Aran's East Ridge as far as a ladder stile. Once over this, turn left to follow a wall descending across a rocky face to Bwlch Cwm Llan. The route now climbs Yr Wyddfa's South Ridge, Sometimes it uses little ledge paths and sometimes the natural slabs of the ridge. After going over a little peak, known as the Saddle, the path is joined by the Rhyd Ddu Path and uses both sides of the ridge before taking a bouldery final course up to the summit.

Opposite: Bwlch Cwm Llan from north-west.

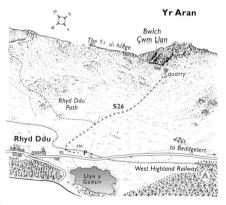

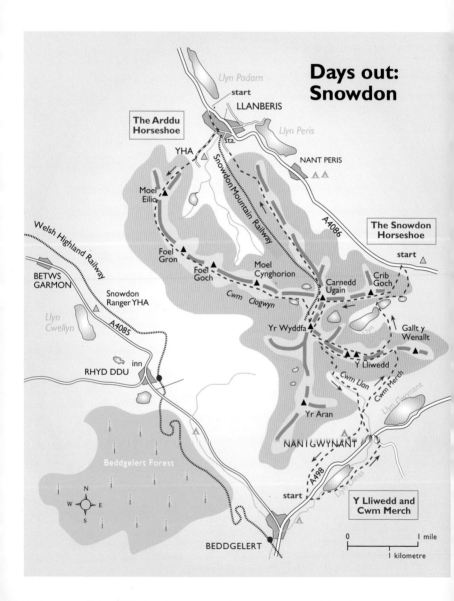

Days out: Snowdon

The Arddu Horseshoe

The Snowdon Horseshoe

Y Lliwedd and Cwm Merch

Llyn Padarn

start

LLANBERIS

Llyn Peris

NANT PERIS

sta.

YHA

Snowdon Mountain Railway

Moel Eilio

A4086

start

Welsh Highland Railway

BETWS GARMON

Foel Gron

Foel Goch

Moel Cynghorion

Carnedd Ugain

Crib Goch

Snowdon Ranger YHA

A4085

Cwm Clogwyn

Yr Wyddfa

Gallt y Wenallt

Llyn Cwellyn

inn

RHYD DDU

Y Lliwedd

Cwm Llan

Cwm Merch

Llyn Gwynant

Yr Aran

NANT GWYNANT

Beddgelert Forest

A498

start

Llyn Dinas

N
W — E
S

BEDDGELERT

0   1 mile

1 kilometre

Days out: Snowdon

The Arddu Horseshoe

Start: Lakeside car park near Electric
   Mountain Centre, Llanberis
   (GR: SH 578605)
Distance: 12½ miles/20km
Height gain: 5180ft/1580m
Time: About 8 hours

---

*Note: Although there's no scrambling, this
roller-coaster of a route is a huge walk with
a lot of ups and downs – don't underestimate
it! There are many escape routes, however,
and by the time you reach Moel Cynghorion
you should have a fair idea if it's going to
be too much. A way of shortening the route
would involve using the bridleway from
Llanberis through Maesgwm (see Route S13
to Moel Cynghorion)*

*Above: The Arddu Valley seen from the
Llanberis Ridge.*

A narrow lane opposite Llyn Padarn's lake-side car park passes the public toilets to reach Llanberis High Street. Turn left here before turning right up Capel Coch Road. By the large chapel turn right up a street known as Fron Goch and climb to a T-junction. By turning left, the houses of Llanberis are left behind as the lane climbs pastured hillsides to the sad ruins of Main-llwyd-isaf. Here the tarmac ends and the lane bends right to pass above the slate heaps of disused quarries. There are fine views into the wild cwm of Arddu to the great cliffs of Clogwyn Du'r Arddu, also back down to Llyn Padarn and the coast.

The winding green lane reaches its summit at Bwlch-y-groes. Here, tractor tracks guide the route up rough grass slopes to a fence-side path up Moel Eilio's northern ridge, Bryn Mawr. After going over a ladder stile at a fence corner, the path joins one from the north-eastern ridge and veers right for Moel Eilio's summit. It's an intricate scene from here across a series of spurs and ridges. At the back lies the massif of Snowdon, fronted by the cliffs and yawning valley of Arddu. The plumes of smoke from the Snowdon Mountain Railway engines will probably be billowing up into the sky as the train chugs alongside the Llanberis path on its 4½-mile journey to the summit.

What follows now is a long series of ups and downs over several rounded grassy tops. At first, the views down rocky cliffs show Llyn Dwythwch to perfection. The OS have a lower peak marked as Foel Gron and a higher one, which is unnamed, although many writers have reversed this for the convenience of their mountain tables. Foel Goch is lower but has a fine long spur framing Llyn Dwythwch on the south side. There's a steep drop down more grass slopes to the pass of Bwlch Maesgwm, where a bridleway between Llanberis and Rhyd Ddu straddles the ridge.

Moel Cynghorion presents the biggest challenge yet, as a steep fence-side path struggles high above the deep valley of Maesgwm to the summit. This is a great place for viewing Clogwyn Du'r Arddu and the bouldery surrounds to its tarn, although you'll have to adjust your eyes to see it through the shadows.

From Cynghorion's summit the route descends in the same fashion as the ascent but the scenery is becoming more spectacular with every footstep.

At the pass you could head towards the

Below: The Llanberis Ridge with Elidir Fawr on the right.

prominent Snowdon Ranger Path, which zigzags up the Clogwyn ridge. But it is better, although a little bouldery in places, to follow the cliff edge – not too near, though – for great views down the cliffs. This means joining the Snowdon Ranger Path high up on Carnedd Ugain's slopes.

After crossing the mountain railway track (with care) the route meets the Llanberis Path, which leads the route to the rim of Cwm Dyli and the monolith at Bwlch Glas. Here you can look down on the Miners' and Pig track routes, which have climbed through the huge corrie of Cwm Dyli. The great Horseshoe ridges, Crib y Ddysgl, Crib Goch and Lliwedd, wrap themselves around the blue lakes of Glaslyn and Llydaw with the dark pyramidal massif of Snowdon at their hub. Wales does not come more wild and wonderful than this.

The path now follows the line of the railway to the summit, where you'll be able to buy refreshments and look out of the huge picture window of the new glass-and-granite summit café with half of Wales in your view. It's a different world from the one to which Wordsworth came for his nocturnal spiritual view in *Prelude Book XIV*:

For instantly a light upon the turf
Fell like a flash, and lo! as I looked up,
The Moon hung naked in a firmament
Of azure without cloud, and at my feet
Rested a silent sea of hoary mist.
A hundred hills their dusky backs upheaved

After retracing your steps to Bwlch Glas, leave the wide Snowdon paths and the railway for a path on the right, which climbs the easy slopes to Carnedd Ugain. An easy grass ridge declines northwards allowing a fine promenade along the rim of Cwm Glas, which offers particularly impressive views across the climbers' grounds of the Llanberis Pass. Two little tarns, Llyn Bach and Llyn Glas, add a little sparkle to their respective craggy cwms.

Where the grass ridge ends above Gyrn Las, descend left on easy grass slopes to join the Llanberis Path at the point where it runs alongside the mountain railway. The path goes under the railway near Clogwyn, and if you're getting weary by this time you can follow it all the way down.

However, there's a better way – a true horseshoe. Don't go under the railway bridge; instead, go around the fence by the bridge and follow the true ridge, keeping clear of the railway trackbed. Keep right of the station and climb half-right to the summit of Llechog (yes, yet another Llechog!). In the upper regions the course will be over boulders, but the view is worth the extra effort: nowhere can you see the rugged Llanberis Pass in such fine form as it squeezes between the towering Esgair Felen and Crib Goch crags and screes.

Overleaf: This view from Moel Eilio to Yr Wyddfa on the skyline includes the velvety spurs of Foel Gron, Foel Goch and Moel Cynghorion.

The route descends back towards the railway line, which does seem to get in the way on these early stages of the ridge. However, the railway soon sidles away, and the route follows the ridge fence over several rocky knolls and squelchy cols (the wet parts of which are easily rounded). The knolls are collectively known as Tryfan, so I suppose that means there are three. The tiny cottages of Nant Peris lie far below the cliffs and are dwarfed further by the steep slopes of the Glyderau on the other side.

Beyond Tryfan's last knoll the ground drops away steeply in terraces of crag. It's time to leave the ridge by taking easier gradients to the left to reach the Llanberis Path. If you leave it later you'll be confronted by precipitous (but not impossible) bracken-infested slopes which descend to the woods of Coed Victoria. Follow the Llanberis Path down to the lane, Victoria Terrace, which descends to the main road through Llanberis. Turn left to pass the railway and take the right fork, the main road, past the Electric Mountain Visitor Centre and back to the car park.

Below: Looking across LLyn Llydaw from Lliwedd Bach.

The Snowdon Horseshoe
Start: Pen y Pass (GR: SH 648557)
Distance: 8 miles/13km
Height gain: 3300ft/1000m
Time: 6–7 hours

The Snowdon Horseshoe is without doubt the most spectacular and exciting route a walker can undertake on the Welsh Mountains. The route is usually done in an anticlockwise direction starting with the ascent of Crib Goch, and I would say it is better this way as the tricky ridge of Crib Goch is much easier in ascent than it is in descent.

The route begins from the top right end of the car park on the Pig Track. The heavily slabbed route winds up the mountainside high above the Llanberis Pass, with Crib Goch directly ahead for much of the way. On reaching the pass, Bwlch Moch, take the right fork track, which climbs directly up the nose of Crib Goch. There are no difficulties until the path comes to a halt beneath a large crag – sometimes a queue develops here, held up by a nervous walker. The rock is solid with good hand-holds, though. Although steep and exposed, the upper section over more broken rock is straightforward all the way to Crib Goch's east summit.

Now the scramble over the exposed knife-edge begins. For those with a head for heights the views are wonderful, down to Cwm Glas and the Pass of Llanberis on the right and across Llyn Llydaw to Yr Wyddfa on the left.

In calm conditions walkers with good balance can go along the crest, but many walkers prefer to take a line just below on the Cwm Dyli (left) side, using the crest as a steadying handrail. Unless you're a competent scrambler, it is better to keep to the left of the Pinnacles before descending a scree gulley down to the grassy col of Bwlch Coch.

The longer climb along Crib y Ddysgl to Carnedd Ugain is easier but still involves a little scrambling, with a few rock steps and short stretches of narrow exposed ridge. Do not be drawn on little paths to the left this time. Eventually the gradient eases and the ridge widens until it reaches Carnedd Ugain's grassy summit.

A path leads the route around the rim of Cwm Dyli to Bwlch Glas, where the Miners' Path, the Pig Track, the Llanberis Path and the Snowdon Ranger route all converge and climb alongside the railway to the summit of Yr Wyddfa.

Now the path follows the Watkin Path for a short way, firstly down the South Ridge, which begins by the far end of the summit café. Follow the ridge path down to a finger of rock on the left, which marks the start of the descent route, a cairned path that slants down the loose, shaley slopes of the summit massif to Bwlch y Saethau, the pass of the arrows, where legend has it that King Arthur fought his last battle.

A fairly level path over rocky terrain continues to the right of the crest to reach a second pass, Bwlch y Ciliau, the pass of the retreat, another reference to Arthur's battle. The Watkin Path, which descends right, should be abandoned for the climb to Y

Lliwedd's West Peak. Keeping to the crest means more scrambling; many walkers follow the path, which stays generally on the right (Cwm Tregalan) side. The views from the West Peak's summit down those 1000ft cliffs to Llyn Llydaw are awe-inspiring, and it is satisfying to scan the horizon back to the ridges you've completed so far.

An easy path descends to a shallow col before tackling the East Peak in similar fashion. A winding path descends the ridge before going around the right side of Lliwedd Bach. A cairn marks the start of the descent to Llyn Llydaw. The route soon becomes a rough clamber down rocky slopes to the left, but as the terrain eases, a slab-and-step path traverses largely grassy slopes down to Llyn Llydaw. After crossing a footbridge over the lake's outflow, the path meets the Miners' Track, which it follows left, passing Llyn Teyrn and its ruined copper mine barracks on an easy course back to Pen y Pass.

Below: The summit of Crib Goch in gloomy mood.

Lliwedd by the Back Door

Start: Craflwyn car park (donations invited)
   (GR: SH 599489)
Distance: 11 miles/17.5km
Height gain: 3350ft/1020m
Time: 6 hours

This route takes a look at Snowdon without going to the highest peak, Yr Wyddfa, and, for most of its course, this is as quiet as the area gets. Y Lliwedd, with its 1000ft/300m cliffs, is the main destination, but the route as a whole shows what a region of contrasting landscapes Snowdonia can be. One moment the walker can be wandering by a sylvan streamside coloured by rhododendrons or bluebells; the next he or she can be climbing among crags and thundering waterfalls.

The walk begins at Craflwyn, part of an estate bought by the National Trust in 1994. The name is derived from the word *criafolen*, Welsh for rowan or mountain ash. In the 13th century, this land was owned by Llewelyn the Great, who probably built the fort on the nearby crag, Dinas Emrys, although romantics would have it as Merlin's castle. Today the Trust has designed a series of short routes around the estate and one long one that links Craflwyn with Cwm Llan. The route starts with a combination of these paths. There are toilets and an information notice board at the back of the car park.

The walk starts by leaving the Craflwyn Estate and turning left along the main road. As you reach the tree-cloaked rocky slopes of Dinas Emrys, turn right at the entrance to the Sygun Copper Mines. After going over the bridge across the Afon Glaslyn, turn past Cae'r Moch cottage and on to a path running parallel to the river. The extremely pleasant path then follows the southern shores of Llyn Dinas before swinging left to hug the lower perimeters of a wooded hillside. Beyond the farm of Llyndy Isaf, a track winds to the Nantmor Road, where you should turn left into Nantgwynant.

Turn right along the main road then left along a narrow lane just before the main road-bridge over the Glaslyn, Pont Bethania. After a few paces go left again on the Watkin Path route, which now goes through the woods of Parc Hafod-y-llan. The well-graded path comes out of the woods and takes a circuitous course around a rocky knoll, marked Castell on the map, then gives a glorious view of some foaming waterfalls backed up by the cliffs of Craig Ddu and the immense stony southern flanks of Lliwedd.

Beyond the falls and an old quarry tramway, take a path on the left down to a small slabbed footbridge across the river. Climb north-east towards the furthest right of two ladder stiles at the bottom of a woodland copse. Beyond this a good path climbs right towards Cwm Merch.

On reaching a fenced enclosure turn left

Overleaf: A bitterly cold day on Lliwedd Bach, with Y Lliwedd on the left and Yr Wyddfa behind it, partially hidden by snow-bearing cloud.

through a gap in the intake wall and follow the zigzags up grassy slopes before the path resumes its NNE course. At this point there are wonderful views of Llyn Gwynant, its beautiful woodland and the fascinating complex heather and rock knolls leading up to Moel Meirch's ruffled crest. Eventually the path ends by some old mine workings but there are no obstacles to a pathless progress to the Gallt y Wenallt–Y Lliwedd ridge.

Descend to cross a stream below a waterfall before climbing away from the mines north-westwards along rocky ribs to reach the col between Lliwedd Bach and Gallt y Wenallt. For the first time you can see into Snowdon's inner heart, with Cwm Dyli and its lake, Llyn Llydaw, taking pride of place in a mountainscape that encompasses Yr Wyddfa, Crib Goch, Carnedd Ugain and Y Lliwedd's East Peak.

Turn left along a narrow ridge path over a couple of subsidiary peaks; the unnamed 694m top has some especially nice cliffs. Soon the route comes to the cairn that marks the path coming up from Llydaw and together the routes tuck behind Lliwedd Bach before tackling Y Lliwedd's East Peak. After a short drop the West Peak is conquered.

Below: Llyn Gwynant seen from Cwm Merch.

Now the route becomes a bit rougher. Generally the path stays to the left of the crest on its way down to Bwlch y Ciliau. At this col, leave the ridge on the Watkin Path route which slants left, before zigzagging down into Cwm Tregalan and down to the quarries of Cwm Llan. The wide path, now dominated by the rocky Yr Aran ridge, stays parallel to the Afon Cwm Llan before passing the Gladstone Rock and coming to the ruins of the quarrymaster's house. Here a bridge takes the route across the river.

On reaching the lower cwm, watch out for a track climbing diagonally up hill slopes to the right. Highlighted by black arrows, this will take you back to Craflwyn. The waterfalls you saw earlier in the day come into view as the path hugs the lower slopes of Clogwyn Brith. Beyond Bwlchau Iertyn the path skirts the edge of a rough prairie-like hollow grazed by cattle. At the far end there's a ladder stile over a cross-wall.

The wall is the ridge wall used to guide Route S25 to Yr Aran. After a short climb, the route descends among heather and craggy knolls into Cwm y Bleiddiaid, the pass of wolves – and it's easy to believe that wolves did once roam this wild terrain. After passing some waterfalls, the path meets a track which leads to the Afon y Cwm. A ladder stile on either bank show where the track should be abandoned and the river forded – there are stepping stones but the crossing can be difficult after periods of heavy rainfall. In such cases walk back upstream to find an easier crossing.

Now on the other side of the river, the path trends westwards across rough terrain beneath the heather-interspersed crags that form Yr Aran's lower south flanks. The whole area is a mix of thick bracken, heather and rough moor grasses, but black arrows on wooden posts keep the narrow path obvious. The crags and rhododendrons of Mynydd Sygun across Nantgwynant make an attractive backdrop to the complex wooded knolls, waterfalls and bracken-filled hollows passed along the final descent into the valley.

After crossing a field of particularly dense bracken, the route meets another National Trust trail, this time marked by a red arrow. Turn left along it. A short way after going over a stile in a fence the path comes across a large wooden throne, from which to admire the view of Nantgwynant. The winding path continues, passing between the mixed woodland copses of the Craflwyn Estate. At another junction, turn left along a path marked with a yellow arrow which takes the route by more woodland down towards the hall. On meeting a stony drive, turn left to follow it between the hall and some cottages back to the car park.

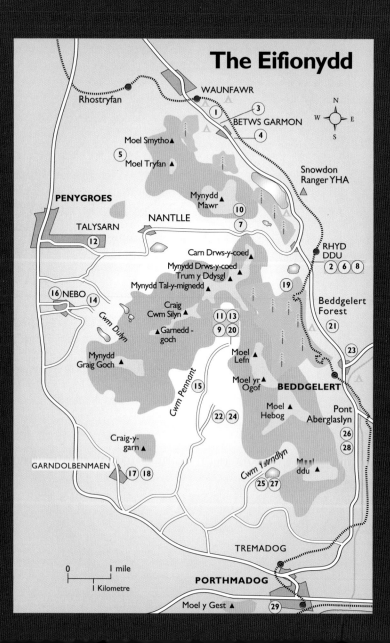

The Eifionydd

Rhostryfan

WAUNFAWR
①
③
BETWS GARMON
④

Moel Smytho▲
⑤
Moel Tryfan ▲

Snowdon
Ranger YHA

PENYGROES

Mynydd
Mawr ▲
⑩
⑦

NANTLLE

TALYSARN

⑫

RHYD
DDU
② ⑥ ⑧

Carn Drws-y-coed ▲
Mynydd Drws-y-coed ▲
Trum y Ddysgl ▲
Mynydd Tal-y-mignedd ▲

⑯ NEBO
⑭

Craig
Cwm Silyn ▲
⑪ ⑬
⑨ ⑳
▲ Garnedd -
goch

Cwm Dulyn

⑲

Beddgelert
Forest

㉑

㉓

Moel ▲
Lefn

Mynydd
Graig Goch ▲

Moel yr ▲
Ogof

BEDDGELERT

Cwm Pennant

⑮

㉒ ㉔

Moel ▲
Hebog

Pont
Aberglaslyn

㉖
㉘

Craig-y-
garn ▲

GARNDOLBENMAEN

⑰ ⑱

Cwm Llyndlyn

Moel
ddu ▲

㉕ ㉗

TREMADOG

0   1 mile

1 Kilometre

PORTHMADOG

Moel y Gest ▲   ㉙

It's a typical Sunday morning in Rhyd Ddu. Walkers are mingling in the huge car park by the Welsh Highland Railway station where a steam engine is billowing smoke into the sky before chugging back to the castle town of Caernarfon. Time passes by. One by one the groups of walkers set off eastwards over the railway track, with eyes only for Snowdon. By eleven the car park is empty of people: the mountains of the Eifionydd, which lie to the west, have once again been forsaken, ignored by all but a few connoisseurs.

THE PEAKS

Main Tops	height	
Moel Hebog	2656ft	782m
Craig Cwm Silyn	2408ft	734m
Trum y Ddysgl	2326ft	709m
Garnedd-goch	2296ft	700m
Mynydd Mawr	2290ft	698m
Mynydd Drws-y-coed	2279ft	695m
Moel yr Ogof	2148ft	655m
Mynydd Tal-y-mignedd	2142ft	653m
Moel Lefn	2094ft	638m
Carn Drws-y-coed (Y Garn)	2076ft	633m
Mynydd Graig Goch	2000ft	610m
Moel-ddu	1814ft	553m
Craig-y-garn	1187ft	362m
Moel Smytho	1125ft	343m
Moel y Gest	861ft	262m

Although not as high as Snowdon, the Eifionydd are noble mountains with exciting ridges and fine craggy corries – but all those rock features are also to be found on the other side, in the seldom-visited Nantlle Valley.

The Eifionydd are laid out in a form rather like an upturned wishbone, with Mynydd Mawr in the north-west as the stem and the two arms of the Nantlle Ridge and Moel Hebog group wrapping around Cwm Pennant. A high road between Rhyd Ddu and Penygroes dissects the group.

I'll start this quick tour of the Eifionydd in the north of the region, from Caernarfon, through the pretty valley of the Gwyfai. Mynydd Moel appears first above the camp-sites and forests. It's dome-shaped with a brooding corrie of heather and splintered cliffs. Passing along the shores of Llyn Cwellyn reveals a second corrie, this time guarded by a narrow defile flanked by the great towers of Castell Cidwm and the cone-shaped peaklet of Foel Rudd. In the calm of early morning, when the crags are etched in gold and reflected to perfection, there are few better sights in Snowdonia.

South of Rhyd Ddu the scene is spoiled by a vast tract of conifers so we'll climb right on the road to Penygroes, passing two lakes – Llyn y Gader and Llyn Dywarchen – before dropping into the Nantlle Valley. On the right skyline are the pinnacled cliffs of Craig y Bera, while to the left a heathery spur rises to the summit of Carn Drws-y-coed, the last peak in the Nantlle Ridge.

Ahead lush emerald fields on the south side of the valley are flanked by slate quarries and mines. These extend up the lower hills behind Mynydd Mawr and are the reasons for the sprouting up of scores of villages including Nantlle itself, Carmel, Fron and Rhosgadfan. The mines, although extensive, were largely unprofitable and have been redundant for many years. The view backwards across Llyn Nantlle includes the fine northern corries of the Nantlle Ridge with Snowdon in the background. The view was immortalised in a well-known oil painting by Richard Wilson.

Below: Nantlle Ridge from above Craig y Bera.

Above: Craig y Bera from Carn Drws-y-coed.

Cultivated farmland with no legal access has meant that, however enticing it may feel, there are few routes to the ridge from this side. Once you reach Tal-y-sarn, however, things change and many walkers doing the ridge start or finish here before climbing to Craig Cwm Silyn, the highest Nantlle peak, or Garnedd Coch. Craig Cwm Silyn and the peaks in the west are rugged, broad-topped and craggy, but walking east soon brings a change. After dropping steeply down crags to Bwlch Dros Bern the ridge narrows and becomes grassy. The going gets delightfully easy, but with one or two exciting bits, including the steep and jagged arête of Mynydd Drws-y-coed.

Moving around to the south of the Nantlle Ridge you come to Garndolbenmaen, a small village lying to the south of Cwm Pennant. The outlier of the Nantlle Ridge is Craig-y-garn just outside the village. It's just a quick saunter to get to the top, but what a view! Here the full beauty of Cwm Pennant is realised.

The vale has a cultivated pastoral beauty and a shade of velvety green to match any in the Emerald Isle. Here, peaceful country lanes lined with hedgerows wind past farmsteads, woodland copses, lively crystal streams and low hills. On the horizon a horseshoe of shapely mountains shuts out the rest of the world – it could be the 1950s were it not for the occasional sounds of gleaming new Japanese tractors in the fields. To the north is the serrated crest of Mynydd Graig Goch, which was long considered to be only 1998ft high. However, a survey of 2008 revealed it to be two feet higher, and thus it became the latest addition to the Welsh 2000-footers.

On the east side of the valley is the Moel Hebog group of mountains. They're more frumpy than those of Nantlle but still interestingly studded with crags. The lowest of the four, Moel Lefn, is definitely the dominant one with fine cliffs and screes. Like Nantlle, Cwm Pennant was given over to slate and copper mines in past centuries and, also like Nantlle, they didn't prove very profitable for long. In Cwm Ciprwthon, the shoulder of Garnedd Goch, walkers can view the copper mine water wheel, which is remarkably intact except for the wooden buckets and the water leat.

An old tramway, which served the huge quarries at the head of Cwm Pennant, runs the length of the valley to a lonely cwm beneath Mynydd Tal-y-mignedd. It is a wonderful way to explore the beauty and majesty of Cwm Pennant, and can be used for approaches to nearly all the surrounding mountains.

The Moel Hebog range overlooks the Pass of Aberglaslyn, a spectacular rocky gorge with a river as white, as violent and thunderously noisy as any in Wales. Moelddu, the most southerly peak, is often tackled from here and there is a devious way to Moel Hebog too. Most walkers begin in Beddgelert though and climb beneath a line of high cliffs to the cairn on the summit.

The circular route described in most books continues along the ridge over Moel yr Ogof, where there's a cave said to have been used by Welsh Prince Owain Glyndwr, and Moel Lefn. The east side of the Hebog ridge is engulfed by Forestry Commission conifer plantations, which make the approaches dull but relatively speedy. These routes are enlivened by the renewal of the narrow-gauge Welsh Highland Railway. From 2009 steam trains will run regularly from Porthmadog through the Pass of Aberglaslyn and Beddgelert, and continue beneath Snowdon to Caernarfon. It should prove to be a great walkers' train – if they can keep the prices reasonable.

Opposite: Mynydd Tal-y-mignedd's east ridge above Blaen Pennant.

MOEL SMYTHO

Moel Smytho is unremarkable in that it rises to only 1125ft/343m above the waters of the Menai Straits, and as a peak it has no exciting mountain form. It also has cultivated green farm pastures and a scattering of farmhouses high on its slopes and a drab spruce forest to look down on, but Moel Smytho is an otherwise marvellous viewing platform.

From the crags on its heathery summit the northern horizon includes the castle at Caernarfon, the Menai Straits with the flat fields of Anglesey stretching into the coastal mist, to the shapely peaks of the Rivals on the Llyn Peninsula. Southern views start with the rather ugly quarried slopes of Moel Tryfan, but things improve, for rearing up behind these are the impressive northern crags of Moelwyn Mawr backed up by the peaks of Snowdon, with the Glyderau trying to get in on the act over the shoulder of Moel Eilio.

Moel Smytho is a fine first-footer for those wanting to make a day walk of Mynydd Mawr, or as a short walk ideal for lovers of great sunsets or sunrises.

Left: Mynydd Mawr from the summit rocks of Moel Smytho.

Route E1

Waunfawr

A pleasant short walk through woodland and
heath – with wide views

Start: Car park/picnic site just south of
Waunfawr (GR: SH 577584)

Distance: 3 miles/2km

Height gain: 690ft/ 210m

Time: ¾–1 hour

Turn left out of the car park on to the main
road then left again opposite the campsite on
to the country lane climbing up the hillside
towards Rhosgadfan. Leave the lane on
the left for a path signed 'Y Fron 3¼ miles'.
The path, waymarked in places, crosses a
meadow then winds up the hill slopes
through a mix of broad-leaved woodland and
meadow with the odd iron ladder climbing
high, mossy stone walls. After emerging from
the woods the right of way, unclear on the

ground, climbs high pastures. After making a
little nick to the left by a drystone wall, the
route resumes its south-westerly direction. It
passes through several small enclosures and
comes to a gate on the edge of open heather
moor (GR 518581). Turn left beyond the gate
to follow the wallside track towards Moel
Smytho.

At the first junction take the right fork
track, which leads to the walled pastures of
Parc-newydd. From here a peaty path continues up the final heather slopes of the hill to
the rocks on its summit.

Other route options

The route could be made even shorter by taking the track from the summit of the Waunfawr–Rhosgadfan road (GR 515584). There's
also a quick route from the road-end east of
Rhosgadfan (GR 519572).

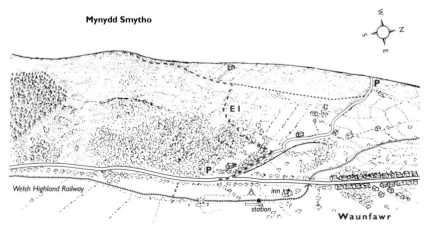

Mynydd Smytho

Welsh Highland Railway

inn

station

Waunfawr

RIDGE ROUTES

Mynydd Mawr

Distance: 2½ miles/4.2km
Height gain: 1380ft/420m
Time: 1½ hours

Follow the path down through heather with Mynydd Mawr dominating the view ahead. After nearing the road-end near Hafod Ruffydd, turn half-left along another path running parallel to the top edge of a large spruce plantation and beneath the quarried sides of Moel Tryfan: occasional red-tipped posts mark the route, which crosses a trial level – this looks like a grassy V-shaped hollow cut through the heather. The path climbing above the western rim of Cwm Du can plainly be seen ahead.

There are several paths that will take you there but to avoid a slight downhill section follow the path with the red-tipped posts to the right to a large isolated crag and towards an old ruin surrounded by a few trees (the ruin is marked 'water works' on the OS Explorer map). On reaching the previously mentioned crag a faint path continues south then arcs left to meet a more prominent route on the heathery saddle between Moel Tryfan and Mynydd Mawr. The path steers a positive course to Mynydd Mawr's north-west spur. Please use the zigzags halfway up to the mine shaft on the spur because the 'straight up' route which has developed in recent years is badly eroded. Keep left of the mine shaft and follow the continuing path by the rim of Cwm Du, whose crags and cliffs can now be seen to perfection. Where the path gives up it's just a matter of maintaining a south-easterly direction to the summit rocks and shelter. For those who like extra guidance when the path fades look out for a cairn on the right, the first of many that will lead to the summit.

Left: The wooded slopes of Moel Smytho from the campsite at Waunfawr.

MOEL TRYFAN

MYNYDD MAWR

Moel Tryfan, the bare hill of the three summits, rises from the slate rooftops of little Rhosgadfan. The three summits are in fact rocky tors that jut out from the surrounding moorland dome. Unfortunately over many centuries the axes and gunpowder of the quarrymen have savaged Moel Tryfan's heart. These quarries are probably some of the oldest in North Wales. Many historians believe the slate was used by the Romans for their fort at Segontium (Caernarfon).

Today, great flooded caverns, old tramways, artificial cliffs and huge spoil heaps litter Moel Tryfan's hill slopes. The tramways and old miners' tracks from Y Fron and Rhosgadfan offer quick ways on to the hill; fascinating ways to those who love industrial history, but for the rest of us they're a bit of an eyesore, a place to be passed on the way to Mynydd Mawr.

Mynydd Mawr, the big mountain, is one of my favourite peaks in Snowdonia. It has many different facets to its character: secluded corners, subtle mountainscapes where heather crowds understated broken crags, and great climbing buttresses – castles of rock. The mountain's summit is scattered with boulders and has a few wind shelters, hollowed out from Iron Age burial cairns. Its exposed position only a few miles from the Irish Sea can make these quite a comforting refuge at times. The view from Mynydd Mawr's summit is dominated by the coast, which can be traced from the Llyn Peninsula and Anglesey through to Caernarfon, where the castle stands out from the waters of the Menai Straits.

Seen from the north, Mynydd Mawr is dome-shaped, but its heather slopes are gouged by a fine shady corrie aptly named Cwm Du. The corrie is ringed by cliffs rather like those of Clogwyn Du'r Arddu on Snowdon, although I will not pretend the scene is quite as spectacular. Drive south along the road to Beddgelert and you come to Llyn Cwellyn. Through the shoreline trees the great crags of Castell

Opposite: The rocky east face of Mynydd Mawr is reflected in the calm waters of Llyn Cwellyn.

Cidwm guard another secret corrie, that of Cwm Planwydd. The inner world of the 'castle' is a dark landscape of screes and waterfalls. Foel Rudd, which lies to the left, is a satellite of Mynydd Mawr, a fine pyramid of a mountain, grassy, but grazed with scree and topped with just enough crags to make it interesting.

Mynydd Mawr's finest face is saved for the head of the Nantlle Valley. Here, the pinnacled buttresses of Craig y Bera, popular with climbers and scramblers alike, are punctuated by scree gulleys, which tumble down to the green fields of Drws-y-coed.

Route E2
Rhyd Ddu and Foel Rudd

The classic route: steep but engrossing
Start: Rhyd Ddu station (GR: SH 572526)
Distance: 3 miles/5km
Height gain: 1830ft/ 560m
Time: 2 hours

Turn right out of the car park and walk through the village, passing the Cwellyn Arms before turning left up the Nantlle B-road. Turn right along the forestry road just beyond the last houses. Where a path from Planwydd crosses the track turn left along it to climb towards the ridge. The conifers were felled in 2008 and the scene is more airy than it normally would be. A stile gives access to a low ridge at Bwlch y Moch (pass of the pigs).

Turn right here and follow a faint path along the forest's top edge towards the boulder-fringed grass peak of Foel Rudd. Behind you the grass ridges of Moel Eilio and Foel

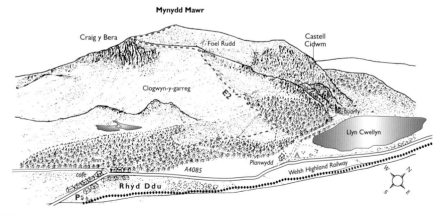

Above: Descending from Foel Rudd to Rhyd Ddu with Snowdon on the left.

Goch hem in the waters of Llyn Cwellyn. There may be the sound of the little steam trains of the Welsh Highland Railway, which runs through the valley between Caernarfon and Beddgelert.

The going gets much tougher as the forest is left behind. A narrow path zigzags up grass slopes before arcing right to Foel Rudd's cairned summit. Now easier, it rounds the rim of Cwm Planwydd, a desolate featureless corrie of heather and grass, then flirts with the top edge of the pinnacled buttresses of Craig y Bera. From this vantage walkers get to look down the spectacular gulleys and crags with an added bonus – stupendous views of the precipitous north face of Carn Drws-y-coed (Y Garn).

Beyond Craig y Bera the path curves right to make an easy climb to the cairns on Mynydd Mawr's summit.

Route E3
Bryn Gloch, Cwm Ddu and the North Ridge

A complex, rather dull start

Start: Betws Garmon (Bryn Gloch)
  (GR: SH 535575)
Distance: 2¾ miles/4.5km
Height gain: 1890ft/575m
Time: 2 hours

Go through the gate to the left of the Bryn Gloch campsite entrance following a well waymarked path. Turn left along a campsite road then right to cross the bridge over the Welsh Highland Railway. Turn left along the next campsite road, then right following more waymarks leading to a footbridge over the Afon Gwyfai. A cross-field path now heads towards the whitewashed house on the right-hand side of a farming hamlet. After going through a kissing gate at the far end of the field, turn left on a farm lane, passing the other houses and turning right past Tyddyn Bach. A grass track heads south-westwards past a small pool and comes to a gate.

Through the gate climb on a narrow grass path through newly planted woods to reach a mature conifer forest. A path of pine needles continues through the woods to emerge in scrubland on the plantation's southern perimeter. A narrow, winding path now climbs through scrub. It meets and follows the heather- and gorse-garnished hollow of a small stream to reach a kissing gate on the edge of open fell.

Turn left alongside the wall. Where the wall turns left watch out for a path raking up the heather slopes ahead. This takes the route up to the rim of Cwm Du. To help reduce the effects of path erosion, follow the short zigzag section on the approach to a huge mine shaft. Keep the mine to the right and continue with the path to the cliff edge of Craig Cwm Du. This leads entertainingly up the mountainside. Above the cwm the path fades but maintain direction on short-cropped grass and mosses to reach the slaty top and its wind-shelters.

Below: The cliffs of Cwm Ddu.

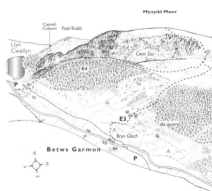

Route E4
Betws Garmon and Cwm Du

An interesting route through woodland,
*   heather slopes and above lonely cliffs*
Start: Lay-by at Betws Garmon
    (GR: SH 547563)
Distance: 2½ miles/4.3km
Height gain: 2000ft/610m
Time: 1½ hours

From the lay-by turn left down the road (in the Caernarfon direction) for a few paces before turning left again along a signed stony track, which crosses a stone bridge over the waterfalls of the Afon Gwy before turning left to the cottage of Pen y Gaer. Another footpath signpost points uphill and a clear path climbs towards the larchwoods ahead. The early and very attractive scenes are dominated by the rugged cone of Craig Cwmbychan and Llyn Cwellyn beyond. The path through the woods is a delightful if slightly slippery one, with a surface of larch needles, tangled tree roots and slatey stones.

The path emerges at a step stile in the fence at the top end of the woods, now dominated by pine and spruce. Ahead and left the rocks of Craig Cwmbychan and the immense cliffs of Craig Cwm Du watch over a sombre cwm.

The path maintains direction to some sheepfolds. Go over a ladder stile in a wall beyond them before angling right on a narrow path up heather slopes. The wall climbs too and rejoins the route higher up the hillside. As the path enters a marshy hollow watch out for a narrow path on the left that climbs the lower slopes of Mynydd Mawr. It joins a wide path that comes in from the right and climbs to reach a fenced-off mine shaft. The required path passes to the left and climbs along the clifftops of Craig Cwm Du before fading on the grass and moss slopes. Maintain a south-easterly direction to the slatey summit.

Below: Nantlle Ridge seen across the slopes of Mynydd Mawr.

Route E5

Y Fron and the North Ridge

The easiest but least spectacular way

Start: Y Fron (parking at end of public road)
   (GR: SH 512548)

Distance: 2¼ miles/3.6km

Height gain: 1410ft/430m

Time: 1½ hours

From the top of the public road just above the village head ENE along the tarred mine road passing derelict buildings and the gaping chasm marked on the map as Fron. After passing between spoil heaps the tarred road descends to a gate, beyond which it becomes an unsurfaced lane that takes the route through high pastures to the open moor to the north of Llyn Ffynhonnau. Mynydd Mawr, from here a domed hill of heather and grass, is straight ahead while the view is enlivened by the cwms and crags of the Nantlle mountains on the right.

Ignore the right fork to the lake but go straight ahead, passing a small, cultivated pasture before climbing to the watershed.

Take the right fork here. This climbs Mynydd Mawr's north ridge, joining Routes E2–4 at a cairn at GR 531556 and following them past the fenced-off mine shaft and alongside Cwm Du's top edge before striking south-east to the summit.

Other route options

There are numerous ways on to the mountain from villages and high lanes in the Rhosgadfan and Y Fron areas. Walkers could take in the quarry-scarred subsidiary peak of Moel Tryfan although I think there is little reward in doing so. Access problems in the Nantlle Valley prevent any approaches from there. A route begins from the road at Betws y Garmon near Tyddyn Syr Huw (Huw is incorrectly spelled 'Hugh' on Explorer maps) and climbs through forest before heading south across heather ridge to join the Bryn Gloch route (Route E5). Another possible route is by way of Castell Cidwm. This would involve taking the forestry track by Llyn Cwellyn to its end, rounding the fence by the stony shoreline, and following a narrow path to the

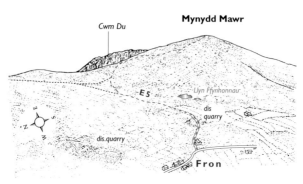

Mynydd Mawr

mouth of the cwm where a primitive stile gets you across the wall.

A very rough and sporty path scrambles up to the right of some waterfalls and leaves you in the wild environs of Cwm Planwydd. By following the stream deep into the cwm you could either go left on to the slopes of Foel Rudd or double back on a rough overgrown path to the heather of Mynydd Mawr's north-east ridge. This would be a bad choice for a descent route, as the path by the falls could be quite testing to all but the seasoned and sure-footed mountain walker.

RIDGE ROUTES

Moel Tryfan

I will not attempt to include a detailed direct ridge route to this peak as there are massive areas of old quarries and spoil heaps to mar acceptable progress. Those who want to bag Moel Tryfan are better advised to approach using mine tracks and tramways from Y Fron or Rhosgadfan.

Moel Smytho

Distance: 2½ miles/4.2km
Height gain: 200ft/61m
Time: 1¼ hours

Descend north-westwards over stony ground following a line of cairns. On reaching the last of these turn NNW (no path on the ground at first) to pick up a good path by around the rim of the Cwm Du cliffs. After passing a huge mine shaft the path zigzags across a heathery spur to reach a saddle of land separating Mynydd Mawr from Moel Tryfan.

Ignore tracks to the left, as they'll leave the ridge for the village of Y Fron. Instead, go straight ahead (NW) on a track aiming for the ruins marked on the map as water works – they're surrounded by a few gaunt trees. On nearing these turn right on a path waymarked with red-topped posts. This heads north-east towards a large conifer plantation before heading north towards the heath of Moel Smytho.

The path nears a road-end between the farms of Tan Gaer and Hafod Ruffydd before climbing north to the crags on Moel Smytho's summit.

Left: Passing Llyn Ffynhonnau with Mynydd Mawr ahead.

CARN DRWS-Y-COED (Y GARN)

This splendid peak, shown simply as Y Garn (the cairn) on all maps, is referred to in George Borrow's *Wild Wales* as Carn Drws-y-coed and by Poucher in *The Welsh Peaks* as Y Garn II. I prefer Carn Drws-y-coed: it is much more likely to be historically accurate and it's certainly more fitting because, geologically speaking, for all its splendour, the peak is little more than Mynydd Drws-y-coed's northern end.

Carn Drws-y-coed is the abrupt northern end of the Nantlle Ridge: a delectable grass ridge plummeting in angular slopes of broken cliffs and scree to the rugged moorland col of Bwlchgylfin at the head of the Nantlle Valley and west of Snowdon. Three cairns crown the summit. The two large ones are ancient, although they have been hollowed out to form wind-shelters, while the third, a small chaotic pile of stones, marks the highest point. The view down and across the gullies are quite spectacular and include the magnificent pinnacled climbing buttresses of Craig y Bera. Looking the other way, most walkers will see the upthrusting rock castles of Mynydd Drws-y-coed and be lured to venture forth in earnest.

Left: Carn Drws-y-coed showing the north-west ridge.

Wandering from the pass into the Nantlle Valley past the mysterious Llyn Dywarchen and the hamlet of Drws-y-coed, Carn Drws-y-coed's north-west ridge comes into view. It ends defiantly in one shapely rocky tor known as Clogwyn y Barcut, the cliff of the kite (the raptor kind, not the sort you fly). The cliffs, like much of the valley beyond, are littered with the relics of old mines as is the shady northern cwm to its right. This last-mentioned place feels enchantingly eerie and isolated and offers some of the best routes to the ridges.

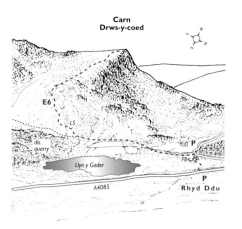

Route E6
Rhyd Ddu and the East Spur
An arduous but quick route
Start: Rhyd Ddu car park (GR: SH 572527)
Distance: 1½ miles/2.4km
Height gain: 1480ft/450m
Time: 1¼ hours

Go through a kissing gate on the far side of the road. A path of slate flags traverses a wet field. On reaching the stream (Afon Gwyrfai) by a cottage it turns left, crosses a bridge, the left one of two. A farm track now takes the route to an elbow in the Nantlle B-road.

Double-back through the gate on a bridle-way track and follow it south-westwards across fields. After turning right just south of Drwsycoed Uchaf Farm, the bridleway resumes its south-westerly course across rough pastureland west of Llyn y Gader with the grass slopes of Carn Drws-y-coed rearing up to the right. A narrow path forks right from the main bridleway and, beyond a ladder stile, toils up steep grassy hill slopes. Magnificent retrospective views over Llyn y Gader to Snowdon and its satellites make the efforts of the day worthwhile.

The gradient eases just after the path reaches the northern cliff-edge. On reaching the rim of the ridge you are confronted with bouldery terrain but much of this can be avoided on the left. A ladder stile in the ridge wall gives access to this summit and its three cairns.

Opposite: Overlooking one of Drwys-y-coed's gullies to Snowdon.

Route E7
Drws-y-coed and the North-West Ridge

A tough but fascinating route for the
connoisseur

Start: Lay-by on the B4418 road at Drws-y-
coed (GR: SH 537533)
Distance: 1½ miles/2.5km
Height gain: 1640ft/500m
Time: 1½ hours

At the entrance to Tal-y-mignedd Farm and campsite road, go through the gate on the left just beyond the cattle grid and skirt the right-hand side of a rushy field beneath the lower crags of Clogwyn y Barcut. Watch out for a ladder stile in a short length of wall where it abuts a crag. This is the key to the route. Climb up grassy banks to reach it. Climb right beyond the stile – you'll come across a series of wooden waymarking posts aiding route-finding along a line following the path marked on the OS Explorer with faint black dashes. The path soon follows the course of an old rush-filled water leat that zigzags up the hillside with the crags of Clogwyn y Bar-cut rearing up to the left. There are two dips in the route as it reaches a ruined farmstead where a track comes in from the right. The place is not shown on maps but it's placed at approximately GR 541530.

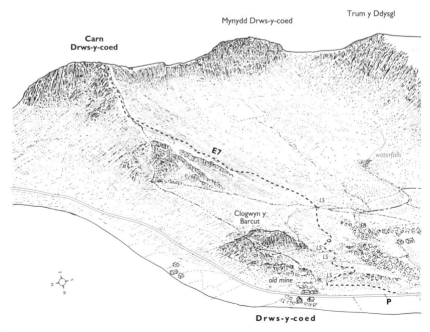

Beyond the ruins head up the cwm on grassy terrain, staying right of the Barcut ridge. Carn Drws-y-coed, Mynydd Drws-y-coed and Trum y Ddysgl now form the horizon. This brings the route up to a ladder stile in a wall at GR 543528. Now the climb to the ridge on the left begins. Follow the grassy line beneath the crags on the left and keep a south-easterly direction all the way to the ridge. Follow the little path on the left side of the tumble-down wall. This feeds through the crags on to a mainly grassy ridge top, all the way to Carn Drws-y-coed's summit rim, where it comes out by one of the huge hollowed-out cairns just south of the true summit.

Below: On the north-west ridge of Carn Drws-y-coed, with Craig y Bera behind.

RIDGE ROUTE

Mynydd Drws-y-coed

Distance: ½ mile/0.85km
Height gain: 295ft/90m
Time: ½ hour

Follow the wall along a narrowing grassy ridge with the crags of Clogwyn Marchnad falling away to the right. The walk soon becomes more craggy underfoot and as the slopes steepen both sides. After rounding a deep gulley the winding route clambers up a boulder-strewn, craggy arête towards the cone that is Mynydd Drws-y-coed. You'll need to use your hands in places but in clement conditions experienced mountain walkers will find the route exhilarating rather than daunting. The difficulties are short-lived and the terrain of the summit turns to grass once more.

129

Above: Mynydd Drws-y-coed and Trum y Ddysgl from the north.

Seen from the ridge Mynydd Drws-y-coed, which means mountain of the forest gap, is an impressive cone of splintered crag, and yet it hardly justifies its mountain status. The peak throws out no ridges and it's not as high as neighbour Trum y Ddysgl, which does. In his fine book *On Foot in North Wales*, Patrick Monkhouse refers to Trum y Ddysgl as the real summit of Mynydd Drws-y-coed.

The climb up the spiky eastern arête is one of the most invigorating sections of the Nantlle Ridge. The view onwards to the triangular crag face of Trum y Ddysgl maintains that mood. While the crags of Clogwyn Marchnad, which plummet down to a high corrie above the Nantlle Valley, give the west face dramatic appeal, the east face, although steep, is grassy and subdued by the spread of Beddgelert Forest's spruce trees.

I haven't listed any routes to Mynydd Drws-y-coed as they would nearly all have to visit one of the neighbouring peaks first. If you were to insist on one try following Route E9 from Drws-y-coed to the waterfalls at GR 543527, then climb directly to the col between Trum y Ddysgl and Mynydd Drws-y-coed on a steep grassy rake. Turn left at the col following the rocky ridge to the summit.

RIDGE ROUTES

Carn Drws-y-coed

Distance: ½ mile/0.85km
Height gain: 100ft/30m
Time: ½ hour

Descend with great care down the winding, rocky route, which in general stays slightly on the right side of the arête. After going round a deep gulley the path follows a drystone wall over a widening grassy ridge to Carn Drws-y-coed's summit.

Trum y Ddysgl

Distance: ⅓ mile/0.5km
Height gain: 230ft/70m
Time: 20 minutes

There's a descent among crags down to the col followed by easier terrain over a smooth grass ridge to the summit of Trum y Ddysgl, whose great cliffs and screes present a spectacular onward view.

Above: Looking across Bwlch-y-Ddwy-elor to Trum y Ddysgl.

This highest peak of the northern part of the Nantlle Ridge is perhaps the finest too, with its abrupt eastern face forming a triangle of precipitous rock and scree. The name Trum y Ddysgl, the ridge of the dish, refers to the northern ridge that encloses a remote corrie high above the Nantlle Valley. To the west of this ridge in the equally remote Cwmyffynnon lies a tiny tarn, Llyn Cwmyffynnon.

The southern slopes, like Mynydd Drws-y-coed, are steep and grassy, with the conifers of Beddgelert Forest masking the huge drop into Cwm Du. Trum y Ddysgl's south ridge, which it shares with Mynydd Tal-y-mignedd, descends to the pass of Bwlch-y-Ddwy-elor and divides the conifers of Cwm Du from the extensive mines and quarries of Cwm Pennant. The bridleway linking Rhyd Ddu and Cwm Pennant is an ancient byway used by miners and ancient traders alike, and now serves walkers well.

Above: Llyn Cwmyffynnon.

Route E8
Rhyd Ddu and Bwlch-y-Ddwy-elor

*A dull start; improves once you get to
    the pass*
Start: Rhyd Ddu car park (GR: SH 572527)
Distance: 3¼ miles/5.2km
Height gain: 1820ft/555m
Time: 1½–2 hours

The route begins through a kissing gate on the far side of the road, where a path of slate flags traverses a wet field. On reaching the stream (Afon Gwyrfai) by a cottage it turns left, crosses the left of two bridges, before continuing on a farm track, which swings right to reach an elbow in the Nantlle road. Here a bridleway doubles back south-westwards across rough pasture After turning right just south of Drwsycoed Uchaf Farm, the bridleway resumes its south-westerly course across rough pastureland west of Llyn y Gader and climbs gradually with the grass slopes of Carn Drws-y-coed rearing up to the right.

The crossing of Cwm Marchnad's stream can be awkward after periods of heavy rain but usually it's straightforward. The path enters the spruce plantations of Beddgelert Forest beyond a gate. A narrow path of peat and stones climbs to cross a forest road before coming to a second one. Here, the forestry road wanted is staggered slightly to the left over a concrete bridge and signed to Cwm Du. It comes to a T-junction where you turn right before leaving the roads for a signed path on the left. This climbs past an old mine before coming to open fell at the edge of the forest. Here the path traverses craggy heather moor to reach a gate on the pass of Bwlch-y-Ddwy-elor where you look down into Cwm Pennant.

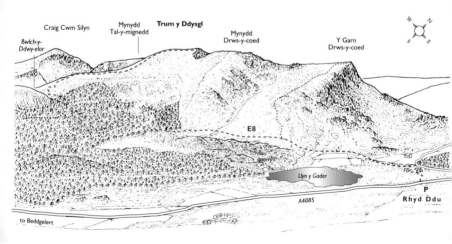

Go though the gate before climbing right up hill slopes with a wall to the right. The initial steep section has convenient steps that have been worn through the grass. Eventually a defined ridge develops, one with a fine view into Cwm Dwyfor, the south faces of Mynydd Tal-y-mignedd and the serrated rock ridge of Craig Cwm Silyn. Halfway up, the path takes to the right side of the ridge overlooking Beddgelert forest, but in the upper section it follows the broad crest to arrive at the main ridge where a right turn on grass leads steadily up to Trum y Ddysgl's summit.

Below: Beddgelert Forest and Trum y Ddysgl's East Ridge.

Route E9
Blaen Pennant and the South Ridge

Fascinating quarry routes to the ridge
Start: End of Cwm Pennant road
 (GR: SH 540492)
Distance: 1¼ miles/2.8km
Height gain: 1900ft/580m
Time: 2 hours

From the car park go over the ladder stile across the bridge over a stream, then turn right on a path climbing rough grassy slopes to the ruins of Cwm-trwsgl and its surrounding quarry slag heaps. Here the path joins an old quarry tramway and follows it right to the ruined dressing sheds of the Prince of Wales Quarries.

Now head up the cwm on a grassy incline taking the route past the terraces of slag, with the small reservoir and the impressive cliffs of Moel Lefn to the right. Carry on through the pass of Bwlch-y-Ddwy-elor.

On reaching the gate at the top of the pass you now follow the same route as E8 by turning left on Trum y Ddysgl's grassy south ridge with a wall to the right. Halfway up, the path takes to the right side of the ridge overlooking Beddgelert forest, but returns to the broad crest to arrive at the main ridge just a short way SSW of Trum y Ddysgl's summit.

Opposite: Trum y Ddysgl's south ridge.

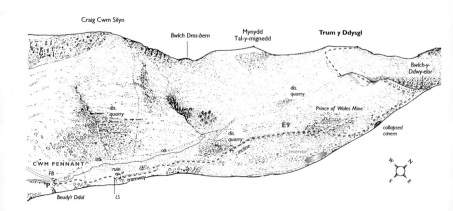

Route E10

Drws-y-coed and the North Ridge

Fine route on steep, seldom-trod ridge

Start: Drws-y-coed (GR: SH 537533)

Distance: 1¼ miles/2.8km

Height gain: 1900ft/580m

Time: 2 hours

At the entrance to Tal-y-mignedd farm and campsite road, go through the gate on the left just beyond the cattle grid and skirt the right-hand side of a rushy field beneath the lower crags of Clogwyn y Barcut. Climb up grassy banks to reach a ladder stile in a short stretch of wall punctuating the fence above. Climb right, guided by a series of wooden waymarking posts, to trace the path marked on OS Explorers with faint black dashes. The path soon follows the course of an old rush-filled water leat in long zigzags up the hillside with the crags of Clogwyn y Barcut rearing up to the left. The path descends slightly to a ruined farmstead (not shown on maps but about GR 541530).

Beyond the ruins head up the cwm on grassy terrain, staying right of the Barcut ridge. Carn Drws-y-coed, Mynydd Drws-y-coed and Trum y Ddysgl now form the horizon. This brings the route up to a ladder stile in a wall at GR 543528.

Turn right here along the line of a rush-filled water leat, which cuts across the hillside. Follow it across the first stream, the Afon Tal-y-mignedd, then climb grass slopes on the left towards some waterfalls at GR 542526. Beyond these you'll join an old grass track. Turn right along it to ford the stream above the falls and head for the Trum y Ddysgl ridge. Climb to the ridge on an easy line just left of the end-of-ridge crags, then gird your loins for the climb ahead. This is steep at first, but the going eases as all heather turns to grass. With splendid views over Craig Trum y Ddysgl to those of Mynydd Drws-y-coed and Carn Drws-y-coed, this is an exhilarating part of the route and all too soon you arrive at the summit.

Opposite: Mynydd Tal-y-mignedd from the nick in Trum y Ddysgl's ridge.

Drws-y-coed

Other route options

A variation of Route E9 would be to leave it above the waterfalls and head up the cwm. A steep grassy rake leads up to the col between Trum y Ddysgl and Mynydd Drws-y-coed. A right turn up the grass ridge to Trum y Ddysgl's summit would follow.

RIDGE ROUTES

Mynydd Drws-y-coed
Distance: ⅓ mile/0.5km
Height gain: 165ft/50m
Time: 20 minutes

A fine grass ridge descends to a col beyond which the path climbs among crags to the grassy summit of Mynydd Drws-y-coed.

Mynydd Tal-y-mignedd
Distance: ⅔ mile/1.1km
Height gain: 345ft/105m
Time: ½ hour

Descend the easy grass slopes to the col beyond which there's a narrow eroded section with a landslip. A good path negotiates this and continues on *terra firma* to a lovely smooth grass ridge that climbs to the column on Mynydd Tal-y-mignedd's summit.

MYNYDD
TAL-Y-MIGNEDD

Although lower than both its neighbours, Mynydd Tal-y-mignedd has a serene form, with graceful ridges and spurs, scraped with a little crag and topped by an impressive chimney-like stone column, which was erected to celebrate Queen Victoria's Jubilee.

The mountain shares its south ridge with Trum y Ddysgl but also has a north ridge declining gently into high corries above the Nantlle Valley and from that northern ridge a steep craggy spur enclosing a tight, craggy and sombre corrie skulking between Mynydd Tal-y-mignedd and Trum y Ddysgl. Deep within the corrie lies a small tarn, Llyn Cwmyffynnon. Seen from here, the mountain has a powerful and menacing presence.

From Cwm Pennant, Mynydd Tal-y-mignedd has a saddleback shape with a little crag and scree breaking through the grasses and heather. The steep slopes plunge into Cwm Dwyfor at the head of Cwm Pennant where the last remnants of old mines crumble into the grasses and a miners' tramway, sunken into marshland in places, sidles into the vale.

The main ridge declines to Bwlch Drosbern, where an old drovers' route, now completely lost on the ground, used to cut across from Cwm Pennant to Nantlle.

Opposite: Mynydd Tal-y-mignedd across the Nantlle Valley.

Route E11

Blaen Pennant

*A tough but entertaining route on old mine
    tracks and a steep, grassy spur*

Start: End of Cwm Pennant road
    (GR: SH 540492)

Distance: 2 miles/3.2km

Height gain: 1770ft/540m

Time: 1½–2 hours

From the car park at the end of the road, take the signed path over the ladder stile and cross the bridge over a stream. Beyond a step stile a clear path develops, highlighted by way-marking posts. It curves to the right and climbs the hillside towards some ruins, partially obscured by a large sycamore tree. On reaching those ruins go over a ladder stile, climb a grassy bank and turn left over an area of slate waste. You're on the course of an old tramway running the length of the valley but it doesn't manifest itself hereabouts. A narrow path weaves between gorse bushes parallel to a slate fence. The tramway becomes clear again and continues towards the head of the valley. Beyond a boggy stretch it swings to the left, passes another ruin and heads towards the grassy slopes at the foot of Mynydd Tal-y-mignedd and the spiky arête of Craig Cwm Silyn. The view is dominated by a deep rocky gorge cut by the Ceunant yr Allt stream.

On nearing a drystone wall at the foot of Cwm Dwyfor the tramway turns right up an incline. At the top of this leave it for the start

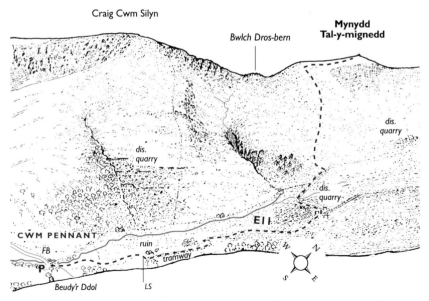

of the climb to Mynydd Tal-y-mignedd. The south-east ridge is ill-defined at this stage and it is better to zigzag up the pathless grassy slopes. There's an old grassed-over wall that looks like a path but this isn't helpful – it's too steep. Gradually a ridge route does become clear and a very narrow path develops, taking the route up it and on to the main Nantlle Ridge to the south of Mynydd Tal-y-mignedd's summit. Head north towards the tall Jubilee Monument, which lies just offset, to the north of the main ridge.

Other route options

A rather circuitous route would start from the hamlet of Drws-y-coed and follow Route E7 to the water leat beyond the stile at GR 543528. The water leat would then need to be followed westwards, cutting across grassland beneath the Trum y Ddysgl ridge to the foot of Mynydd Tal-y-mignedd's north ridge. Beyond a stream crossing around GR 535523 climb to the mines before rounding the cliffs on the right to gain the ridge. A ridge wall will guide the route to the summit obelisk.

RIDGE ROUTES

Trum y Ddysgl

Distance: ⅔ mile/1.1km
Height gain: 200ft/60m
Time: ½ hour

Descend the grass slopes with steep craggy drops to Cwmyffynnon on the left and to Cwm Dwyfor on the right. The path is joined by a narrow path that has climbed a grassy ridge from Bwlch-y-Ddwy-elor. From here there's a short climb to Trum y Ddysgl's summit, which comes to an abrupt end on the cliff edge of Craig Trum y Ddysgl.

Craig Cwm Silyn

Distance: 1 mile/1.7km
Height gain: 755ft/230m
Time: ¾–1 hour

A grassy ridge descends steadily SSW then WSW to reach the deep pass of Bwlch Drosbern. Ahead, the rocky arête above Craig Pennant can be tackled head on in an entertaining scramble but it might be more prudent to take the easier path, which angles right to skirt the steepest crags before continuing on the bouldery terrain of a broad ridge which culminates on an equally bouldery summit plateau. A cairned route leads to the summit cairn.

Left: The Jubilee Monument.

CRAIG CWM SILYN

Craig Cwm Silyn, which dominates the scenery in the central regions of the Nantlle Ridge, is the highest of that group and second only to Moel Hebog in the Eifionydd.

Walkers doing the Nantlle Ridge from Rhyd Ddu will have noticed a change as they climb on to the mountain's rugged slopes from Bwlch y Dros-bern. The narrow grassy inter-connecting ridges of the northern end have gone, replaced by this broad, boulder-heaped summit. The change is due to vol-canic activity and the rocks are rhyolitic tuffs and lava flows. This is explained in more detail in the description of Craig y Garn. Heather has taken hold In the cwms, smoth-ering the boulders and peat beneath its tan-gled stems. But this is not a moorland scene, for cliffs predominate on both sides of the high slopes. Craig Cwm Pennant, a serrated triangle of crags, towers above Bwlch y Dros-bern.

The mountain's pride, however, lies on the north side, above the three lakes of Cwm Silyn. Craig yr Ogof and the Great Slab have provided climbers with excellent rock choices from the days of the pioneers such as Menlove Evans and Colin Kirkus. The cliffs of Craig Cwm Silyn were also the scene of a

Left: Cwm Silyn and Craig Cwm Silyn.

145

fatal wartime air crash. In November 1942, quarrymen who were working in the vicinity of the cwm heard the sound of a low-flying aeroplane, then an almighty bang as it hit the cliffs. Rescue teams were unable to locate the wreck of the RAF Hawker Henley and returned to the valley as darkness fell. The next day, locals found first the tail-plane near the bottom of the Great Slab, then the fuselage wedged in a groove high on Craig yr Ogof. After the wreck was cleared the engine was rolled into the top lake, where in all probability it still lies.

In times gone by, drovers straddled the high pass of Bwlch y Dros-bern to the north of Craig Cwm Silyn on their way from the Nantlle Valley into Cwm Pennant before continuing to the markets of England. Unfortunately for modern walkers, only small traces of their route are evident today but, in all but clement weather, they can imagine the awe-inspiring sight of those drovers struggling to drive cattle in such a harsh environment.

Route E12
Tanyrallt and Llynnau Cwm Silyn

A classic route with a long preamble
Start: Talysarn (see note below)
Distance: 4½ miles/7.2km
Height gain: 2200ft/670m
Time: 2½ hours

Note: Although many guidebooks say that there is parking through the gate at the beginning of the Cwm Silyn cart track at GR 495511 and cars can usually be seen here, there have been quite a lot of reported break-ins. An alternative is to park the car at Talysarn – there's a handy car park at GR 488529 just off the B-road as it bends to cross the Afon Llyfni – or catch the No. 80 bus there which runs from Caernarfon via Penygroes

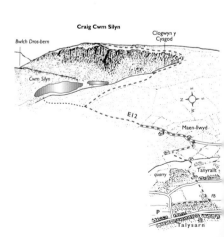

Opposite: Craig Cwm Silyn's fine climbing slabs.

146

For the extended walk, follow the B-road southwards to the bridge over the Afon Llyfni. Take the footpath on the right. This follows the river's north bank. Go over a footbridge before following the path climbing south to Tanyrallt, where an impressive old chapel has been turned into an outdoor centre.

A stony quarry road to the left of the centre climbs the hillside ahead. Leave the track at the foot of the quarry workings to go right, through a kissing gate, beyond which another track passes between slag heaps. After a short way this track is abandoned for a narrow path on the left, which climbs parallel to the road you left. It climbs high pastures alongside a drystone wall and passes the whitewashed cottage of Fron-oleu, where an arrow highlights the change to the right side of the wall. On reaching the farmhouse of Glangors, turn right along the drive and follow it out to a narrow lane, then turn left to its terminus.

The mountain walk proper begins at the road-end at Maen-llwyd (GR 495511). Here a cart track leads across the shoulder of the mountainside. The cliffs of Craig Cwm Silyn are peeping over its grassy north-west ridge but the lakes lie hidden until the last moment. Where the track divides take the right fork through a gate in the drystone wall. Beyond a gate in the top wall, a narrower path zigzags uphill and flirts with the cliffs of Clogwyn y Cysgod.

The lakes are now seen to good advantage, with the mighty Cwm Silyn slab and Craig yr Ogof dominating the shoreline. The path arcs left around the rim of the cwm giving airy views of the cliffs. Beyond a step stile in a broken-down fence, the path makes for the ridge proper. Glimpses into the wide Pennant Valley include Moel Hebog, but from here it is overshadowed by the lower but spectacularly craggy Moel Lefn. After straddling two bouldery tops the path comes to the highest point marked by a wind shelter. The views onwards to the ridges of Mynydd Tal-y-mignedd and Trim y Ddysgl are made all the more spectacular by the cavernous drop to Bwlch Dros-bach.

Route E13

Blaen y Pennant

A tough but stunningly beautiful route

Start: End of Cwm Pennant Road
    (GR SH 540492)

Distance: 2⅓ miles/3.7km

Height gain: 2070ft/630m

Time: 2 hours

From the Blaen Pennant car park at the end of the road, a signed path over the ladder stile crosses a bridge over a stream before curving right on a clear path, highlighted by way-marking posts. It climbs grass hill slopes towards some ruins partially hidden by a large sycamore tree. A ladder stile by the ruins gives access to the course of an old tramway, obscured hereabouts by areas of slate waste. Turn left on a narrow path that weaves between gorse bushes parallel to a slate fence. The tramway soon becomes clear and continues towards the head of the valley.

Beyond a boggy stretch it swings to the left, passes another ruin and heads towards a dry-stone wall at the foot of the grassy slopes of Mynydd Tal-y-mignedd and Craig Cwm Silyn. Leave the tramway as it inclines half-right and pass through a gap in the crumbling wall. Angle left up pathless grass slopes keeping clear of the deep rocky gorge of the Ceunant yr Allt stream. The ground levels out as you enter a lonely cwm separating Craig Cwm Silyn and Mynydd Tal-y-mignedd. Ahead, the buttresses and serrated arête of Craig Pennant tower above the pass of Bwlch Dros-bern.

Follow the stream through the cwm until the ground steepens again. The slopes are slightly easier if you angle left then turn right beneath the screes below Craig Pennant. On reaching the pass take the little path skirting the craggy crest on the right-hand side. It soon slants back to a broad rocky ridge before coming to the equally rocky summit.

Other route options

It is feasible to climb from Braich-y-Dinas into Cwm Braich-y-ddinas before climbing on to the broad spur on the right. I did note that the access land by the farm was disputed in the CROW consultation process, so you might not be popular.

Craig Cwm Silyn

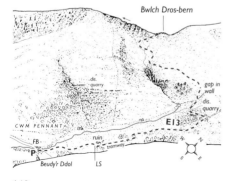

Opposite: The top of the path descending to Bwlch Dros-bern.

RIDGE ROUTES

Mynydd Tal-y-mignedd
Distance: 1 mile/1.7km
Height gain: 490ft/150m
Time: ¼–1 hour

Descend the broad, bouldery north-east ridge and keep left on a path to avoid the most severe of the lower crags. The pass of Bwlch Dros-bern is grassy, as is the succeeding ridge climbing steadily to the column on the summit of Mynydd Tal-y-mignedd.

Garnedd-goch
Distance: 1 mile/1.7km
Height gain: 115ft/35m
Time: ½ hour

Head west across bouldery ground at first. After passing two subsidiary tops, grass takes root. Beyond a step stile in a fence ignore the path arcing right as it's the descent path into Cwm Silyn. Instead, stay with the fence then the ridge wall to reach what has from a distance looked like a stone man, but is in fact quite an ordinary summit cairn.

GARNEDD-GOCH

Garnedd-goch, which means the red cairns, is the penultimate 2000-foot peak in the Nantlle Ridge. It's almost an extension of Craig Cwm Silyn but, unlike Craig Cwm Silyn, it's a little bit more moorland than mountain, a little more domed than peaked, and with a more confusing, less defined ridge. The summit is bouldery, and when seen form the north exhibits a little stone man – on close inspection this becomes a quite unremarkable wallside cairn.

Garnedd-goch's southern scree slopes descend precipitously to a deep, narrow pass between the reservoir-filled Cwm Dulyn in the west and the wild corrie of Cwm Ciprwth in the east. The gentle eastern slopes are cloaked with thick heather and scattered with boulder and rocky knolls – such a contrast to the verdant pastures of Cwm Pennant below. The north-eastern slopes above Cwm Dulyn and the fields of Nebo are bleak and largely featureless, with heather and rough grassland dominant. Only on the north-west side, where the crags of Clogwyn y Cysgod curve around Llynnau Cwm Silyn, does Garnedd-goch offer a little excitement.

Opposite: Mine wheel, Cwm Ciprwth.

Route E14
Cors-y-llyn and Cwm Dulyn

An uneventful but easy way on to the Nantlle Ridge

Start: Roadside parking on Ffordd Cors-y-llyn east of Nebo (GR: SH 490505)

Distance: 2 miles/3km

Height gain: 1310ft/400m

Time: 1½ hours

From the road-end turn right along a rough grassy track ending at a gate and ladder stile. Beyond this, a more faint unenclosed grassy track veers left with the dome-shaped Garnedd-goch on the horizon and the crags of Cwm Silyn peeping over its shoulder. Watch out for a faint path arcing right across rough grassland to a wall corner at GR 498501. Keep the wall to the left until the next wall corner, where the path reaches open hill. The path is sketchy in the early stages but soon you should notice upright marker stones as the route climbs towards the head of Cwm Dulyn. Llyn Cwm Dulyn appears on the right, beneath the sullen rocky slopes of Mynydd Graig Goch. On reaching the wall at GR 507492 climb left up the steep, sometimes stony slopes of Garnedd-goch. The narrow path winds up to the little stone man marking the boulder-strewn summit.

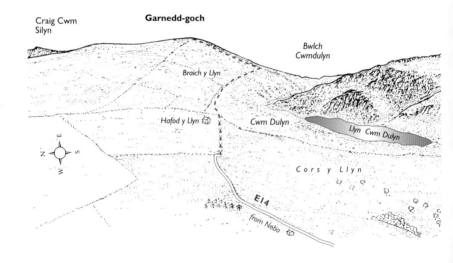

Opposite: Descending into Cwm Dulyn from Garnedd-goch.

Route E15

Cwm Pennant and Cwm Ciprwth

A tough route but full of interest – has that wilderness appeal

Start: The bridge at GR: SH 532476; limited parking. If full there is more at the next bridge (toll)

Distance: 2½ miles/4km

Height gain: 2060ft/628m

Time: 2 hours

Go through the roadside gate on the left and cross the field to a ladder stile at the lower edge of woodland. A faint path marked by yellow posts winds though this conserved broad-leaved plantation to exit at a stile on the upper perimeter. A steep stony path rakes right to reach an old mine shaft and into the lower regions of Cwm Ciprwth. The yellow marker posts continue to guide the route across the hillside to a mine wheel just off-route on the far side of the stream.

The route, still aided by yellow arrows, continues by the lively stream, whose cataracts and waterfalls have now cut themselves a fine rocky gorge. Beyond a ladder stile in a tall cross-wall (GR 520479) the arrows and the path give up. Cwm Ciprwth reveals its wilderness side, with dark heather and pallid moor grasses cloaking a shallow cwm. The stony high slopes of Garnedd-goch slowly reveal themselves above the mountain's craggy south-east ridge.

Sheep tracks by the north bank of the stream – don't cross this – offer the easiest progress through heather. Although the tracks occasionally give up, the really serious heather needn't spoil your route for too long as there are usually tracts of rough moor grass to help you to the horizon. You should reach the ridge just to the north-east of Bwlch Cwmdulyn's nick. There's a narrow path just short of the ridge wall. By turning right along it you will come to a gap in the wall. (Hope-

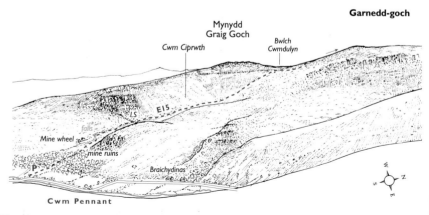

fully at some time stiles will be erected.) Go through it and head north-west. After 50 paces you will come to the footpath marked on the map. Occasional upright stones mark this old byway as it heads for the wall descending Garnedd-goch's west flanks. Once through the gap in this wall, turn right on a path climbing the steep bouldery flanks to arrive on the equally bouldery summit.

Other route options

Walkers who want to get high soon can leave Cwm Ciprwth earlier than in Route E14. Beyond the ladder stile in the cross-wall (GR 520479) climb north (no path) to join the ridge where a wall leads to the main Nantlle Ridge just east of Garnedd-goch's summit.

RIDGE ROUTES

Craig Cwm Silyn

Distance: 1 mile/1.7km
Height gain: 200ft/60m
Time: ½ hour

Follow the ridge wall north-eastwards. After going over a step stile in a continuing fence and straddling two bouldery tops, the path comes to the highest point marked by a wind shelter.

Mynydd Graig Goch

Distance: 1 mile/2.5km
Height gain: 260ft/80m
Time: ¾ hour

The descent alongside a stone wall is steep and rough. Don't follow the wall down into the bottom of the cwm but turn left through a gap in the wall using the marked footpath to Bwlch Cwmdulyn. Now climb south-westwards across boulder-strewn slopes to reach a cairn (GR498483). Turn right (NW) across slopes to the summit crags and the tall stone wall dissecting the mountain.

Left: Conservation woodland beneath Cwm Ciprwth.

MYNYDD GRAIG GOCH

I originally wrote that the peaks of the Nantlle Ridge slipped below the 2000-foot mark for the first time at Mynydd Graig Goch, but in September 2008 – after I had made my ascents – Myrddyn Phillips, John Barnard and Graham Jackson used a state-of-the-art satellite positioning system to find that the mountain rose to a height of 609.75 metres or 2000.49 feet.

Mynydd Graig Goch, the mountain of the red crag, continues the wild craggy moorland theme of Garnedd-goch, although the tiered cliffs above Cwm Dulyn defy this definition, as do the great rocky summit tors, which form a semicircle of serrated crag divided by a tall, almost insurmountable drystone wall.

To the south, vast featureless slopes of heather, peat and cotton grass descend to the rocks of Llwyd Mawr, which overlook a rough complex terrain of bracken and pool-scattered marshland dividing Mynydd Mawr and the lower outlier of Craig y Garn. To the east of the peak is Cwm Ciprwth, a shapely hollow whose surrounding peaks and tors seem to shut out the world. Lower in the cwm there's a renovated water-wheel by a splendid stream whose waterfalls splash through a rocky gorge.

The nature of the mountain's vast southern slopes has meant that the rights of way promised on the map are, in reality, very hard to find and lead the walker through unspectacular country. Geologists may find it fascinating though, for the rocks of Llwyd Mawr were the centre of a great volcanic catastrophe resulting in a 2300ft/700m layer of tuffs, some of the thickest accumulations in the British Isles.

Opposite: Mynydd Craig Goch and a break in the storm.
Below: On the summit of Mynydd Graig Goch looking to Garnedd-goch.

Route E16

Nebo

The best way up but steep from lake to summit

Start: Nebo (GR: SH 479505)

Distance: 1¾ miles/2.85km

Height gain: 1310ft/400m

Time: 1½ hours

From the centre of the village take the lane Ffordd y Llyn heading south-east past the school towards Cors y Llyn. Where the lane turns sharp right (there is also space for a few cars here – but it might not be convenient if you want to come down a different way) go straight ahead on a stony track that comes to the outflow of Llyn Cwm Dulyn. Now go straight ahead across grassland to a stile.

Ignore the narrow path ahead but instead make a bold ascent parallel to the wall you've just crossed – there's no real path, just faint tracks. Gradually arc left, climbing the grass and bilberry slopes above the crags of Cwm Dulyn.

A shepherd's quad bike track helps navigation for a while, weaving its way through rocks towards the summit, whose serrated crags are now in view. Where the track veers left, leave it and tackle the bouldery terrain to the first summit rocks. Unfortunately, at the moment, there's no stile over a tall drystone wall dividing the first summit from the highest of the rocky tors. Until one is erected the easiest crossing is where the wall abuts a large crag. Take care: it's a bit of a scramble, but preferable to damaging the wall.

Mynydd Graig Goch

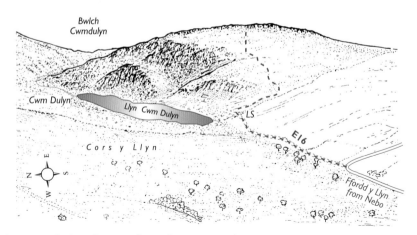

Opposite: Climbing the steep slopes above Cwm Dulyn.

Route E17

Garndolbenmaen

A very hard to follow and slightly dull route
Start: Garndolbenmaen (GR: SH 497442)
Distance: 3½ miles/5.6km
Height gain: 1640ft/500m
Time: 2–2½ hours

From the crossroads in the village centre take the lane heading north-east past the school play area. Ignore all turn-offs and climb until the house of Bryn Tirion, where you take the right fork (the left is signed unsuitable for motor vehicles), which climbs the pastoral spur of Pen y Braich before dropping down into an equally pastoral valley. The lane becomes stony and turns sharp right before swinging left towards the house at Bryn-eithin. Leave the track here and go through a gate in a field to pass in front of the house. Beyond this rejoin the track, cross a bridge and climb the hillside on a delightful grassy walled lane to the top gate. Beyond this you are confronted by undulating moorland slopes of bracken and heather punctuated by craggy hillocks.

Mynydd Graig Goch

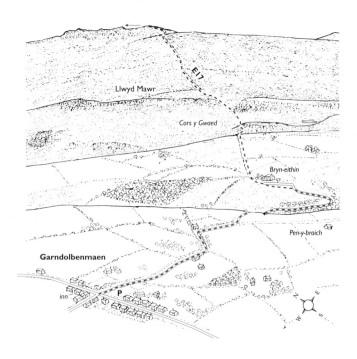

The next section of the walk will be on very easily lost sheep-tracks, and I've added photographs to help navigation. Circumvent the large sheepfolds beyond the gate on the left and head north keeping just to the left of a squat unnamed crag-topped hill. The large crags of Llwyd Mawr will be dominant on the horizon by now. Continue northwards with the marshy hollow of Cors y Gwaen well to the right. Not long after crossing the equally narrow east–west path to the small tarns, the path gets lost in heather. Aim for a heathery hollow to the right of the largest crags – you may spot a lonely rhododendron bush along

the way – and climb to a heathery plateau by the previously mentioned crags of Llwyd Mawr. The rocks are particularly interesting to geologists as they represent the thickest accumulations of welded rhyolitic ash-flow tuffs related to an individual volcanic centre in the whole of the British Isles.

Next, head for a wall corner at GR 503466 – again it's a trackless route. Go through a gap in the partially collapsed wall and stay on the left-hand side of the wall climbing the eastern shoulder of the mountain. Now the craggy top of Mynydd Graig Goch looms large across slopes of heather and cotton

Below: Mynydd Graig Goch from the wallside part of Route E17 from Garndolbenmaen.

grass. A grassy ribbon by the wall makes the going easy, although there are a few boggy stretches to negotiate.

High on the shoulder of the mountain, just to the left of the wall, are some dominant crags. Climb the easy heather slopes to reach them before continuing on a pathless route WNW to the highest summit tors.

Descent

The descent is straightforward at first: just follow the lines of the summit tors ESE and follow the wall down to the wall corner at GR 503466. From there maintain direction with Llwyd Mawr's gigantic boulder-like rocks ahead (GR 502463). Veer left down a small hollow with a rhododendron bush among the heather and bracken. Also keep an eye open at this stage for a walled grass track next to a sheepfold on the edge of the moor – this will eventually be the one to take you back to civilization.

On reaching levellish ground beneath Llwyd Mawr, try to locate a very narrow path heading south towards the right side of a squat rock-topped hill. From here the previously mentioned track should have reappeared. Head south towards it and go through the iron gate by a large sheepfold, Now the pleasant grass track leads the way back to Bryn-eithin, where lanes return you to Garndolbenmaen.

RIDGE ROUTES

Garnedd-goch
Distance: 1 mile/2.5km
Height gain: 575ft/175m
Time: ¼ hour

Head east to the cairn at GR498483 before descending north-east to Bwlch Cwmdulyn. Now climb on the cairned path across heather and grass to the wall cutting across the hillside. Go through the gap in the wall and climb the rough bouldery slopes alongside the wall to reach the cairn on Garnedd-goch's summit.

Opposite: On the north ridge of Mynydd Graig Goch, with Garnedd-goch ahead.

Craig-y-garn, which means cairn crag, is a bit of a tiddler as far as mountain status goes, but it is an interesting tiddler, quite broad and, as you might expect with its name, quite craggy too. Being slightly offset from the main ridges, Craig-y-garn commands the best position by far to view the beautiful Cwm Pennant and its ring of mountains. It's also well placed for an expansive maritime panorama from Porthmadog to Anglesey and the sweep of Cardigan Bay. The hill is separated from the Nantlle Ridge at Mynydd Graig Goch by a rocky pass, Bwlch y Bedol, and Cors y Gwaed, a marshy tract of land studded with several shallow pools.

In geological terms Craig-y-garn is very important, for studies show it to have been formed by a bed of volcanic welded ash flow tuffs, known as the Llwyd Mawr ignimbrites. Llwyd Mawr, the line of crags just to the north of Craig-y-garn, was the centre of a great volcanic eruption which formed a huge caldera or collapsed crater. The tuffs confined within this are around 700m, some of the thickest accumulations in the British Isles.

Craig-y-garn dominates the village of Garndolbenmaen and the mouth of Cwm Pennant from where it hides the bigger mountains behind its modest mass. On the mid slopes above the village are the remains of an old fort, Castell Caerau, while on the east side the disused Hendre quarries and mines are being reclaimed and landscaped with trees. On this east side, sheltered by two rocky knolls, is Llanfihangel-y-pennant, the only village in Cwm Pennant. It is little more than a scattering of cottages but has a stone-built church, beautifully sited by the Dwyfor river and its pastures.

Below: Cwm Pennant from the summit of Craig-y-garn.

Route E18
Garndolbenmaen

A pleasant stroll through village pasture and crag

Start: Garndolbenmaen (GR: SH 497442)
Distance: 1 ¼ miles/2 km
Height gain: 660ft/200m
Time: ¾ hour

From the crossroads in the village centre take the lane heading north-east past the school play area. Ignore all turn-offs and climb until you reach the house of Bryn Tirion, where you take the right fork (the left is signed unsuitable for motor vehicles), which climbs the pastoral spur of Pen y Braich. At the top of the road turn right through a gate on to a farm lane with a grass island running through the middle. Beyond a second gate there's a junction. Take the right-hand track and go over a ladder stile by another gate. A second ladder stile beyond it marks the start of a narrow grass path that climbs half-left towards the rocky hillside. Just short of the low ridge, by an area of cotton grass, the path divides. Take the right fork for a bolder course up the rocks and onwards to the twin summit shelters. The path going straight ahead past the cotton grass takes a slightly more circuitous route round the back to reach the summit.

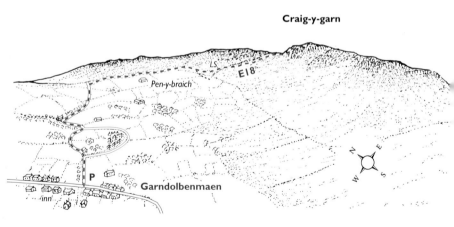

Craig-y-garn

Pen-y-braich

Garndolbenmaen

Opposite: The final climb to Craig-y-garn with Mynydd Graig Goch in the background.

MOEL LEFN

This most northerly of the Hebog peaks rises from the far end of Cwm Pennant. Seen from Bwlch-y-Ddwy-elor, the pass at the head of Cwm Pennant, Moel Lefn is a truly magnificent spectacle, far more so than Moel Hebog, which appears as a large but uninspiring mound. The angular peak is a conglomeration of bare broken rock and screes fringed by precipitous cliffs. The scars of past industries have accentuated the ruggedness, for miners and quarrymen have created precipices of their own, as well as cavernous pits and a small lake. Moel Lefn carries these scars like an embattled but still magnificent prizefighter.

Seen from the west, Moel Lefn is still eye-catching with its bold angular outlines, but the vast spread of Beddgelert Forest's conifers appear almost to engulf its crags. Climbing from this direction by way of the high pass of Bwlch Cwm-trwsgl, the walker may be surprised to see the huge chasm of the Princess Quarry so high on its slopes. Heather and lush bilberry are now tempering the mountainscape hereabouts, but this must have been a scene of devastation in its 19th-century heyday.

Left: A storm over Moel Lefn and Cwm Pennant.

The summit of Moel Lefn is largely grassy, with a scattering of rocky tors and outcrops, the highest one of which is cairned. The views across the verdant pastures of Cwm Pennant to the Nantlle Ridge are tremendous, especially towards Craig Cwm Silyn with its conical bouldery top and spiky arête.

Route E19
Beddgelert Forest

An entertaining climb once the forest section is done

Start: Pont Cae'r-gors forestry car park (GR: SH 574503)

Distance: 3 miles/4.85km

Height gain: 1640ft/500m

Time: 2 hours

From the car park head back to the approach road and turn left. Leave the road for a bull-dozed forestry road through large double gates on the left. Immediately the road crosses the Welsh Highland Railway (take care). It gradually arcs left, passing marker posts 64 and 65. Ignore the right fork (heading towards the Nantlle Ridge) but stay with the main track with the bold peak of Moel Hebog directly ahead.

Moel Lefn

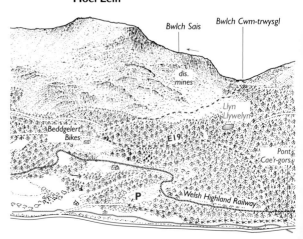

Opposite: The key to the descent northwards from Moel Lefn is to take a faint left fork path, which reaches the rim of the summit just left of the end crags – note the position of the walker.

170

At post 77 above the farmhouse of Hafod Rhuffydd Ganol (the Beddgelert Bikes hire shop), take a right fork. Watch out for a narrow path on the right: this is the public footpath marked on the maps. Follow this uphill as it crosses and recrosses the zigzagging forestry road before emerging on an open hillside of heather and impressive crag. The ground slopes away to the right, with forestry hiding Llyn Llywelyn in the early stages. The peaty path re-enters the forest for a short while before re-emerging from the trees at Bwlch Cwm-trwsgl.

Turn left by the wall on a stony path passing close to a mine entrance before climbing further to the huge chasm of the Princess Quarry. A path rakes up slopes of bilberry to the right of the pit and comes across a shallow pool (maybe dry in summer) at Bwlch Sais. The narrow but clear path stays above the steep crag and scree slopes on the right but below some rocky buttresses on the left.

Eventually it tackles the rocky upper slopes to arrive on the north-west end of Moel Lefn's summit ridge. A short easy rise on grass leads to the summit rocks, which are slightly to the left of the path.

Descent

Finding the path down the steep craggy north-west slopes of Moel Lefn can be tricky, especially in mist. A cairn used to mark the spot but cairn wreckers, unable to distinguish between the useful and the superfluous, have removed it. The photograph below gives a visual key. Basically go NNW on a faint left fork path, which comes to a slightly angular knoll slightly to the left of the rocky summit crest. Look down and you'll see the path descending to Bwlch Sais and further downward on bilberry slopes to the Princess Quarry. Keep the deep pit to the right before following the fence/wall down to the stile allowing entry into Beddgelert Forest.

Route E20

Blaen Pennant

The classic route – stimulating all the way

Start: Blaen Pennant car park
  (GR: SH 574503)

Distance: 3 miles/4.85km

Height gain: 1660ft/505m

Time: 2 hours

From the car park go over the ladder stile across the bridge over a stream, then turn right on a path climbing rough grassy slopes to the ruins of Cwm-trwsgl and its surrounding quarry slag heaps (GR 544494). Here the path joins an old quarry tramway and follows it right to the ruined dressing sheds of the Prince of Wales Quarries (GR 545493).

Beyond this, at a right-hand bend in the tramway, climb left on an overgrown grassy incline before turning right along an old dam. A path on the far side veers left and climbs to the Bwlch Cwm-trwsgl path where a right turn will eventually lead to the pass by Beddgelert Forest. Ignore the stile into the forest and instead stay with a wallside path passing a mine entrance before coming to the huge pit of the Princess Mine.

A path climbs slopes of bilberry to the right of the pit to the shallow pool (maybe dry in summer) at Bwlch Sais. The narrow but clear path climbs above steep crag and scree slopes but below some rocky buttresses on the left. In the upper stages it winds though craggy slopes to reach the north-west end of

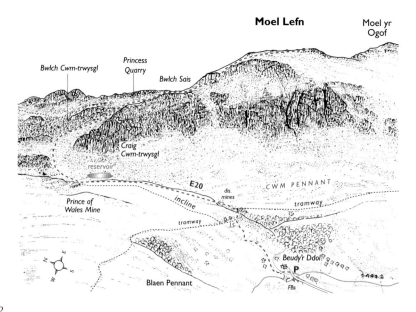

Moel Lefn's summit ridge. A short easy rise on grass leads to the summit rocks, which are slightly to the left of the path.

Descent

See the Route E19 descent for route-finding off Moel Lefn. At the col, Bwlch Cwm-trwsgl, turn left on a path that descends to the terraced slag of the Prince of Wales Quarries. Go across the lowest of these terraces and turn left at the far end. A grassy incline then takes the route down to a quarry tramway near the apex of a bend. Turn right here and pass through the old dressing sheds. The tramway continues to another bend by the ruins of Cwm-trwsgl. Go over a ladder stile below left of the ruins and follow the way-marked path down grassy slopes back down to the car park, which lies over a river bridge.

RIDGE ROUTE

Moel Yr Ogof

Distance: ½ mile/0.8km
Height gain: 250ft/75m
Time: 20 minutes

There's not much descent between these craggy tops and the going is relatively straightforward: descend on a clear path down the summit boulders, continue on a grass path to the shallow depression, go over the ladder stile in a cross wall, then climb to the cairn on Moel yr Ogof's highest rocks.

Below: The head of Cwm Pennant from Bwlch Sais.

The 'hill of the cave' is gnarled with crags and, seen from both Cwm Pennant and Beddgelert Forest, has a ruffled, rather unkempt look. The volcanic rocks are of dark basalt. The cave referred to in the mountain's name lies high in crags on the east flanks, overlooking the spruce trees. Legend has it that the 15th-century Owain Glyndwr took refuge here in order to escape the attentions of the English troops of Prince Henry, the young man who would eventually become Henry V.

Moel yr Ogof is one of four peaks in a ridge rising from Rhyd Ddu to its zenith on Moel Hebog before dropping down to the plains of Tremadog. There's only a slight dip between Moel yr Ogof and Moel Lefn to the north, but there's a deep pass, Bwlch Meillionen (clover pass) before the rise to Hebog. On the down-slopes to the second-mentioned col the path enters a short defile in the rocks. Close inspection of these rocks reveals pillow lavas, formed under the ocean when the white-hot basalt oozed though cracks to be immediately cooled by the cold waters.

Just above the defile are a couple of shallow pools formed in the Ice Age. In spring there are tadpoles swimming in this seemingly inhospitable place. You would think the frogs wouldn't be able to find enough to eat up here, but they do.

Another 'step' of crags leads to the next shelf, that of Moel yr Ogof's summit plateau, which is grassy with a scattering of boulders and rock outcrops and with the highest point marked by a small cairn. From it you can look east across the plantations of Beddgelert to Snowdon and its satellites and across sullen western flanks that sink gradually into the brighter environs of Cwm Pennant.

Opposite: On the summit of Moel yr Ogof looking north across the rugged ridge to Moel Lefn.

Route E21

Beddgelert Forest

A dull plod through forest improves on the
crag-scattered climb to the top

Start: Lay-by opposite Beddgelert forestry
campsite entrance (GR: SH 588483)

Distance: 3 miles/5km

Height gain: 1970ft/600m

Time: 2 hours

From the lay-by cross the road on to the
driveway of the forestry campsite. After passing the reception, keep to the road with the
Afon Meillionen to the right. Cross the Welsh
Highland Railway track, and turn left along a
forestry road. Take the next right fork, which

gradually rakes up the hillsides and swings
right to double back above the fields of Meillionen.

Beyond a concrete bridge over the Afon
Meillionen the road meets a waymarked footpath. This climbs over tree roots to another
forest road where you turn right until another
waymark by another bridge points the way
uphill. Recent felling has made the route by
the banks of the Meillionen rather messy,
although there are more open views to the
crags and knolls of Moel Hebog and Moel yr
Ogof.

More forest roads are crossed before the
route finally comes to a ladder stile at the
plantation edge. The path gives up beyond

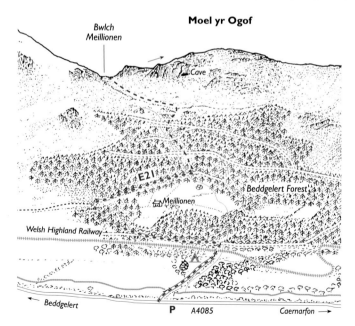

Moel yr Ogof

the stile, but a stiff climb threads through a grassy corridor in the crags to reach a crumbling drystone wall. Go though one of the many gaps to locate a good path on the other side. The wall and path lead to the ridge at Bwlch Meillionen, where views open up to Cwm Pennant. Now a narrow path slants right into a defile between two great crags. A stony chute between the crags takes the route up to a grassy shelf where a wall on the left leads to a small shallow pool. Further on another steep climb on bouldery slopes levels out before the final climb to the rocky summit tors and the summit cairn.

Below: Approaching Moel yr Ogof from Beddgelert Forest.
Bottom: At Bwlch Meillionen climbing towards Moel yr Ogof.

Route E22

Cwm Pennant

A steady plod through old mining grounds

Start: Cwrt Isaf, Cwm Pennant
    (GR: SH 539463)

Distance: 2 miles/3.2km

Height gain: 1510ft/460m

Time: 1½ hours

From the road-end near the farm, follow the track northwards and go over a ladder stile to the right of a complex of barns and cattle pens before going through a gate at the far side into a field. Look for a ladder stile at the top end of the field, and another beyond a small rush-covered enclosure. A track now leads the route up grassy hillsides with the Afon Cwm-llefrith and a wire fence to the right. It crosses the old quarry tramway by a half-demolished bridge before continuing the climb by the fence and stream. The path becomes intermittent but the pass between Moel Hebog and Moel yr Ogof should always be straight ahead on the craggy skyline.

Beyond another ladder stile, the path passes well to the left of a complex of mine shafts, slag heaps and old stone buildings, scattered across the slopes of Moel Hebog.

On reaching the pass and scaling the ladder stile in the ridge wall, turn left on a path slanting up to the bottom of the defile separating two great crags. Follow the stony chute through it, eventually to reach a small tarn. The clear path passes to the left of this and climbs the craggy, sometimes steep, terrain to the cairn on Moel yr Ogof's summit.

Moel yr Ogof

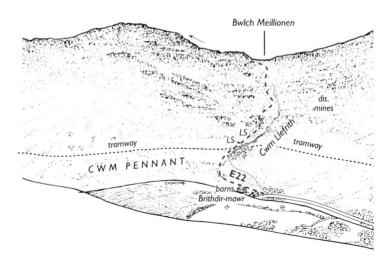

RIDGE ROUTES

Moel Lefn
Distance: ½ mile/0.8km
Height gain: 165ft/50m
Time: 20 minutes

Descend northwards to a ladder stile in a cross-wall and continue across grass to the final bouldery rise to Moel Lefn's cairned summit rocks.

Below: Brithdir-mawr at the start of the Cwm Pennant route.

Moel Hebog
Distance: 1 mile/1.4km
Height gain: 790ft/240m
Time: ¾ hour

A clear path goes from the cairn southwards to a craggy edge, where a stony path clambers down a craggy slope, then levels off before descending another rocky slope. The path comes to a wall, which passes to the right of a shallow pool before descending into a rocky defile that leads down to the col, Bwlch Meillionen. What follows is a stiff climb near the ridge-wall all the way to Hebog's summit trig point.

MOEL HEBOG

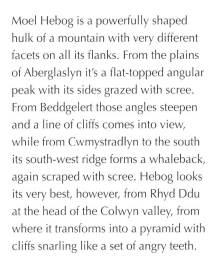

Moel Hebog is a powerfully shaped hulk of a mountain with very different facets on all its flanks. From the plains of Aberglaslyn it's a flat-topped angular peak with its sides grazed with scree. From Beddgelert those angles steepen and a line of cliffs comes into view, while from Cwmystradlyn to the south its south-west ridge forms a whaleback, again scraped with scree. Hebog looks its very best, however, from Rhyd Ddu at the head of the Colwyn valley, from where it transforms into a pyramid with cliffs snarling like a set of angry teeth.

Only from Cwm Pennant does Hebog disappoint, for its great girth is not complemented by great architecture: its crags are chaotic, with easy gradients and great swathes of sombre moor grass belying its mountain status.

Moel Hebog means hill of the haw, which is quite apt as I have often seen hawks at last light soaring above the cliffs above the forest of Beddgelert. The mountain was formed from distinct strata over eons of time. The lower slopes are of mudstone, laid down in deep seas. These are the rocks providing the grey slate, quarried above Ystradlyn. The

Left: Moel Hebog from the Nantlle Ridge.

newer sandstones were laid down on top of the mudstones in shallow seas and a later river delta. The crags and outcrops of Hebog were formed by great volcanic eruptions: welded Pitts Head tuffs, which are in places marbled due to hot lavas being suddenly cooled by the ocean, and the reddish rhyolitic breccias, seen on the high slopes and the rocky outcrops of the summit.

The mountain is separated from Moel yr Ogof by a deep pass, Bwlch Meillionen, but the connection with Moel-ddu, the southern outlier of the Hebog range, is more complex. Beneath its blunt southern spur are a series of low shelves and ridges culminating in Banog, a craggy north–south ridge that ends with a steep grass slope to Bwlch Oerddwr, a marshy pass dividing Cwm Ystradlyn and Cwm Oer Dwr on the Glaslyn side. In poor visibility, a walk in this direction would be a real test of navigational skills.

Route E23
Cwm Cloch

The natural and the best way to this fine summit

Start: Beddgelert (GR: SH 589483)
Distance: 2¼ miles/3.5km
Height gain: 2500ft/760m
Time: 1½ –2 hours

From the main bridge in the centre of the village take the Caernarfon road to Pont Alyn. Turn left along a farm track leading the route over the bridge spanning the Afon Colwyn, a splendid tree-shaded river swirling round smooth moss-clad rocks. Loops in the newly reconstructed Welsh Highland Railway mean that the route has to cross its path three times, the first time under a bridge.

At the upper farm a signed bridleway leads the route to the right through a gate. Take the left fork path soon after for Moel Hebog. This

Moel Hebog

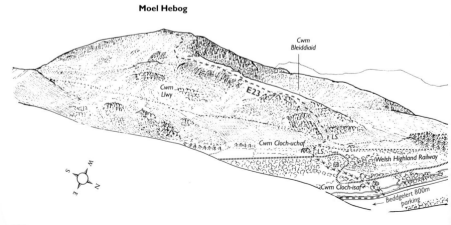

crosses a tiny footbridge over a streamlet, crosses a wall at a ladder stile and climbs steadily through slopes of grass bracken, mountain ash and rocky bluffs. The steepness of the route becomes unrelenting as the path climbs south-west towards high cliffs. In the upper reaches of the route the path avoids the cliffs on a devious course over crag and reddish scree. On reaching the grass plateau the cairned route leads to the stone-built trig crowning Hebog's summit, where views across Cwm Pennant to the Nantlle Ridge should provide due recompense for all the effort.

Right: The Afon Colwyn near Cwm Cloch.

Route E24
Cwm Llefrith

*A seldom-used approach, dull for all but
    industrial archaeologists*
Start: Cwrt Isaf, Cwm Pennant
    (GR: SH 539463)
Distance: 2 miles/3.3km
Height gain: 1970ft/600m
Time: 1½ –2 hours

At the road-end take the track heading north beyond the farmhouse and go over a ladder stile by the barns and cattle pens before continuing through a gate at the far side into a field. Look for a ladder stile at the top of this, and another beyond a small rush-covered enclosure. A track now leads the route up grassy hillsides with the Afon Cwm-llefrith and a wire fence to the right.

The path crosses the old quarry railway by a half-demolished bridge before continuing the climb parallel to fence and stream. Another ladder stile in a high cross wall helps keep you in the right direction as the path

becomes intermittent, but the pass between Moel Hebog and Moel yr Ogof is always straight ahead on the craggy skyline. To the right, on the slopes of Moel Hebog, are the remnants of past copper mines – shafts, slag heaps and old stone buildings. Eventually the route reaches the ladder stile over the ridge wall. Cross it and turn right up the steep slopes of Hebog. The wall guides you all the way to the summit trig point but you'll need frequent stops to admire the view back to Moel yr Ogof.

Below: Mine buildings on Moel Hebog.

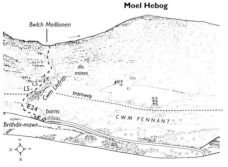

Route E25
Cwm Ystradlyn

A steady pull up a grass ridge – rather dull but better in descent

Start: Car park by Llyn Cwmystradlyn dam (GR: SH 557441)

Distance: 2¼ miles/3.5km

Height gain: 1900ft/580m

Time: 1½ –2 hours

From the car park go back along the road and turn right on the signed track by the cottage of Tyddyn Mawr. Take the main left fork track shortly after and follow it to a gate between a line of trees. Through the gate leave the track and climb half-left (NNE) over rough marshy terrain (no path on the ground), cross a broken-down wall and watch out for a ladder stile in the next wall.

The route will now cross cow pastures with ladder stiles in the intervening walls. Beyond the second of these stiles it turns half-left towards the ridge to locate the next stile, which lies just on the south side. Stay on the

Above: Moel Hebog seen from the Cwm Ystradlyn ascent.

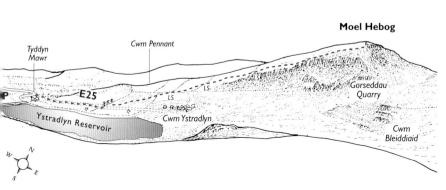

south side of the ridge to locate more stiles at GR 557457 and GR 560459. You're now free of cross-walls and can climb open grass mountainside. By heading north-east you should locate a cairn on the south end of Hebog's ridge, where the summit trig point should be visible beyond an intervening wind break.

Descent

Head south along the grass ridge to the last cairn before the slopes fall away to Cwm Ystradlyn. Now descend right (no path as yet) keeping on the Ystradlyn side of the broad grassy ridge to locate the first ladder stile. The stiles in the intervening ridge *do* come into view when required for navigation. Beyond the last one before reaching the valley, head towards a stand of conifers before following the farm track out to the road. If you've parked in Cwm Pennant, the old mining tramway, which leads out of Ystradlyn, is a useful way and saves road-walking.

Route E26
Aberglaslyn Hall and Banog

*A complex route in the early stages and a
    stiff climb to the summit*
Start: Pont Aberglaslyn car park, Nantmor
    (GR: SH 597462)
Distance: 3½ miles/5.2km
Height gain: 2820ft/860 m
Time: 2½–3 hours

Follow the little path from the west side of the car park down to the bridge, Pont Aberglaslyn. The view from the bridge is awe-inspiring, with the white-water torrents of the river framed by the immense tree-lined cliffs of the gorge. Turn right to cross the road bridge (with care) and then left on the Porthmadog road. Leave the road on a signed woodland path on the right running alongside the entrance to Aberglaslyn Hall. Ignore the waymarked right fork path and instead go left over a footbridge. The succeeding path, bound by crumbling moss-covered walls, winds up woodland slopes. Be careful not to miss a left turn – doing so will lead you back to the stream with nowhere to go but back.

A stile allows you to leave the woods on to bracken-clad hill slopes. In the early stages a narrow path curves right to follow the edge of the woods for a short way before veering half-left (south-west) to pass to the right of two low knolls. Note here that the extension to the forest's perimeter wall climbing the hillside will eventually guide you over confusing territory where paths are no bigger than sheep-tracks – but don't lose sight of it. The

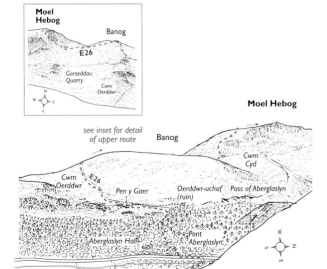

*Above: Climbing the
steep section to Fridd
y Bwlch.*

187

route stays well to the south of the old buildings of Oerddwr-uchaf.

Beyond the second knoll, the narrow path goes through a gap in a wall on the right and crosses more bracken towards a tree which marks the site of an old ruin, Pen y Gaer. On reaching the ruin, turn right alongside a wall, then left by a small stream. You've now returned to the previously mentioned wall. The path soon crosses a wide farm track from Oerddwr-uchaf and stays by the wall until reaching the pass of Bwlch Oerddwr. The primitive stile here takes the form of a crossstone in the wall. Beyond this, climb the steep grass slopes of Ffridd Uchaf up to the ridge of Banog. The ridge wall eventually veers off right and ceases to be of any use as a guide.

There's no need to make the circuitous detour to the northern end of Banog but there is a drop between you and the direct path up to Moel Hebog, whose scree-scraped slopes rear up in intimidating fashion. By gradually arcing left around the grassy bowl at the head of Cwm Ystradlyn you arrive at a shallow pool covered in early summer with bogbean. Go to the left of this and either follow a scree path or contour the steep grassy rake to the right of it. Both routes are sporty, to say the least – very steep and gruelling.

Eventually the gradient eases and the best way forward is to angle right to gain the grassy summit ridge – you should reach it somewhere near an outlying cairn. A straightforward promenade on short-cropped grass now leads past a windbreak towards the rocks and the trig point on Moel Hebog's summit.

Other route options

Those daunted by the steep south-east flanks of Hebog can contour right across the rocky shelf beneath the east face, then climb on the well-defined Cwm Cloch route.

There is a waymarked path from the Aberglaslyn Hall route that climbs to Bryn Du, where there is a superb view of the Pass of Aberglaslyn. This could give access to the east side of Hebog, where the final climbs of Routes E23 or E26 could be undertaken via the craggy spur of Y Dduallt, the black heights.

RIDGE ROUTES

Moel Yr Ogof

Distance: 1 mile/1.5km
Height gain: 360ft/110m
Time: ¾ hour

From the summit follow the right-hand side of the ridge-wall as it descends south-westwards down very steep slopes to Bwlch Meillionen. A path slants up the other side to a defile between two gigantic crags. Climb on the stony path through the defile and by a wall to pass to the left of a large shallow pool. A stony path veers away from the wall to climb on rocky slopes to the next grassy shelf before continuing over more rock to reach the cairned summit.

Moel-ddu

Distance: 2½ miles/4.1km
Height gain: 870ft/265m
Time: 1½ hours

Head south on the broad grassy ridge to the last cairn, the angle half-left SSE (no path), making sure you steer clear of the mountain's loose and precipitous west flank. Mid-way down these slopes of grass and rock outcrops there's a steep grassy ramp leading down to a shallow pool. Zigzag down this before reaching that pool. Now contour around Cwm Clyd before arcing around right on a slight climb to the Banog ridge.

Eventually you meet a wall, which leads over the ridge and steeply down to Bwlch Oerdrws. The stone steps in the wall are not easily seen but, once over them, traverse the marshy col before crossing the ladder stile at the far end. Beyond this go though a gate in the fence running beneath Moel-ddu's lower slopes. A faint path now winds up steep slopes of grass, bilberry and broken rock. The gradient eases beyond a wall junction, beyond which the path swings left parallel with the wall. Through a gate by the next wall junction the path enters a channel between the two peaks. Turn left over a ladder stile and climb the path among crags for the slightly higher northern summit.

Opposite: Moel Hebog from Gorseddau Quarry.

Above: Moel-ddu from the east.
Opposite: Approaching the twin peaks of Moel-ddu.

Although it's next to Moel Hebog, the equally craggy Moel-ddu, the black bare hill, is made of different stuff – mudstone topped by sandstone conglomerates. The vast walls of the Llwyd Mawr caldera stopped the fiery flow of those Pitts Head tuffs from reaching this twin-peaked mountain.

If you searched anywhere south of the Scottish border you'd be hard-pressed to find a mountain of such modest height offering such a panorama as Moel-ddu. It not only encompasses the great expanse of the west coast of Wales; beyond the rooftops of Porthmadog, the Rhinog mountains are backed up by those of Cadair Idris, while the shapely outlines of the Llyn Peninsula's Rivals lead the eye further afield to Anglesey and, if it's a clear day, the distant mountains of Wicklow in Ireland. To the north and east across Aberglaslyn, the magnificent mountainscapes of Cnicht and the Moelwynion are complemented on the left side by Snowdon and Moel Siabod.

Moel-ddu's main claim to fame is in its lower reaches, where there's a series of gracefully shaped dolerite cliffs among the woodland copses of Tremadog. The chimneys, arêtes and overhanging slabs make these some of the most popular climbing crags in Snowdonia, especially on the many days when it's raining in the heart of Snowdonia and it's sunny near the coast. The Bwlch y Moch café in the village is owned by famous climber Eric Jones; it's known locally as 'Eric's Caff'.

Route E27

Cwmystradlyn Reservoir

*A pleasant route once the marshy lakeside
  path has been left behind*

Start: Car park, Llyn Cwmystradlyn dam
  (GR: SH 557441)

Distance: 2½ miles/4km

Height gain: 1310ft/400m

Time: 1½ hours

Cross the dam and follow the lakeside path over a stile at its far end. The path, which is quite damp underfoot in places, crosses to the other side of the fence at a step stile and continues to round the far end of the lake. Now little more than a sheep-track, the right of way crosses a stream at GR 565445 and maintains its direction through the next crumbling wall before climbing bracken- and bluebell-clad hillsides beneath the crags of Ffolt Fawr. The slag heaps of the Gorseddau Quarry beneath Moel Hebog will be directly ahead at this time.

A gap in the wall by a streamlet (GR 568 448) leads to another sheep-track of a path to a ladder stile in the top wall of a bracken-infested enclosure. Beyond this, a faint grassy vehicle track leads the route through a shallow valley, with the rocky flanks of Moel-ddu closing in.

Just before reaching the ladder stile in the wall at the top of the pass, climb right. A gate in the fence, hidden from the main route, marks the start of a faint (at times) path that winds up steep slopes of grass, bilberry and broken rock. The gradient eases beyond a wall junction, beyond which the path swings left, parallel with the wall. The craggy twin peaks of Moel-ddu are in view ahead. Through a gate by the next wall junction the path enters a channel of land between the two peaks. Turn left over a ladder stile and climb the path among crags for the slightly higher northern summit: climb right among similar rocks for the south summit.

*Opposite: Looking from the summit to
Moel Hebog.*

Moel-ddu

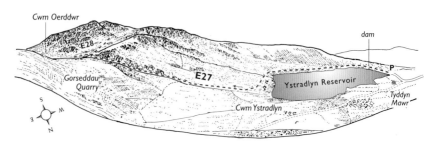

Route E28
Aberglaslyn Hall

A complex route

Start: Car park, Pont Aberglaslyn
  (GR: SH 597462)

Distance: 2½ miles/4.1km

Height gain: 1890ft/575m

Time: 2 hours

Follow the little path from the toilets at the west end of the car park, through woodland to the bridge, Pont Aberglaslyn. Up-river views through the trees and the tall cliffs of the Pass of Aberglaslyn are stunning, enlivened further by the white-water river that bounds over huge boulders.

After crossing the bridge, turn left on the Porthmadog road before leaving it on a signed path running alongside the entrance to Aberglaslyn Hall. Ignore the signed right fork in paths soon after (which climb to Bryn Du) but take the left fork over the footbridge. The path, bound by crumbled walls covered

and smoothed by coatings of lichen and moss, winds and climbs through woodland. Be careful not to miss a left turn – doing so will lead you back to the stream with nowhere to go but back. A stile allows an exit to hill slopes of bracken.

In the early stages, a narrow path veers right to follow the edge of the woods for a short way before veering half-left (south-west) to pass to the right of two low knolls. Note here that the extension to the forest's perimeter wall climbing the hillside will eventually guide you over confusing territory where paths are no bigger than sheep tracks, so don't lose sight of it. Also worthy of note is that the route stays well to the south of the old buildings of Oerddwr-uchaf.

Beyond the second knoll, the narrow path goes through a gap in a wall on the right and crosses more bracken towards a tree marking the site of the ruins of the Pen y Gaer smallholding. On reaching the ruins, turn right alongside a wall, then left by a small stream.

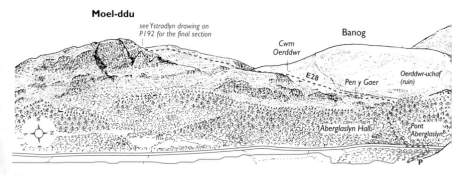

Here, turn right by a wall, then left by a stream – you're now following the previously mentioned wall. The path soon crosses a wide farm track from Oerddwr-uchaf and stays by the wall until it passes a crag in Cwm Oerddwr. Here it angles slightly left across marshy grassland, passing small and shallow pools to reach a ladder stile in a cross-wall. If in any doubt, the wall will lead to the top of the pass, but you'll have to descend left alongside a top wall to locate the ladder stile.

Once over the stile turn left to locate a gate in a fence (hidden until the last moment). This marks the start of a path that climbs steep slopes of grass, bilberry and crag. The gradient eases beyond a wall junction, beyond which the path swings left, parallel to the wall before going through a gate by a wall junction. Now the route threads through a grassy channel between Moel-ddu's twin peaks. Turn left over a ladder stile and climb the path among crags for the slightly higher northern summit.

Below: Bwlch Oerddwr with Cnicht and the Moelwyn range on the skyline.

RIDGE ROUTE

Moel Hebog

Distance: 2½ miles/4.1km
Height gain: 1660ft/505m
Time: 2 hours

From the north peak summit cairn, descend south among crags. After climbing a ladder stile in a wall at the base of the crags turn right and follow a grassy channel. Go through a gate at a wall intersection and continue on easy gradients before swinging right by another wall junction and going more steeply downhill on a path that winds down grass and bilberry slopes to a gate in a cross-wall. Once through this follow the wall that traverses the pass of Bwlch Oerddwr. Go across the wall at the ladder stile and turn left to follow the other side of the wall.

Climb the steep slopes of Banog using stone steps in the high cross wall. Follow the ridge wall over the summit ridge of Banog. The ridge wall eventually veers off right and ceases to be of any use as a guide. There is a slight descent between here and the south-west flanks of Moel Hebog. By gradually arcing around the grassy bowl at the head of Cwm Ystradlyn, you will come across a shallow pool. Go to the left of this and either follow a scree path or the grassy rake to the right of it – both are very steep and gruelling.

As the gradient eases, angle right to gain the grassy summit ridge. A straightforward promenade on easy grass now leads past a windbreak towards the rocks and the trig point on Moel Hebog's summit.

Below: Climbing away from Aberglaslyn above Pen y Gaer.

Visitors to Criccieth, Porthmadog or Borth y Gest will know this little peak if not its name, for its bold craggy form makes it a landmark for miles. The 'bare hill of the paunch' seems a misnomer as it's not bare and the dolerite rocks give it quite a distinctive angular profile. The hill rears up from the rooftops of Porthmadog's town centre, its lower slopes cloaked with both broadleaved and coniferous woodland. Good crags, with maritime names such as Mainmast and Foremast Buttresses, lie on the south side of the mountain and are popular with climbers, as are the twenty or so routes in the quarry on the north side.

There are numerous walking routes up to the top of Moel y Gest, including the one listed here and a variant from a lay-by on the A487 just outside Porthmadog. They are all entertaining, with little paths climbing through oakwoods, weaving among rocks and heather and taking in expansive coastal views, including Criccieth and its castle, Black Rock and the yawning Llyn Peninsula. The ups and downs of the ridge, the scrambling rocks and that pure breeze-blown air make this little hill an exhilarating place to be.

Below: Moel y Gest from the north.

Route E29
Porthmadog

A splendid route through woodland and over a delightful craggy ridge

Start: Porthmadog town centre
(GR: SH 568387)
Distance: 1¼ miles/2.8km
Height gain: 1000ft/305m
Time: 1 hour

From Porthmadog's busy High Street (Stryd Fawr) follow Banc Place (signed 'Borth y Gest') before taking the right fork road signed 'Morfa Bychan'. Turn right down the drive of the campsite and hotel at Tyddyn Llwyn, passing to the right of the hotel. Where the track turns left go straight ahead to a gate on the campsite's perimeter. A clear path continues through a meadow with thickets of bramble and towards the craggy peak of Moel y Gest. At the top of the path turn left off it on to a narrow path threading through delightful oak woodland to emerge on the hill slopes. It climbs among rocky bluffs with the highest ground to the left, and reaches the rocky ridge just beyond the first peak. It's worth detouring left for the views of Porthmadog and its harbour before continuing along the ridge.

There's soon a dip in the ridge but without much effort the path transports you along the crest to the last and highest summit, crowned by a trig point.

Opposite: from the summit of Moel y Gest looking across the Llyn Peninsula, with Criccieth and its castle in the mid distance.

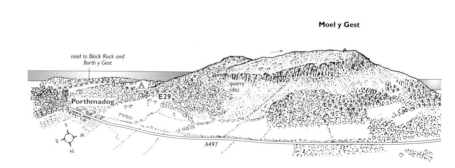

road to Black Rock and
Borth y Gest

Moel y Gest

quarry
(dis)

Porthmadog

E29

A497

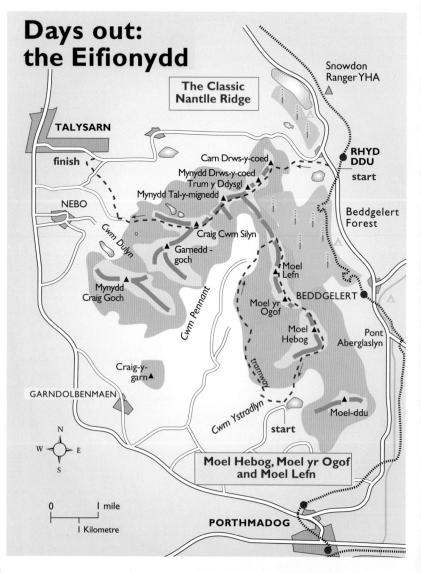

Days out:
the Eifionydd

The Classic Nantlle Ridge

Snowdon Ranger YHA

TALYSARN

finish

RHYD DDU

start

NEBO

Carn Drws-y-coed
Mynydd Drws-y-coed
Trum y Ddysgl
Mynydd Tal-y-mignedd

Beddgelert Forest

Cwm Dulyn

Craig Cwm Silyn

Garnedd-goch

Mynydd Craig Goch

Cwm Pennant

Moel Lefn

Moel yr Ogof

BEDDGELERT

Moel Hebog

Pont Aberglaslyn

Craig-y-garn

GARNDOLBENMAEN

tramway

Moel-ddu

Cwm Ystradlyn

start

Moel Hebog, Moel yr Ogof and Moel Lefn

N
W — E
S

0   1 mile
1 Kilometre

PORTHMADOG

Days out: the Eifionydd

Moel Hebog, Moel yr Ogof and Moel Lefn

A long but splendid route that will introduce you to the beauty of Cwm Pennant and the splendid Moel Lefn–Moel Hebog ridge

Start: Car park, Llyn Cwmystradlyn dam (GR: SH 557441)

Distance: 9¼ miles/15km

Height gain: 2890ft/880m

Time: 4½ –5½ hours

Below: Cwm Pennant.

From the dam-side car park follow the road back past Tyddyn Mawr where it turns left. A footpath on the right (GR 553441) angles half-right past the second of two newish plantations to join a farm track beyond a footbridge. Take the right fork (the left goes to the farm). You have been following an old mine tramway, one that will take you the length of Cwm Pennant. It will be quite faint sometimes, but very prominent at others. Beyond a wide left-hand bend the track almost disappears as it traverses a large field.

Don't be lured off route on to farm tracks but trace the course of the old tramway, which makes another wide loop to avoid a small hill and the more cultivated pastures of Cae-bach before heading north through the valley under the rugged west slopes of Moel Hebog and into the shallow side valley of Cwm Llefrith. By now the whole of Cwm Pennant is in view. In late spring the white blossoms of the wind-bent hawthorn trees will be adding delicacy to a rugged landscape. The Nantlle peaks arc around the head of the valley. Although not endowed with great glacial corries on this side, the graceful slopes and finely sculpted crags of these mountains must have inspired the shepherd poet, Eifion Wyn, who wrote: 'O God, why did'st thou make Cwm Pennant so beautiful and the life of an old shepherd so short?'

The old tramway bridge over the Afon Llefrith has been dismantled but a brief detour to the right leads you across a footbridge and up the far banks to rejoin the trackbed. The track stays above the farm pastures and the scattered farmhouses and makes another loop to the left before swinging right again above the farm at Tyddyn-mawr. Now the route tucks under the shattered cliffs of Moel Lefn and draws near to the valley head at the ruins of some old dressing sheds. Here the tramway breaks off sharp left but the route to be used leaves it to go straight and climb an over-

grown grassy incline, which takes the route to the heart of the Prince of Wales mines. Slag heaps and tumble-down barracks cover the hillsides above you. Moel Lefn looks massive from here, and its crags and precipices impenetrable. But there is a way.

Turn right along an old dam – it's the lowest of several shelves. A path on the far side veers left and climbs to the Bwlch Cwm-trwsgl path. Take the right turn among heather and crag to reach the pass and the edge of Beddgelert Forest.

Ignore the stile into the forest but climb alongside the wall and the forest's edge to reach the huge pit of the Princess Mine. A path on the right climbs relatively verdant slopes of bilberry to a shallow pool at Bwlch Sais. The narrow but clear path climbs above steep crag and scree slopes but below some rocky buttresses on the left. In the upper stages it winds though craggy slopes to reach the north-west end of Moel Lefn's summit ridge. A short easy rise on grass leads to the summit rocks, which are slightly to the left of the path. By now the views across Cwm Pennant are breathtaking, with Craig Cwm Silyn's serrated arête taking centre-stage.

Clamber down the rocky path to the shallow depression between Moel Lefn and Moel yr Ogof before climbing on grass to the ladder stile in a cross-wall straddling the ridge. Soon the path takes you on more crags to this second summit. Now Moel Hebog, the high point of the day, looms large ahead. From here it is powerfully shaped, if unspectacular, with a craggy spur rising from the conifers of Beddgelert Forest to the steep steel-grey screes and crags of the summit's north face.

Descend over two rocky shelves down to a shallow pool with marshy surrounds. After tiptoeing around the right side of the pool, continue the descent down a gully between two huge crags to reach the col of Bwlch Meillionen (clover pass).

Moel Hebog, the high point of the day, comes with a price. Ahead of you lies an immense steep slope of boulder and grass. It's hard going but you are rewarded on reaching the trig point, for Hebog has wonderful uninterrupted views of Snowdon, Cnicht, the Moelwynion and most of the Cambrian coast, including the Llyn Peninsula. If it's clear and fine you'll feel as if you're standing at the centre of the whole of Wales.

A pleasant broad, grassy ridge heads south to a cairn overlooking Cwm Ystradlyn. Here the ridge turns south-westwards. By now there's now no trace of a path. Be content to follow the grassy ridge downhill. The first of several ladder stiles in cross-walls lies just to the left side of the ridge, the next slightly further left. The stiles guide you down towards Ystradlyn. Beyond the last one you'll see a stand of conifers. Head for them to locate a farm road taking you past the lake and the house at Tyddyn Mawr to the road. Turn left to return to the car park and the end of a long but memorable journey.

Opposite: On the old quarry railway trackbed towards the head of Cwm Pennant.

The Nantlle Ridge

*The classic linear route taking in all of these
    delightful ridges*

Start: Rhyd Ddu (Snowdon car park, Rhyd
    Ddu railway station) (GR: SH 572527)

End: Talysarn (car park off junction of
    Station Rd and B4418) (GR: SH 488529)

Finish: Tal-y-sarn

Distance: 8 miles/13km

Height gain: 3020ft/920m

Time: 4½–5½ hours

The walk can be done with cars parked either end. Alternatively, you could base your start from Caernarfon where there are regular buses to and from Talysarn (service 80a, Silver Star) and Rhyd Ddu (service S4). A slightly more expensive but excellent option is to use the Welsh Highland Railway between Caernarfon and Rhyd Ddu. If you want to park one car at Rhyd Ddu there is an on-demand service from Penygroes and Talysarn to Rhyd Ddu, run by Huw's Taxi Service. This should be booked in advance and confirmed on the day (tel. 01286 676767).

Most of the walkers in the big Rhyd Ddu car park will be either catching the little narrow-gauge Welsh Highland Railway steam train or they will have their hearts set on climbing Snowdon. You will be turning your back on this and crossing the road to those shapely mountains on the other side.

Through a kissing gate a path of slate flags cuts across a wet field. On reaching the Afon Gwyrfai stream by a cottage it turns left to cross the second of two bridges. A winding farm track crosses more rough pasture to reach an elbow in the Nantlle road.

Turn left through the adjacent roadside gate to follow the bridleway track south-westwards across fields. After turning right just south of Drwsycoed Uchaf Farm, the bridleway resumes its south-westerly course across rough grassland west of Llyn y Gader, with the grassy slopes of Carn Drws-y-coed rearing up to the right.

A narrow path forks right from the main bridleway and, beyond a ladder stile, toils unrelentingly up steep grassy hill slopes. After a tough climb the path attains the ridge just south of Carn Drws-y-coed's summit cairns. A ladder stile in the ridge wall gives access to this summit. The view down Carn Drws-y-coed's plummeting northern cliffs and across to the climbing grounds of Craig y Bera is worth all the effort, as is the view southwards along the ridge to the shattered craggy pyramid of Drws-y-coed and the north face of the next peak, Trum y Ddysgl.

Follow the wide path alongside the wall on a narrowing grassy ridge with the crags of Clogwyn Marchnad falling away to the right. The grass gives way to crag and boulder and the gradients steepen. A winding path clambers up the nose of Mynydd Drws-y-coed, mostly keeping left of the edge. You'll need to use your hands in places but in clement conditions experienced mountain walkers will

Opposite: On the nick of the ridge between Tal-y-mignedd and Trum-y-Ddysgl.

find the route exhilarating rather than daunting. The difficulties are short-lived and soon you're on the summit.

A descent among crags down to the col leads to a fine grass ridge rising steadily to the summit of Trum y Ddysgl, whose great cliffs and screes have been offering an increasingly spectacular and more intimate onward view.

You're now heading for Mynydd Tal-y-mignedd on a pleasing grass ridge, which narrows in the middle section. Beneath the craggy slopes on the right a tiny tarn, Llyn Cwmyffynnon, shelters from the elements in its sullen, seldom-trod corrie. Beyond the col there's a nick in the ridge, the result of a landslip. A narrow muddy path negotiates this before the route continues along a velvety grass ridge climbing to Mynydd Tal-y-

Below: Looking north across the Nantlle Ridge from Craig Cwm Silyn.

mignedd's summit. The chimney-like column on the summit celebrates Queen Victoria's Jubilee. Looking across to the next peak, Craig Cwm Silyn, it is obvious that there is a change in the hills for the peaks beyond are broad, rough and bouldery. They have in fact been topped by the volcanic ash flows (Pitts Head tuffs) from the ancient Llwyd Mawr eruptions.

A grassy ridge descends steadily SSW then WSW to reach the deep pass, Bwlch Drosbern. An old drovers' route used to cross the ridge here but today there seems to be no trace of their passage. Ahead, the rocky arête above Craig Pennant can be tackled head on but it would be better to take the easier path angling right to skirt the steepest crags before continuing on the bouldery terrain of a broad ridge.

Once you're on the summit plateau, a cairned path will lead over bouldery ground to the summit cairn. The expansiveness of the summit means that you have to walk to the edge for views into Cwm Pennant and the Nantlle Valley. Rocky Moel Lefn and its mines and quarries dominate the former valley, while the latter leads the eye further afield to the numerous hillside mining villages west of Mynydd Mawr.

Head west across the boulders, passing two subsidiary tops before continuing across grassland. Beyond a step stile in a fence, leave the main ridge to follow a course around the rocky rim of Cwm Silyn, where there are fine views of the lakes, slabs and buttresses of Cwm Silyn.

On reaching a large enclosure, continue along the right side of a wall and on the crest of the grassy north-west ridge. On nearing the cross-wall at the bottom of the ridge just beyond the outflow of the lowest lake, veer left to cross a ladder stile before turning left along a wide track. This leads to the road-end at Maen-llwyd. Follow the road past the farmhouse and then the cottage of Maen-y-gaseg before turning right along a farm track leading towards Glangors. Turn left on the waymarked path in front of this farmhouse towards a small wood. Keep the wall on the right and follow it towards the next cottage, Fron-oleu.

Go right through a gateway before reaching the farmhouse and turn left again in the next field – highlighted by arrows. This now passes Fron-oleu and goes downhill, still by the wall, to the quarry on the right. Turn right on meeting a quarry track and go through a kissing gate to reach the quarry's approach road. Follow this downhill past slag heaps and cottages to Tanyrallt, where an impressive old chapel has been turned into an outdoor centre.

Immediately opposite, a signed footpath takes the route across fields and down to the tree-lined banks of the Afon Llyfni. Go over the footbridge and turn right along the riverside path to reach the Nantlle road. Turn left along it and into Talysarn.

Overleaf: Looking across Llyn Dywarchen into the Nantlle Valley.

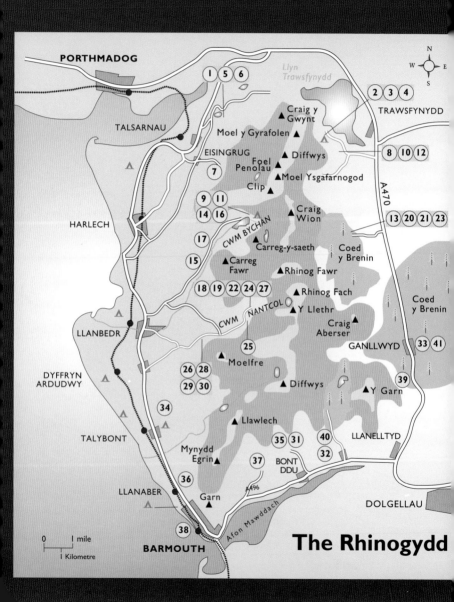

The Rhinogydd

Stand on the southern shores of Llyn Trawsfynydd when the early morning sun sheds its golden light on the bare rock faces to the west and you could swear you were in Utah's Canyonlands. Walk the winding trail to the heather paths on the other side of the ridge and you could be forgiven for thinking you had been transported into Scotland's Northern Highlands. Descend though oak woods to the verdant pastures, the pretty tarn, the crags and the stone-built cottages of Cwm Bychan and you could be in the heart of the Lake District.

Yet this is Wales; the mountains are the Rhinogydd; and, although they're spectacularly good rock peaks, they have not yet been discovered by the masses.

The mountains, part of what is known to geologists as the Harlech Dome, span 22 miles/35km from Maentwrog and the Vale of Ffestiniog in the north to Barmouth and the Mawddach Estuary in the south. The range, which took its name from the central two peaks, Rhinog Fawr and Rhinog Fach, consists of thick beds of gritstone and shale formed in the Cambrian era over 500 million years ago, much older than Snowdon. The much-faulted rocks are riven by deep transverse canyons creating repeated obstacles to hikers walking the 'ridge'.

THE PEAKS

Main Tops	height	
Y Llethr	2480ft	756m
Diffwys (south)	2460ft	750m
Rhinog Fawr	2362ft	720m
Rhinog Fach	2335ft	712m
Y Garn		
(above Llanelltyd)	2063ft	629m
Moel Ysgafarnogod	2043ft	623m
Foel Penolau	2014ft	614m
Clip	1937ft	590m
Moelfre	1932ft	589m
Llawlech	1930ft	588m
Diffwys (north)	1876ft	572m
Craig Wion	1853ft	566m
Moel y Gyrafolen	1754ft	535m
Mynydd Egryn	1695ft	517m
Carreg-y-saeth	1482ft	452m
Craig Aberserw	1444ft	445m
Craig y Gwynt	1444ft	431m
Carreg Fawr	1066ft	325m
Garn (Barmouth)	720ft	220m

Above: Rhinog Fach and Rhinog Fawr at sunset.

You would think the harshness of the terrain would make the Rhinogydd an un-attractive proposition. But this is far from the truth, for on these fine distinctive moun-tains you can still pioneer your own pathless routes to the summits or clamber up anonymous rocky bluffs – and you can scramble over the rocks without resorting to rope. There are more rocks per Rhinog than any other Welsh mountain, except perhaps Tryfan.

To the east of the Rhinog ridges, the land slopes away in drab grassy moorland which has now been cloaked in the inevitable plantations of Sitka spruce. There are quick and easy walks from here to the tops, but quick and easy is often quick and boring – and, more often than not, the first hour of walks from this direction are very forgettable.

In the west there are three main valleys, each with their own special characteristics. The Afon Artro, which begins life as a peaty stream beneath Clip in the north, flows out to the sea at Llanbedr and Shell Island. A pretty little road from Llanbedr weaves among little knolls and oak woodland before turning into Cwm Bychan at the head of the valley. Hereabouts there's a dead-end road with a car park in a field beyond Llyn Cwm Bychan. On one side of the lake are the impressive buttresses of Clip, on the other the equally impressive Carreg-y-saeth (rock of the arrows).

Cwm Bychan is the place for walking the northernmost peaks from Clip to Craig y Gwynt, and the Rhinogydd's roughest terrain on Craig Wion, whose jagged ridge extends to the bell-like massif of Rhinog Fawr. These days, the northern peaks, the highest of which are Moel Ysgafarnogod and Foel Penolau, are unfrequented. There are no real paths to speak of, and if you're following a track it will have been made either by feral goats or by miners of centuries past. One such track, the Roman Steps, climbs out of Cwm Bychan and crosses the range at Bwlch Tyddiad north of Rhinog Fawr. In the upper reaches it has been paved with great gritstone slabs forming a spectacular stairway to the mountains. To call this Roman is fanciful, however: it's medieval in its origins, and would have been used by cattle drovers,

Right: Bwlch Drws Ardudwy in its stunning late summer colours.

And yet there are signs everywhere of ancient civilizations: the cairn circle at Bryn Cader Faner is particularly impressive, as are the earthwork remains of the old fort on Moel Goedog. In times when the Roman soldiers from Caernarfon patrolled their Sarn Helen road around Trawsfynydd, these hills would have been alive to the sounds of ancient tribesmen who worked the rough pastures hereabouts.

The Afon Cwmnantcol is a southern tributary of the Artro. It's a lively stream, tumbling down from the rocks of Rhinog Fawr and Rhinog Fach. The river and its country lane wriggle beneath the slopes of Foel Wen and Moelfre, through cow pastures and woodland copses to enter upper Cwm Nantcol. This is wilder than Cwm Bychan, with less woodland and with even more heather growing out of the thin subsoils.

Maes-y-garnedd, which lies at the end of the road in Nantcol, had an important roll in the British Civil War. It was then home to Colonel John Jones. The Barmouth and Harlech areas were strong supporters of the Crown, Harlech being one of the last strongholds to surrender to the Parliamentarians. But Jones wasn't one of the Royalists. He married Cromwell's sister and took an active part in the war, being one of the signatories of Charles I's death warrant. The Restoration was untimely for Jones, for Charles II remembered him and condemned him to death. Diarist Samuel Pepys noted that the steaming remains of Jones's hung, drawn and quartered body were dragged all over the streets of London.

Beyond Maes-y-garnedd, Rhinog Fawr and Rhinog Fach act as sentries at the head of the cwm, separated by a dark defile known as Bwlch Drws Ardudwy. An old drovers' route climbs into its shadows, making it one of the most spectacular approaches for walkers, who are confronted by great walls of rock and steep slopes of heather.

The Kingdom of Ardudwy, the heart of the Rhinogydd, was once feared both for its tough fighting men and for its rough uncompromising terrain. Ancient highways threaded meekly through the shadows of lonely mountain passes on their journey to and from Harlech.

Ysgethin, the next valley to the south, has as colourful a history of murder and treachery as anywhere in Ardudwy: bandits and highwaymen would hide from their victims behind crags. No man would dare to pass through without a fast horse, a pistol, or both! Ysgethin is wide and, although the hill slopes above the lakes of Bodlyn and Llyn Erddyn have craggy faces, most of the rocks of the north are gone, replaced by windblown rushes in the valley bottom and gaunt, grassy, whale-backed hillsides. Even Diffwys and Y Llethr, the highest two peaks in the whole range, hide their best sides from Ysgethin but, in spite of this, the sheer drama and mystery of the valley draw devotees back time after time.

Beneath Moelfre on the old Harlech–London mail coach road are the ruins of Ty-newydd, a haunt not only of drovers but those bandits and highwaymen. Just beyond the inn, the old road crosses the river at Pont Scethin, a low, one-arched packhorse bridge that skulks in reeds and rushes.

By following the old mail coach road you would reach the grassy ridges north of Llawlech, from where the road makes its escape to the more civilized environs of Bont Ddu and the Mawddach valley. There's an easy grass ridge to Diffwys, which has perhaps the finest summit of the group, with precipitous rocky sides and a gob-smacking view across the sandbars of the Mawddach to Cadair Idris.

Across the conifers of Cwm Mynach (the monks' valley), Y Garn, a rugged rough diamond of a peak, throws out a long, knobbly ridge southwards towards the Mawd-dach. It's a fine, seldom-walked ridge but the one in front of you, from Diffwys through Crib-y-rhiw to Y Llethr, is one of the most splendid in Wales. It's grassy and easy-paced on the ridge-top, with craggy flanks and a host of jewel-like small lakes coming into view as one cwm gives way to another.

It's a world apart from the ups-and-downs, the delightfully horrible canyons, tangled heather and loose boulders north of Nantcol, but the contrast makes the Rhinogydd more intriguing, more invigorating to walk among, and more rewarding when tired limbs have relaxed into the creature comforts of the day's end.

Overleaf: Foel Penolau and Moel Ysgafarnogod seen across Tremadog Bay.

CRAIG Y GWYNT

Craig y Gwynt, the white crag, is the most northerly peak of the main Rhinog ridge. Separated from its neighbour Moel y Gyrafolen by the wide hollow of Cwm Moch, the valley of the pigs, it's an amiable fell, and unlike most Rhinog peaks is largely grassy with pale rock terraces and very little heather. Although there are no paths, the hill can be approached and climbed with ease from almost any direction, and the views are good.

The Moelwyn peaks, fronted by the rocky Moelwyn Bach, look particularly impressive from here, as does the dome-like Manod Mawr. Craig y Gwynt is almost a maritime peak and has great views out to sea, where the Llyn Peninsular yawns out to the distant hazy outlines of Anglesey.

The hill is a bit too much out on a limb to be included in a large itinerary, but it makes a fine half-day walk and offers splendid shaded corners for a summer's picnic which may be refreshed by bracing sea breezes.

Left: Craig y Gwynt from Llyn Trawsfynydd.

3. THE RHINOGYDD

Route R1
Llyn Tecwyn Isaf and Cwm Moch

*A beautiful route with changes and contrasts
    at every turn*

Start: Llyn Tecwyn Isaf (GR: SH 630371)
Distance: 3 miles/5km
Height gain: 1377ft/ 420m
Time: 1¼ hours

The walk begins in the idyllic scenery of Bryn
Bwbach, a tiny hamlet overlooking a tree-
shaded, lily-lined lake, Llyn Tecwyn Isaf. The
ruffled and rugged ridgeline of the northern
Rhinogydd, which stretches across the horizon, seems a world away from such lush
greenery.

From the roadside parking spaces along
the northern shoreline of Llyn Tecwyn Isaf,
follow the lane as it winds around the east
side of the lake and turns sharp left. Leave the
lane for the tarred farm lane that climbs to
Caerwych Farm. Beyond the house the lane
becomes a stony track, climbing eastwards
with a wooded valley on the left. Where the
track divides take the left fork, which leads to
the high farmhouse of Nant Pasgan-bach.

By the house the signed path goes half
right and across bracken-infested pastures to
reach some ruins. After crossing a streamlet
on a primitive slab bridge beyond the ruins,
the path turns left above a drystone wall. It
fords another stream beneath a small water-

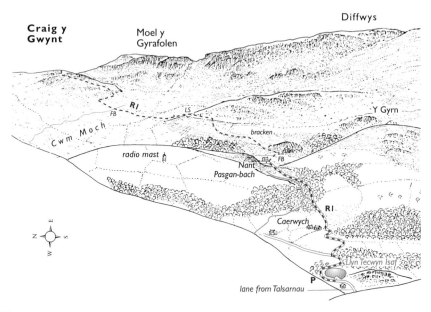

fall and rakes across bracken slopes above the austere medieval farmhouse of Nant Pas-gan-mawr, which is visible among the fields below.

After bending right near a wall corner, the path goes through a gap in a wall to a path junction. Turn left, then go over a ladder stile, beyond which Cwm Moch is laid out before you, with the dark crags of Diffwys and Moel y Gyrafolen dominating the valley head.

Craig y Gwynt's paler crags rise from the far side of the valley and, after dipping down to cross the stream on a slab bridge, the path traverses its lower slopes. On reaching a flat marshy section near the top of the pass – the cairn marked on the map hereabouts has been flattened – climb left, keeping an eye out for a quad bike track, which guides the route NNE towards the summit. Cross the low fence near the top to reach the 431m spot height shown on current OS Explorer maps.

Below: Arriving on Craig y Gwynt summit.

Route R2
Llyn Trawsfynydd

A surprisingly pleasant approach past one of Wales's most infamous buildings

Start: Trawsfynydd Power Station public car park (GR: SH 696384) (see note)

Distance: 3 miles/4.8km

Height gain: 950ft/290m

Time: 1½ hours

Note: Many walkers are parking their cars near the dam at the north-west side of the reservoir and local people tell me that this is tolerated, but check first because the long-term decommissioning of the power station may well change this

---

Follow the tarred access road past the ominous concrete shells of the decommissioned Magnox power station. Beyond this the road passes through attractive woodland to the huge concrete dam, which was rebuilt in 1992 and towers above the wooded gorge of the Afon Prysor. At the far end turn right on a cart track that follows a water leat for a short way. Watch out for a gate on the left. This marks the start of a public footpath winding across moorland. Note that the line of this is actually to the west of that marked on current OS maps. There are fine views across the lake and back to the Moelwyn mountains, especially from where the path nears some woodland.

Craig y Gwynt

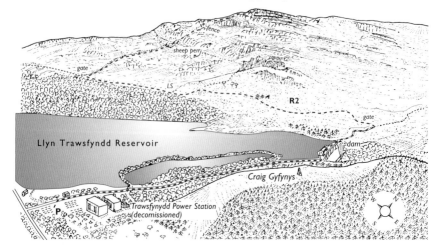

When the path reaches its high point by a gateway in a cross-wall and fence, leave it to climb right up steep slopes of grass and crag – there's no path at present but the going, although steepish, is easy enough. Ignore the first step stile in a fence to the left but take the second by sheep pens. A barricaded gate in the top wall here presents difficulties but can be climbed with care. Now climb by a fence to the upper hillside. A cairned top will be seen to the right. Where the low fence bends left go over it to reach the cairned summit crags.

Other route options

The route can be done from Tyn Twll in the east following the path used in Route R3. This joins Route R1 at GR 671359.

RIDGE ROUTES

Moel y Gyrofolen

Distance: ¾ mile/1.2km
Height gain: 525ft/160m
Time: ½ hour

Descend SSW on trackless grass to the flattened cairn at GR 671359, where you meet the marked Cwm Moch footpath. From here head east along the path, descending slightly to the wall at the foot of Moel y Gyrafolen. Don't cross the ladder stile in front of you, but follow the wall right to the next stile. Over this a narrow path climbs among crags to the summit of Moel y Gyrafolen.

Below: The summit of Craig y Gwynt looking across Trawsfynydd.

MOEL Y GYRAFOLEN

A northern outlier of the real Rhinogydd heather and grit, Moel y Gyrafolen looks down on the great twin concrete cubes of Trawsfynydd's Magnox power station. Though the lake no longer steams as it used to when warmed by the cooling pipes of the power station (now decommissioned), most walkers prefer to look the other way. Indeed, Moel y Gyrafolen turns its back on the unhappy scene to show its best face to Cwm Moch and the west.

Although today the whole of this northern range is laid bare of cultivation, except for the tall drystone walls built in Napoleonic times, the region around the hill was highly populated in the Iron and Bronze ages. A look at the map reveals hut circles, ancient cairns and standing stones. Moel y Gyrafolen must have sheltered these tribes from the cold winds from the east.

Only the narrowest of paths climb to this peak, but if time is short you can get the full essence of the Rhinogydd, the ruggedness of their tangled heather and bilberry slopes, the low and gnarled gritstone cliffs and crags, and the soothing silence that comes from their inexplicable but delightful lack of popularity.

Left: Moel y Gyrafolen.

Route R3
Tyn Twll

A pleasant short route with superb views

Start: Tyn Twll, off the east shores of Llyn
   Trawsfynydd (GR: SH 684358)
Distance: 1¼ miles/2km
Height gain: 1050ft/ 320m
Time: 1 hour

A signed walled track beyond the smaller of
two adjacent gates is lined by trees as it
climbs away from the shores of Llyn
Trawsfynydd. Beyond a ladder stile the path
climbs rough hillside pastures. Bog myrtle
gives a clue to the fact that the route can be
quite marshy after wet periods or in winter.
The crags and heather of Moel y Gyrafolen
rear up to the left and the path soon reaches
the top of the pass at a ladder stile in a tall
drystone wall.

Turn left once over the stile and go alongside the wall to another ladder stile. Beyond
this a narrow path climbs slopes of grass and
bilberry, then through crags to Moel y
Gyrafolen's summit.

Other route options

It's possible to leave Route R2 earlier and
zigzag up Gyrafolen's heathery north-eastern
slopes, although this route is definitely
tougher. Longer approaches can also be
made through Cwm Moch, starting at Llyn
Tecwyn Isaf above Talsarnau (see Route R1).

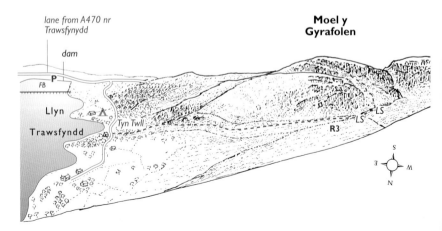

RIDGE ROUTES

Craig y Gwynt

Distance: ¾ mile/1.2km
Height gain: 150ft/45m
Time: ½ hour

Descend on a narrow path northwards down to a ladder stile in a drystone wall. Once over this follow the wall to the right to another stile but don't go over it. Here turn left to follow the Cwm Moch path to a collapsed cairn (GR 671359). Climb right on grassy slopes, keeping an eye out for a quad bike track, which guides the route NNE towards the summit. Cross the low fence near the top to reach the 431m spot height shown on current OS Explorer maps.

Diffwys

Distance: ⅔ mile/1km
Height gain: 230ft/70m
Time: ½ hour

A little path descends south-west to a narrow col. Go over a ladder stile in a cross-wall before climbing a rough, steep path alongside another wall. As this levels out leave it and climb right (west) towards the summit plateau of Diffwys. Turn left to traverse a series of rock slabs to reach the summit cairn.

Below: The medieval cottage of Nant Pasgan Fach, seen on the approach routes from Cwm Moch.

DIFFWYS
(NORTHERN RHINOGYDD)

This Diffwys, not to be confused with the hill of the same name to the south of the range, rises from the western shore of the huge enlarged lake of Llyn Trawsfynydd. Its remoteness and lack of stature – it fails to make 2000ft by a considerable margin – means that Diffwys is seldom visited for its own sake. More often than not it is a minor peak for intrepid souls undertaking the serious task of the complete Rhinog ridge, from Trawsfynydd to Barmouth.

Diffwys hasn't any great mountain architecture: it's more of a flat-topped hill of boulder, crag, grass and heather. Pride of Diffwys though are the dark northern cliffs which overlook Cwm Moch (valley of the pigs) and give the hill its name, which means the precipice. The expansive summit area consists of a series of slightly inclined slabs of Cambrian grit. Unlike the sides, the vegetation of heather between the crags is short-cropped and allows easy walking. The eastern flanks above Trawsfynydd are more chaotic, with squat cliffs and frequent rock outcrops protruding from expansive wooded slopes tangled with bracken heather. They are attractive to look at but the roughness of the terrain makes direct approaches unattractive.

Left: The slabs of the Diffwys North summit.

Route R4
Llyn Trawsfynydd and Head of Cwm Moch

A pleasant route ending with a tough climb

Start: Near Tyn Twll (off Llyn Trawsfynydd's
   west shore) (GR: SH 684358)

Distance: 2 miles/3km

Height gain: 1210ft/ 370m

Time: 1½ hours

A signed walled track lined by trees takes the route away from the shores of Llyn Trawsfynydd. Beyond a ladder stile a path continues the climb over rough hillside pastures, which are marshy in places and dotted with bog myrtle. The crags and heather of Moel y Gyrafolen close in from the left and the path soon reaches the top of the pass at a ladder stile in a tall drystone wall.

Turn left beyond this and straddle the low ridge before rounding the foot of Moel y Gyrafolen's north-west slopes. Soon the dark crags of Diffwys appear beyond them and the grassy valley of Cwm Moch slithers away right towards the coast. A steep bracken-filled hollow between Gyrafolen and Dyffwys offers a way up.

The bracken is thin enough at first to find easy ways through and soon a little track reveals itself and takes you all the way to the ridge. Don't go over the ladder stile in the wall to the left here but climb right by the wall to gain the south-east side of the Diffwys ridge. Where an easy channel breaks right (no path), follow it to the crest. There's no real path over the crest either, with rocky slabs interspersed with short-cropped heather. The summit and its small cairn lie on the east side beyond a shallow pool-like tarn.

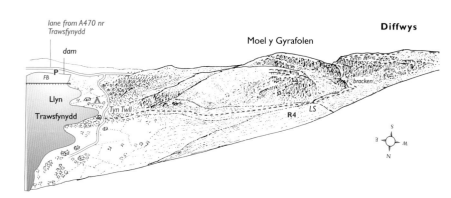

Opposite: The northern cliffs of Diffwys at the head of Cwm Moch.

Route R5
Llyn Tecwyn Isaf and Cwm Moch

A pleasant route ending with a tough climb
Start: Llyn Tecwyn Isaf (GR: SH 630371)
Distance: 4 miles/6.4km
Height gain: 1800ft/ 550m
Time: 2–2½ hours

From the roadside parking spaces along the northern shoreline of Llyn Tecwyn Isaf, follow the lane as it winds around the east side of the lake and turns sharp left. Leave the lane for a tarred winding lane climbing past woodland to Caerwych Farm. Beyond the house the lane becomes a stony track climbing eastwards with a wooded valley on the left. Where the track divides take the left fork, which leads to the high farmhouse of Nant Pasgan-bach.

By the house the signed path goes half-right and across bracken-infested pastures to reach some ruins. After crossing a primitive slab bridge spanning the streamlet beyond the ruins, the path turns left above a drystone wall. It fords another stream beneath a small waterfall and rakes across bracken slopes above the austere farmhouse of Nant Pasgan-mawr, which is visible in the fields below. After bending right near a wall corner the path goes through a gap in a wall to a path junction. Turn left, then go over a ladder stile beyond which Cwm Moch is laid out before you, with the dark crags of Diffwys and Moel y Gyrafolen dominating the valley head. Make a note of the steep ravine dividing the two peaks: this will be your route to the summit.

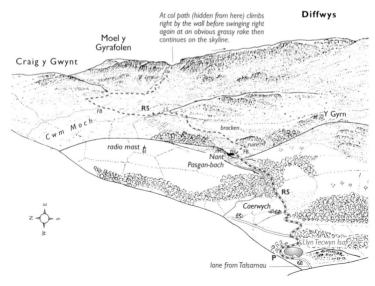

At col path (hidden from here) climbs right by the wall before swinging right again at an obvious grassy rake then continues on the skyline.

Diffwys

Moel y Gyrafolen

Craig y Gwynt

FB   R5

Cwm Moch

Y Gyrn

bracken

radio mast

ruins   FB

Nant Pasgan-bach

R5

Caerwych

Llyn Tecwyn Isaf

P

lane from Talsarnau

The path descends to the valley floor to cross the stream on a slab bridge, then climbs the low hill slopes of Craig y Gwynt. On reaching a ladder stile in a wall beneath Moel y Gyrafolen, turn right along the near side of that wall before climbing among the bracken of the previously described ravine.

A winding path soon develops and takes the route to a narrow col and a cross-wall. Turn right here and climb steeply by the wall. The path soon reaches the southern edge of the summit plateau of Diffwys. The wall ceases to be of any use as a guide – it will skirt the southern slopes of the range for the next few miles – so head westwards across heather and ribbed gritstone crags to reach the small summit cairn that lies at the western end of the mountain.

Other route options

It's feasible to make an approach via the Nant Pasgan cottages and Bryn Cader Faner but this would be a bit contrived. The approach from Trawsfynydd Power Station by way of Craig y Gwynt would be a better bet (see Route R2).

RIDGE ROUTES

Moel y Gyrofolen

Distance: ⅔ mile/1km
Height gain: 80ft/25m
Time: ½ hour

The northern cliffs of Diffwys need to be rounded to the east, so when traversing the angular rock slabs and pools of the summit aim for the Trawsfynydd side of the ridge. Make for a drystone wall which runs alongside the eastern rim and follow it down to the tight col between the two peaks. Go over a ladder stile in the cross-wall before climbing on a narrow path up the eastern side of the fell before reaching the summit.

Foel Penolau

Distance: ¼ mile/400m
Height gain: 197ft/60m
Time: ¼ hour

There's just a slight descent to be made before angling slightly left to a drystone wall running along the eastern side of the ridge. Climb beside this and go through a gap at a wall junction. Follow the wall to a weakness in Foel Penolau's crags. Here, turn right to climb up a grassy rake with Foel Penolau's higher south-western summit to the left, a short scramble up a low terraced crag.

Left: Llyn Tecwyn Isaf.

The distinctively ruffled crest of Foel Penolau, the hill of the white summit, lies at the centre of the Northern Rhinogydd. Ringed by a terraced wall of low cliffs and boulders, it is engaged in a permanent face-off with the more amiable but slightly higher grass-and-boulder peak of Moel Ysgafnogod, which lies across a grassy saddle. Penolau's remarkable summit is roofed by huge flat slabs of ancient Cambrian gritstone, and is divided into two by a narrow grassy ravine.

As would be expected of the second-highest peak in the northern Rhinogydd, Foel Penolau offers a great viewing platform, with distinctive peaks of Snowdonia ringed around the horizon – Snowdon, the Moelwynion and the Eifionydd are wrapped around the blue waters of Tremadog Bay, while the more distant Aran and Arenig and Cadair Idris ranges lie behind the rolling, anonymous hills of the Migneint and the Upper Mawddach.

Opposite: Foel Penolau's cliffs seen from the final stages of Route R6.

Route R6
Llyn Tecwyn Isaf and Bryn Cader Faner
A fine, easy-paced route
Start: Llyn Tecwyn Isaf (GR: SH 630371)
Distance: 4½ miles/7.3km
Height gain: 2100ft/ 640m
Time: 2½ hours

Follow the narrow lane around the north and east shores of the pretty Llyn Tecwyn Isaf which soon turns sharp left through woodland. Leave the lane for a tarred winding lane climbing through more woodland before zigzagging to Caerwych Farm. Beyond the house the lane becomes a stony track climbing eastwards, with a wooded valley on the left and the shapely crags of Moel Tecwyn beyond.

Where the track divides take the left fork, which leads to the high farmhouse of Nant Pasgan-bach. By the house, the path goes half-right and across bracken-covered pastures to reach some ruins. After crossing a primitive slab bridge over a streamlet beyond the ruins, the path turns left above a drystone wall. It fords another stream beneath a small waterfall and rakes across bracken slopes above the austere farmhouse of Nant Pasgan-mawr, visible in the fields below.

After bending right near a wall corner, the path goes through a gap in a wall to a path junction. Turn right here along an undulating path – part of an ancient route linking Trawsfynydd and Harlech – which stays parallel to the wall. After passing beneath the squat cliffs of Moel Ddinas the going gets a little marshier and the wall disappears down the hillside on the right. A GPS unit will be handy at this point because if you follow the exact line of the path you'll miss the wonderful stone circle at Bryn Cader Faner (it's marked as a cairn on the OS Explorer Map).

A faint vehicle track to the left of the line of the now indistinct path does take the route in the right direction, though – this is the one marked with thin black dashes on the Explorer map. A distant shallow lake will be seen directly ahead lying amid marshland. Follow the track for a short way before taking a right fork (GR 650355), which eases through a shallow depression between the low slopes of Ysgafnarnogod and a low grass ridge on the right. The circle lies on the top of the latter and is just a few minutes away.

The remoteness of its position is one of the most dramatic imaginable, overlooking the sweep of Tremadog Bay and standing defiantly on the inhospitable, windswept Rhinog mountainside. The circle, which is believed to date back to the 3rd century BC, is quite small – 28ft/8.5m in diameter with fifteen 6ft/2m-tall outward-leaning pillars ringing the burial cairn. It has been aptly described as resembling a crown of thorns. Treasure hunters have over the years vandalised the site by making excavations exposing the burial chamber, but this is nothing compared to the British Army, who in 1940 used Bryn Cader Faner as an artillery target – there were originally thirty pillars in the circle.

Return northwards to the track and follow it back to the previously mentioned junction. Turn right here and climb the hill slopes. The path will arrive on a grassy brow (GR

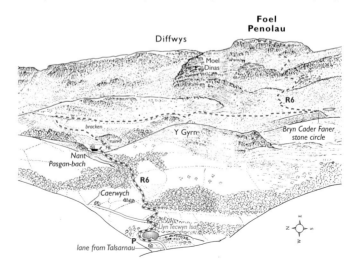

655353). Beyond a marshy dip with a small shallow lake you'll see the cliffs of Foel Penolau on the left side of the horizon and, just peeping out from a nearby series of tiered crags, the rounded grassy summit of Moel Ysgafarnogod on the right.

Work your way around to the right of the marsh and climb up a craggy hollow to reach the grassy saddle between the two peaks. Now head for the obvious breach in Foel Penolau's western cliffs. Over bilberry and boulders you'll come to a narrow ravine between the mountain's twin summits. Both summits are worth visiting and you'll need to pick your way over the terraced crags – easy scrambles unless wintry conditions prevail.

Other route options

Almost any route used for Moel Ysgafarnogod can be used for Foel Penolau – they are so close.

Below: The stone circle on Bryn Cader Faner.

RIDGE ROUTES

Diffwys

Distance: ¼ mile/400m
Height gain: 65ft/20m
Time: ½ hour

Clamber down the rocks to the gap between the north and south tops before turning right through the gap to reach the drystone wall running along the east side of the ridge. Follow the rough course to the saddle between Penolau and Diffwys, where it's just a short climb to the cairn on the latter's summit slabs.

Moel Ysgafarnogod

Distance: ¼ mile/450m
Height gain: 165ft/50m
Time: 20 minutes

Clamber down the rocks to the gap between the north and south tops then head southwest down a weakness in Foel Penolau's low cliffs to a wide grassy saddle. A faint path climbs the easy grass slopes to Moel Ysgafarnogod's summit trig point.

MOEL YSGAFARNOGOD

The highest of the northern Rhinogydd peaks at 2043ft/623m, Moel Ysgafarnogod, the bare hill of the hare, is a domed peak with a craggy south face but with amiable north-eastern flanks of grass and sparse rock outcrops.

To the north-west lies Llyn Dywarchen, a horseshoe-shaped rushy lake languishing in a lonely cwm. To the south, amid an area of old manganese mines and overgrown tracks, lies another little lake, Llyn Du. The triangular lake's dark waters are hemmed in by crags that help to justify its name (black lake), which is especially apt on a day when clouds hang low or when a mountain mist engulfs the mountainsides.

Unlike Foel Penolau, easy ascents of Ysgafarnogod are plentiful, although few real paths exist. The comfy grass ridge, topped by a cairn and a stone-built trig point, may mean that the urge to wander further may be replaced by a desire to repose on the grass and watch the waves of Tremadog Bay lap over its wide beaches, or perhaps just lie back to survey the fluffy white clouds scudding across the pale blue heavens.

Left: The summit cairn of Moel Ysgafarnogod looking to Foel Penolau.

Route R7
Eisingrug and Llyn Du

A fine, easy-paced route on miners' tracks

Start: Road-end east of Eisingrug (toll for parking) (GR: SH 629342)

Distance: 2¾ miles/4.5km

Height gain: 1295ft/ 395m

Time: 1½–2 hours

From the car parking space at the end of the road take the right fork track beyond the gate. This winding track heads roughly in a south-easterly direction before being joined by an old drovers' route which has traversed the slopes of Moel Goedog. Now the track turns left and heads north-east to pass the dam at the southern end of Llyn Eiddew-bach. By now the grass slopes are interspersed with heather and boulders and the much-faulted gritstone of Moel Ysgafarnogod's slopes rear up behind.

At a track junction turn right on a gently inclining track climbing past old manganese mine workings to reach the shores of Llyn Du. The track ends on the north shores of the small triangular lake, but a faint path stays on fairly level ground at first to round the low cliffs on the left. Reassuringly, the bouldery dome of Moel Ysgafarnogod soon appears beyond a grassy depression ahead. The best way to the summit is to climb the easier grassy slopes to the south-west.

Above: Llyn Du beneath Moel Ysgafarnogod.

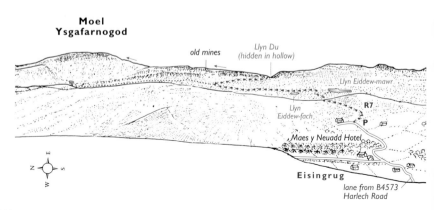

Route R8
Cefn Clawdd and the Old Mine Road

An easy but attractive way on an old miners' track

Start: Manganese mines, Cefn Clawdd (GR: SH 684336)

Distance: 2 miles/3.3km

Height gain: 1150ft/ 350m

Time: 1¼ hours

From the old mine continue up the tarred road with the rugged northern Rhinogydd directly ahead. Just before reaching the farmhouse of Cefn Clawdd turn off right on a stony miners' track. This winds and climbs over rough grassland at first, then around craggy slopes. After passing a ruined mine building, the track becomes a bit marshy. Beyond a small conifer plantation it veers left and eventually ends.

A narrow and faint path climbs right over some rocks. On the skyline you'll notice a gap in a prominent drystone wall (the gate in it is usually lying adjacent on the ground). Climb the pathless grass slopes to go through this. A faint path on a low ridge to the left offers an easy way over grass and bilberry. This disappears half-way up but just continue to climb in the same direction to the trig point on Moel Ysgafarnogod's summit. For views of Llyn Dywarchen, a rushy, horseshoe-shaped tarn, detour westwards along a grassy ridge.

Note: If you want to visit Foel Penolau first, turn right after going through the gap in the wall and follow the wall past the guarding cliffs. A grassy rake descends from the left and this leads up to the gap between Penolau's north and south tops. Thread through the crags on the left to reach the slabbed summit.

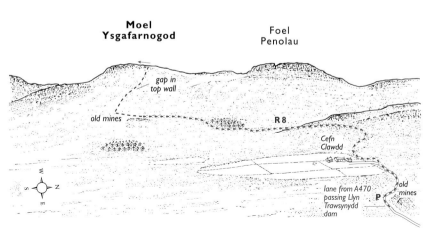

241

Other route options

Approaches could be made from Llyn Tecwyn Isaf via either the stone circle of Bryn Cader Faner (Route R6) or directly up the hil slopes above Nant Pasgan-bach to Foel Penolau.

RIDGE ROUTES

Foel Penolau

Distance: ¼ mile/450m
Height gain: 150ft/45m
Time: 20 minutes

From the trig point a faint path descends the grassy northern slopes and cuts across the equally grassy saddle between the two peaks. Aim for the weakness in Foel Penolau's cliffs – this lies in the south-west corner. Climb among boulders and crags to reach the ravine between north and south tops, then scramble up among boulder and crag to the gigantic horizontal summit slabs.

Clip

Distance: 1⅓ miles/2.1km
Height gain: 395ft/120m
Time: ¾ hour

There are infinite routes that could be used here, as any one of the minor tops could be included or circumvented left or right. From the summit of Ysgafarnogod head westwards towards an outlying western summit. Just before reaching this a faint track descends a grassy bowl to an equally grassy depression with a line of low gritstone cliffs ahead. Keep to the left of these to pick up eventually a path that leads to the shoreline of Llyn Du, which has been hiding in a deep hollow.

Follow an old miners' track along the east shores of the little lake, then go through a gap in the cross-wall just beyond and rake left up an obvious grassy ledge. After approximately 50 yards, the ledge becomes indistinct and a short scramble up a rock terrace takes the route to the next level – a traverse of the left side of the tor. A sheep-track of a path has developed again by now and leads to another lake, Llyn Corn-ystwc, which appears beneath a craggy knoll on the right.

Beyond some marshy ground and yet more horizontal rock-slabs, the path continues over heather cotton grass and bilberry on the east side of a cairned peak: the summit, marked on the map with a spot height of 596m, is sometimes referred to as Craig Ddwrg, although this name really refers to the crags flanking the east side of the ridge hereabouts. Skirt the right side of this with Clip now large in the view ahead. A narrow path drops to a rugged boulder-ridden ravine overlooking the pass between Clip and Craig Wion – Bwlch Gwylim. Now it's just a short climb to reach the huge horizontal slabs which form the summit of Clip.

Opposite: On Cefn Clawdd miners' track, with Craig Dwrg cliffs ahead.

CLIP

Clip, which means the sharp edge, towers above the head of Cwm Bychan in the form of a steely grey cone of tiered rock and scree, contrasting starkly with the lush pasture woodland and lake of the valley. The mountain sends down a complex craggy south-western ridge to the shores of Llyn Cwm Bychan but it's not for walkers – there's just too much vegetation and tall walls to negotiate. Clip's east slopes, known as Craig Ddrwg, are almost as impressive when seen from the sullen moors of Crawcwellt or above the spruce plantations of Coed y Brenin. Most direct routes to Clip involve the climbing of a wild boulder-strewn ravine climbing from the lonely pass, Bwlch Gwylim, to the ridge.

Like several of the northern Rhinogydd peaks, Clip's summit is characterised by gigantic horizontal rock slabs, one of which supports the large summit cairn. The view south from the summit is exquisite with the pasture and oak woods of the valley leading the onlooker's gaze up the Roman Steps path, through the Cambrian canyonlands to the big Rhinog.

Left: Clip from Cwm Bychan.

Route R9
Cwm Bychan and Bwlch Gwylim

The most popular and most interesting route
Start: Cwm Bychan (GR: SH 647315))
Distance: 1½ miles/2.5km
Height gain: 1410ft/ 430m
Time: 1¼ hours

From the barn at the east end of the car park, follow a signed shortcut 'to Clip'. After going through a gate into a field, climb half-right up rough slopes of crag and bracken to the marked footpath at GR 646318. The path now rakes north-east before threading through the narrow pass, Bwlch Gwylim, between Clip in the north and Craig Wion to the south.

A few paces beyond the summit of the pass you should see a rough bouldery hollow to the left. After going over the stile in the wall climb left into the hollow, where a path does develop and climbs to the ridge. Climb left over the rough undulating ridge to the cairn on Clip's summit.

Above: Start of Route R9 from Cwm Bychan.

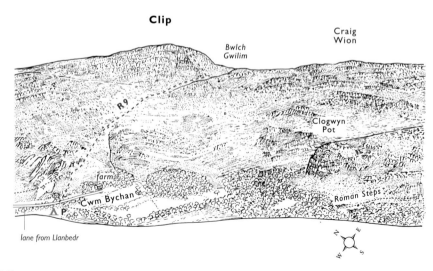

Route R10

Crawcwellt and Bwlch Gwylim

A rather dull way

Start: Cefn Clawdd Manganese Mines
    (GR: SH 684336)

Distance: 2½ miles/4.2km

Height gain: 1115ft/340m

Time: 1½ hours

Turn right from the mines back down the lane towards Trawsfynydd, then double back up the stony track descending towards the cottage of Wern Fach. Where the track divides take the left track, which crosses the Afon Crawcwellt using a concrete bridge. Go over the stile by the farm. Turn right to the next stile (one of many on this route) on a marshy streamside path that passes the house Wern Uchaf (Wern Cyfrdwy on current maps). The knobbly ridge from Clip to Moel Ysgafarnogod, including the terraced rock wall of Craig Ddrwg, is imposing from here and the sense of drama increases as Craig Wion's crags also cast their shadow. Gradually the mountainsides close in and the path enters the pass of Bwlch Gwylim.

Just before the rock knoll at the summit of the pass turn right and climb up a rough bouldery gully to the ridge. It's a steep route with an uncertain start but a path soon develops and takes you to the ridge. As in Route R9, turn left towards the cairn on Clip's summit.

This route could be combined with Route R8 up Moel Ysgafarnogod for a good day out.

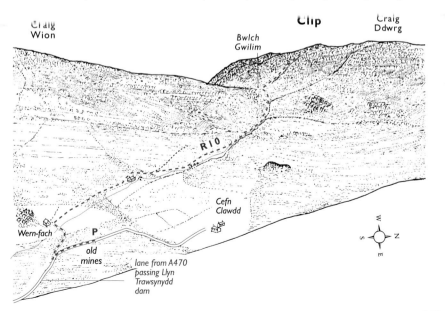

Other route options

Most other routes would be tough and involve scaling tall cross-walls. The easiest of the routes with no walls to climb would be from the Eisingrug road end to Llyn Eiddew-mawr, where a climb south-eastwards up one of the vegetated gullies would lead to the ridge just to the north of the summit.

RIDGE ROUTES

Moel Ysgafarnogod

Distance: 1⅓ miles/2.1km
Height gain 460ft/140m
Time: ¾ hour

Descend to the top of the gully above Bwlch Gwylim then keep to the left side of a rock tor marked as Craig Ddrwg on the map (spot height 518m). A narrow path continues along the right side of the crest knolls to reach the first of two small tarns, Llyn Corn-ystwc. After traversing more slopes of heather and crag, still to the right of the crest, Llyn Du comes into view. You will need to clamber down tiered crags before raking left along a grassy shelf down to the miners' track by the tarn. Beyond the track a little path continues around the east side of the ridge with Moel Ysgafarnogod's rocky slopes clearly in view

beyond a grassy depression. Aim for Ysga-farnogod's south-west slopes, the grassy slopes overlooking Llyn Dywarchen, a horse-shoe-shaped lake on the west side of the ridge. This will lead to a grassy ridge, an easy promenade away from Moel Ysgafarnogod's summit trig point and cairn.

Craig Wion

Distance: 1¼ miles/2km
Height gain: 360ft/110m
Time: ¾ hour

Again, descend to the top of the gully. This time descend the gully to Bwlch Gwylim. A wallside path on the south side of the pass scrambles up rocks and heather. Veer left away from the wall, keeping to high ground to avoid the tallest crags and stay on the ridge west of a C-shaped tarn, Llyn Twr-glas. A cairned route continues over heather and slabs of rock to the highest point, the 566m spot height, which overlooks another lake, Llyn Pryfed.

Opposite: The crag and heather slopes of Clip and Llyn Eiddew-mawr.

CRAIG WION

This low rakish peak of terraced crag lies immediately south of Bwlch Gwylim and overlooking Cwm Bychan in the west, with the marshes of Crawcwellt and the conifers of Coed y Brenin to the east. Craig Wion forms part of a ridge described by Harold Drasdo in his classic *Big Walks* as a 'splendid mile of Celtic badlands'. The summit itself is clad with amazing flat rock slabs and flanked by two fine tarns, Llyn Pryfed and Llyn Twr-glas.

Many approaches to it are guarded by thick heather, boulder and crag, but don't let that put you off Craig Wion, for here is a peak that typifies all that is good about the Rhinogydd: it's an unspoiled wilderness where you can wander with only the constraints that your own limbs put upon you.

The ruggedness of Craig Wion contrasts with the verdant beauty of the western panorama, which encompasses the pastures and lovely oak woods surrounding Cwm Bychan's lake. This, in turn, is punctuated by the striated rock peaks of Carreg-y-saeth and Clip. To the north Rhinog Fawr beckons. However, between here and that grand peak, the intervening ridge is cut deep by transverse canyons that would make Utah proud.

Opposite: Craig Wion from near Coed y Brenin.

Route R11
Cwm Bychan and Bwlch Gwylim

A rugged climb
Start: Cwm Bychan (GR: SH 645315)
Distance: 2 miles/3.1 km
Height gain: 1310ft/400m
Time: 1½ hours

From the barn at the east end of the car park, follow a signed shortcut on the left 'to Clip'. After going through a gate on the right climb northwards up rough slopes of crag and bracken to the marked footpath at GR 646318. As you gain height the views south towards Rhinog Fawr reveal a dramatic contrast between the verdant fields and oak woods and the fierce heather-cloaked craggy terraces and ravines.

The path rakes north-east to a narrow rugged pass between Clip and Craig Wion. At the col, just beyond the cross-wall and ladder stile, turn right to gain the Craig Wion ridge where you should keep to the wide crest. There's one short scramble before a cairned path heads south on heather and crag. A small C-shaped tarn, Llyn Twr-glas, appears to the left. The narrow path continues over crags, heather and slabs to reach Craig Wion's summit cairn, where a larger lake, Llyn Pryfed, comes into view.

Opposite: Llyn Pryfed from the summit of Craig Wion.

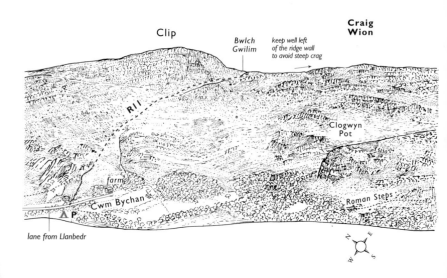

Route R12

Crawcwellt and Bwlch Gwylim

A sombre start across wet moorland

Start: Manganese mines, Cefn Clawdd
  (GR: SH 684336)

Distance: 2¼ miles/4.4km

Height gain: 1015ft/ 310m

Time: 1½ hours

Go back along the lane from the mines towards Trawsfynydd, but after about 300 yards double back along the stony track descending towards the cottage of Wern Fach. Where the track divides take the left track, which crosses the Afon Crawcwellt on a concrete bridge. As you draw level with the right side of the house, turn right across marshy fields parallel to the river.

Pass to the left of the next house, marked Wern Cyfrdwy on the map but known locally as Wern Uchaf. You'll see the remains of an old water wheel. Beyond the house go right

to return to the riverside, where you go through a gate and climb damp moorland. Don't be led away from the river by a shepherd's track, which veers half-left towards Craig Wion's east slopes.

Eventually the sombre moorland scenes are left behind as the rocky flanks of Craig Wion and Clip close in to form the pass of Bwlch Gwylim. Turn left along a grassy channel made by a streamlet just before reaching the col and its cross-wall to gain the Craig Wion ridge. Gradually rake up low slopes to the right to gain the ridge crest but stay well clear of the wall running along the western edge of the ridge – the scramble would be harder by this wall.

A sketchy path, highlighted by several cairns, continues with views on the left towards two lakes. First to appear is Llyn Twrglas, then, as you reach the summit, the larger Llyn Pryfed.

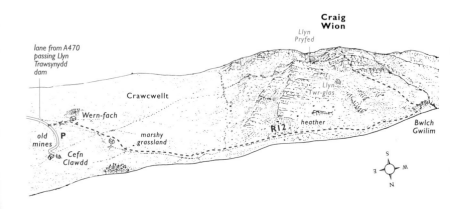

Above: The rugged crags
and canyons of Craig
Wion, seen from Carreg-
y-saeth.
Right: The old mill by
the banks of the Afon
Crawcwellt.

Route R13

Coed y Brenin and Hafod Gynfal

A hardly walked route through forest and a
   fine little hollow of heather and crag

Start: Coed y Brenin – the terminus of the
   Crawcwellt lane (GR: SH 685302)

Distance: 2½ miles/4km

Height gain: 1050ft/ 320m

Time: 1½ hours

From the car park just inside the forestry boundaries take the right fork flinted road, then turn right again to head north. The road swings left after about ½ mile/800m. Watch out for a footpath waymarker pointing right: this is the route out of the forest. In 2008 the trees had been felled but expect a new crop of saplings within a year of this. The way-marked path, which is further east than the one shown on OS maps, heads north, goes through a gap in the wall and passes to the right of a ruined farmstead, Hafod Gynfal (ignore the arrow on the left side of the ruin – that was the line of the old path). The path

reaches a ladder stile on the edge of the plan-tation (GR 677315).

Over the stile, climb left alongside the boundary of the forest – the ground is marshy in places and there are no paths. Turn left with the boundary, which is now ill-defined as the trees have been felled inside the perimeter and a scattering of young trees have seeded themselves outside.

In fine weather you could clamber up rocks to the ridge from almost any point, but the easiest line lies just across the outflow of Llyn Pryfed (GR 672312) – an impressive angular rocky bluff looks down on the spot. A short way up the hollow a sketchy path goes through a gap in the wall and continues a climb through a heather-and-grass channel cutting into the mountain with the crags of the Craig Wion ridge on the left. In the upper stages the stream goes subterranean.

On reaching the shores of Llyn Pryfed, climb left by a substantial drystone wall to the cairn on the summit.

Craig Wion

Llyn Pryfed

R 13

Crawcwellt

Coed y Brenin

LS

ruin

P

waymarked
path off road

lane from A470 Llanaber

Other route options

Any which way you can – a short-cut from the Roman Steps and Llyn Morwynion or perhaps a direct route from Coed y Brenin – but be prepared for a slog through heather, thick bilberry, bracken and loose rock, which is not to everyone's taste.

RIDGE ROUTES

Clip

Distance: 1 mile/1.7km
Height gain: 425ft/130m
Time: ½ hour

Head north along the slabbed crest, scrambling down a bouldery slope to another flat section. Keep right of the wall to find an easy way down to the path at Bwlch Gwylim col then climb the rough bouldery hollow ahead to reach the northern Rhinogydd ridge. A left turn will lead across more crag and heather to Clip's summit.

Rhinog Fawr

Distance: 1¾ miles/2.7km
Height gain: 1150ft/350m
Time: 1–1½ hours

After following the cairned crest path the complex route descends a heathery slope to a depression where the ridge changes from a southerly to a south-westerly direction. Various paths lead over or round the crests – take your pick – with frequent canyons working against the grain. It's spectacular stuff, but it can be energy-sapping in the context of a long journey. Llyn Morwynion is a gem of a tarn, set deep among a complex of crags.

A route descends to Bwlch Tyddiad– yet another canyon! This is where the so-called Roman Steps take walkers across the range; maybe the first walkers you'll have seen all day. Follow this well-defined drovers' track to the left for a short way, but take the first narrow path on the right when the spruce trees of Coed y Brenin come into view. This winds around rocky terraces to reach Llyn Du, a small tarn set spectacularly beneath the fragmented cliffs of Rhinog Fawr. You can walk around either shore to reach the gulley slanting right up the slopes. At the top of the gulley a cairned path climbs left up stony slopes to reach Rhinog Fawr's summit trig point.

Left: The crag that marks the start of the climb to Llyn Pryfed above Coed y Brenin.

This low but impressive rugged peak, translated as the arrow rock, towers above the south shores of Llyn Cwm Bychan, as proud as any Rhinog. It's an angular rock ridge with tiered and much-faulted gritstone crags, many upthrusted diagonally. While its northern flanks rise from the stunningly beautiful verdant pasture and crag surrounding Llyn Cwm Bychan, those of the south decline to the wilder environs of Gloywlyn, which is a long narrow tarn set in a landscape of faulted slabs and heather.

Any gaps and crannies in Carreg-y-saeth's crags are filled with the tangled roots of heather and bilberry, mingled with bracken and loose rock. Unlike other peaks it has no paths to its summit areas. Those tackling Carreg-y-saeth will have to be on their guard as the terrain is as ankle-twisting as it is exhilarating. The ascent is worthwhile, though, especially if you like peace on your hills.

The peak has two summits: the higher is to the east, while the one to the west is known as Castell Carreg-y-saeth. Both are topped by slabs of crag and small cairns. The views are incredible. Gloywlyn now hides beneath the upper crags but Rhinog Fawr looks menacingly good. The drum-shaped Clogwyn y Pot fronts a mountainscape that looks a bit like Arizona, with added purple and green bits of vegetation. To the west the sweep of Cardigan Bay leads the eye to the Llyn Peninsula and the Isle of Anglesey. You're close enough to see the waves!

Opposite: Carreg-y-saeth from Cwm Bychan in the west.
Below: Carreg-y-saeth and Gloywlyn from Rhinog Fawr.

Route R14

Cwm Bychan and Gloywlyn

A wonderful Rhinog experience, but a very tough final climb

Start: Cwm Bychan (GR: SH 646315)

Distance: 1¼ miles/2.1km

Height gain: 950ft/ 290 m

Time: 1¼ hours

Go through the gate at the east end of the car park and turn right on a track that goes across a bridge/causeway spanning the Afon Artro, which has divided into three streams hereabouts. Where the track veers left across pastureland, leave it to follow a path going straight ahead by a fence. After crossing a ladder stile, the splendid little route climbs under the canopy of oak woodland before re-emerging into a rugged valley of bracken and boulder. All around you are the typical Rhinogydd tiered gritstone crags. The path crosses a nice packhorse-type stone bridge and continues through the valley with the surrounding crags closing in. Most walkers will be

heading for the Roman Steps, so you'll need to watch out for the Gloywlyn path junction.

If the cairn wreckers haven't been active, a small cairn marks the spot beyond a slab bridge and adjacent to a netted rock flood barrier. The path now climbs right over a low craggy spur, then through a bracken-filled hollow to another ladder stile at GR 649305. A narrow peaty path continues through a narrow bracken-filled hollow before climbing through heather and rock. Where the path divides take the right fork, which will soon bring you to the northern shore of Gloywlyn. The magnificently placed rushy lake has marvellous views to Rhinog Fawr. It makes an ideal refreshment stop before tackling Carreg-y-saeth.

Take the path rounding the western shores of the lake, then the first right fork, climbing to a heathery shoulder overlooking the marshy bowl of the Afon Gloyw-lyn. The rest of the climb is trackless and on rough steep slopes of heather, crag outcrops and loose boulders. The hill throws out a rugged arm to your right. Follow the route of least resistance on this before scrambling left (westwards) among the crags – watching out for loose boulders. The rigours of the route are short-lived and soon you'll find yourself on the cairned summit, which is topped by slabs of crag and small cairns.

Other route options

The peak could also be accessed from the west – from Pont Crafnant or Cwm yr Afon lower down in Cwm Bychan.

Above: The little packhorse bridge on the beautiful Cwm Bychan route to Carreg-y-saeth (Route R14). Clip is the prominent peak on the horizon.

CARREG FAWR

Rising steeply from the oak woodland and rushing waters of the Afon Artro in slopes of shattered rock and heather and topped by much-faulted rocky bluffs rising in tiers to the summit, Carreg Fawr, the big rock, looks far bigger and more important than it is. Although the peak is everything that a real Rhinog peak should be, everything has been scaled down by a half.

Walk up from the banks of the Artro, above the forest and the vegetation proliferates. The path is always there but delights in ducking for the cover of heather, bracken and bilberry. Above this the breezy summit is topped by a little cairn with a fine maritime view of Harlech and Tremadog Bay. Look east and the rugged mountainscape starts with a ruffled blanket of heather criss-crossed by tall stone walls built in Napoleonic times and culminates in the shapely peaks of Carreg-y-saeth and Rhinog Fawr.

Left: Carreg Fawr seen across the rough vegetated slopes traversed by the Route R15 path from Crafnant.

Route R15
Pont Crafnant
A rather devious and seldom-used path
Start: Pont Crafnant (GR: SH 617289), car
   park a short way north along the road
   (GR 619295)
Distance: 1½ miles/2.4km (from car park)
Height gain: 850ft/260m
Time: 1 hour

Go over the bridge, Pont Crafnant, spanning the Afon Artro and follow the track over the field, past the barn and on to the wooded slopes at the east side of the Artro valley. The track, now of coarse stone, rakes up the shaded slopes. Watch out for a right fork on a grass path climbing away from the track at GR 623289.

This sticks close to the wall on the right, passing a ruin before making a small zigzag (not as large as that shown on the map). It leaves the woods beyond a ladder stile and gate and the route moves into typically rugged Rhino country. It veers left, with the crags of Carreg Fawr dominant in the view ahead and the broken stone of old quarry workings to the right. As height is gained the path becomes sketchier and, in summer, overgrown with bracken. To make it easier to locate the gap in the drystone wall at GR 627291, stick with the path through the bracken rather than the more open but marshy grassland to the left.

Once through the gap the path stays parallel to the wall on the left as it ploughs through thick heather to reach a ladder stile at the highpoint of the right of way. From here you are looking down into the valley of the Afon Gloyw-lyn. Twenty yards or so beyond the stile, immediately beyond low crags on the left, climb left on rough heather slopes. After a few paces a narrow path develops, taking the route up to the little cairn on the summit.

Other route options
The peak could also be accessed from Cwm yr Afon higher up in Cwm Bychan but the right of way marked doesn't exist on the ground.

Carreg Fawr

Opposite: The summit cairn on Carreg Fawr.

In the middle of the range and separated by the passes of Bwlch Tyddiad and Bwlch Drws Ardudwy, the big Rhinog has the most distinctive outlines of the whole range. W. P. Haskett Smith, often referred to as the father of rock climbing, said of Rhinog Fawr: 'It is one of the barest and most rocky mountains in all Wales, and yet it has hardly anywhere on it a crag of respectable height.'

Seen from the busy A470 road across the vast bare moorland of Crawcwellt and the conifers of Coed y Brenin, Rhinog Fawr is almost bell-shaped; from the shores of little Llyn Du its northern face is rugged, with scree-scraped gullies biting deep into the crag. The most impressive face, however, is the one seen from slopes above Bwlch Drws Ardudwy, for the mountain is now powerfully angular in profile and riven by diagonal scree-filled gullies and tilted rock strata.

Strangely, the top is an amiable place with a nice wind shelter – there are even carpets of bilberry on the unfrequented edges. To the south Y Llethr blocks the view but otherwise it's quite spectacular, with the Cambrian grit peaks and heather beds punctuated with scores of lakes, the most prominent being Gloywlyn and Llyn Cwm Bychan in the north, and Llyn Hywel, half-hidden but lying precariously in a high rocky cwm between Rhinog Fach and Y Llethr. Cardigan Bay parades itself along the western horizon – and if it's really clear you may pick out the hills of Wicklow in Ireland.

Opposite: Rhinog Fawr and Cwm Nantcol from Moelfre.
Below: On the summit of Rhinog Fawr.

Route R16
Cwm Bychan and the Roman Steps

*The most popular route through varied and
attractive scenery*

Start: Cwm Bychan (GR: SH 646315)
Distance: 2⅓ miles/ 3.7km
Height gain: 2000ft/610m
Time: 2 hours

Go through the gate at the east side of the car
park and turn right along a causeway over the
three streams of the Afon Artro. Where the
track you're on curves left go straight ahead
on a path which soon enters and climbs
southwards through pretty woodland. As the
path emerges on the hillsides and gains
height, it climbs on the slabbed Roman Steps
path, which weaves through impressive rocky
tors. Just beyond the pass of Bwlch Tyddiad
you arrive at a grassy hollow overlooking the
spruce woods of Coed y Brenin.

Here, leave the main path for a narrow
right fork track traversing the heather and
boulders of the eastern flanks of the range
before climbing right to Llyn Du. Go around
the lake's east shores before climbing a bouldery gully slanting right from the far shores.
At the top of the gully a cairned path swings
left over stony ground to climb to the summit.

*Above: Rhinog Fawr seen across the oak
woods of Cwm Bychan.*

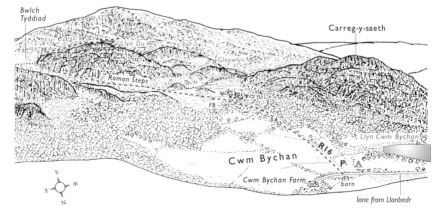

Rhinog Fawr

Route R17
Cwm-yr-afon and Gloywlyn

A rather devious and seldom-used path

Start: Cwm-yr-afon car park a short way
    north along the road (GR: SH 619296)

Distance: 3½ miles/5.5km

Height gain: 2030ft/620m

Time: 2–2½ hours

Head north along the road from the car park
before turning right over Pont Cwm-yr-afon, a
one-arched stone bridge spanning the tree-
enshrouded Afon Artro. A stony track takes
the route past Cwm-yr-afon Farm and cuts
across its surrounding fields. Watch out for
the less distinct track climbing away from the
pastures by some larch trees on the right.
After crossing and briefly following a boister-
ous stream the track climbs among rough
pasture with rushes and bracken.

To the left are the impressive crags of
Carreg-y-saeth, while to the right rough
slopes of heather and bracken swell to the
rocky fringe of Carreg Fawr. The track
becomes a pleasant grassy swath through
bracken. Don't go through the large gate in
the wall at GR 637294 but follow the path
ahead going through a small gate before

Above: Pont Cwm-yr-afon.

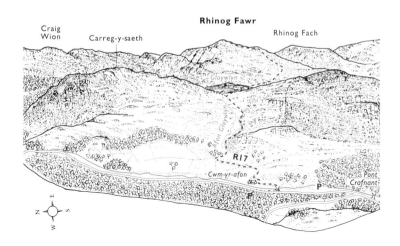

269

coming across the Afon Gloyw-lyn (a mere stream, despite the name).

The path climbs the stream's grassy hollow all the way to Gloywlyn's western shore. Turn right here on a peaty path that climbs a rocky spur to reach the heathery western flanks of Rhinog Fawr. Head south-east here (pathless) to locate a ladder stile in a tall drystone wall (GR 652288). Now a well-defined stone and peat path climbs steadily if unspectacularly up the south-west ridge to Rhinog Fawr's summit.

Route R18
Cwm Nantcol and Bwlch Drws Ardudwy

A dramatic entry and a nice rocky ascent

Start: Maes-y-garnedd (GR: SH 641270), parking by farm (small charge)

Distance: 2½ miles/4 km

Height gain: 1770ft/540m

Time: 2 hours

From the road-end at Maes-y-garnedd a path climbs gently into the defile of Bwlch Drws Ardudwy between Rhinogs Fawr and Fach. The defile widens briefly to form a marshy amphitheatre, then narrows as it nears the top of the pass. By the cairn at the col, leave the main path and climb northwards on a faint path to a hole in a drystone wall.

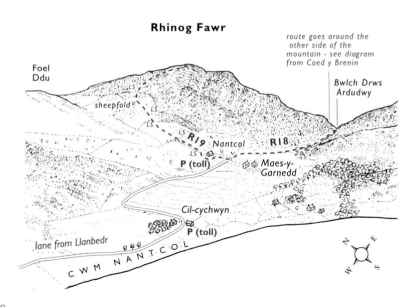

Rhinog Fawr

Beyond this the path disappears for a while – you can see by the screes above that some walkers (and many more wild goats) have made a direct ascent of the slopes, but this isn't the best way. Instead, maintain your direction on to a shelf above and below prominent crags and angle up left on easier crags and heather to reach the first of several cairns, which should appear on the horizon. It is important hereabouts not to stray too far left on to the slabbed southern slopes above the amphitheatre.

After the boulder scrambles of the early stages the route flattens out on a slabbed arm to the right of a marshy hollow with the steep slopes of the summit massif directly ahead. A few cairns mark the way to Rhinog Fawr's eastern side where a narrow path zigzags up to a large cairn on the east side of the summit plateau. A bold track now heads west to the trig point.

Descent

The descent route can be a quite tricky one to locate. From the summit head east, passing the eastern cairn and descending slightly to the level grassy summit rim where the left fork path is the best option. Beyond the rim this winds down among rocks and heather before turning right along another level section. The route has the odd cairn hereabouts, and you should watch out for the one on the edge to the left, overlooking the plantations of Coed y Brenin.

Descending slightly left from here helps you to avoid the steepest of the crag and loose boulder slopes overlooking Bwlch Drws Ardudwy. Eventually the route veers right to join a wall, which leads down to the top of the pass. Turn right along the clear path. This will lead back to Maes-y-garnedd at the head of Cwm Nantcol.

Below: The way off Rhinog Fawr to Bwlch Drws Ardudwy.
Overleaf: Bwlch Drws Ardudwy, just to the west of the col.

Route R19
Cwm Nantcol and the South-west Ridge
An easy if slightly dull route (better in
*   descent)*
Start: Maes-y-garnedd (GR: SH 641270),
    parking by farm (small charge)
Distance: 2 miles/3km
Height gain: 1770ft/540m
Time: 1½–2 hours

Another route from the road-end at Maes-y-garnedd, this one follows the signed track on the left to Nantcol farm where waymarker posts guide the way left of the farmhouse. After scaling a ladder stile on the right, then another to the north of the farm, continue across rough rushy ground to another ladder stile. The path you're on lies slightly to the west of the one marked on current OS maps. Flattened beds of rushes are a giveaway to the line of the path, which heads north at first, then north-west from a ruined stone barn.

Watch out for a sheepfold on the skyline (GR 646285). As the path approaches this it suddenly disappears in a jumble of heather and loose boulders. Keep well to the right of the sheepfold and aim for the stony slopes ahead. The path resumes as a narrow one of peat and stone furrowing through the heather to a primitive stile in the wall at GR 651287. If you cannot locate this there is a ladder stile about 100 yards to the north. Once over both stiles, the route enters the Rhinog Fawr Nature Reserve, beyond which well-defined paths, which meet very soon afterwards, climb easy slopes to Rhinog Fawr's summit.

Below: Above Nantcol on the route to Rhinog Fawr.

Route R20
Coed y Brenin and Bwlch Tyddiad

A route which improves after a dull forest walk

Start: Coed y Brenin (GR: SH 685302) car park at entrance to forest

Distance: 2½ miles/4km

Height gain: 1575ft/480m

Time: 1½–2 hours

Take the right fork forestry road before turning left to pass the neat farmhouse of Graigddu-isaf Farm, where you may be greeted by the sound of ducks. Beyond the farm leave the road for a path along a track signed 'Bwlch Tyddiad, Roman Steps'. The track becomes a path and leads through a forest ride cutting through an area of broad-leaved trees and past a waterfall. The path can be marshy in places. After crossing another flinted forestry road it maintains direction to reach the plantation's western edge at GR 666298. Here you look out across a heath and grass basin in the shadow of Rhinog Fawr.

A sketchy footpath crosses the basin towards the pass, Bwlch Tyddiad, which lies to the right of Rhinog Fawr. As you reach the rocky bluffs watch out for a path on the left. This rakes across the Rhinog ridge's eastern flanks to reach the shores of Llyn Du. Skirt around the eastern shoreline before climbing a bouldery gully slanting right up Rhinog Fawr's bold north face. At the top of the gully a cairned path swings left over rocky ground to climb to the summit.

Rhinog Fawr

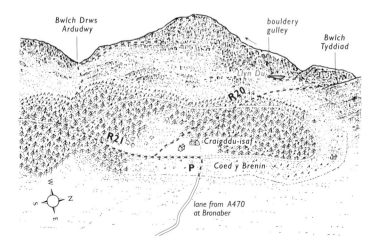

Route R21
Coed y Brenin and Bwlch Drws Ardudwy

An entertaining scramble follows a dull forest walk

Start: Coed y Brenin (GR: SH 685302) car park at entrance to forest

Distance: 2¼ miles/4.5km

Height gain: 1575ft/480m

Time: 2 hours

Take the right fork track from the car park then turn left along the flinted track that heads southwards past Graigddu-isaf farm. Stay with this track all the way to a bridge over the Afon Gau. Turn right following the stream's north bank on a forest ride. After going through a gate at the plantation's edge, a good path rakes half-left towards Bwlch Drws Ardudwy, the gap between Rhinog Fach and Rhinog Fawr.

On reaching a drystone wall just short of the cairn at the col, leave the main path to follow the wall up right to an opening rather like a rough fireplace – this is where you meet Route R18. From here you can see by the screes above that some have made a direct ascent up the slopes ahead, but this isn't the best way. Instead angle half-right (still pathless) on to a shelf between prominent crags. From here climb the easier crags and heather on the left to reach the first of several cairns,

Left: Pistyll Gwyn waterfalls seen on the Roman Steps route.

which should appear on the horizon. It is important hereabouts not to stray too far left on to the slabbed southern slopes above the amphitheatre.

After the boulder scrambles of the early stages the route flattens out on a slabbed arm to the right of a marshy hollow. The steep slopes of the summit massif are directly ahead. A few cairns mark the way to Rhinog Fawr's eastern side where a narrow path zig-zags up to a large cairn on the east side of the summit plateau. A bold track now heads west to the trig point.

Descent

See the descent for Route R18 for the route down to Bwlch Drws Ardudwy, but turn left along the clear path towards the conifers of Coed y Brenin. Although the left fork path encountered soon after joining this route is usable the right fork path is slightly quicker.

Other route options

With no restrictions of access and few real paths, Rhinog Fawr has numerous informal approaches. Most are rough and require a high degree of mountain experience. Direct routes up the north and south faces are possible but for the inexperienced walker they could be dangerous. A long route from the mouth of Cwm Bychan up Mynydd Llanbedr and Foel Ddu would lead to the south-west ridge route and could be combined with a descent via Gloywlyn and Cwm-yr-afon.

RIDGE ROUTES

Craig Wion

Distance: 2½ miles/4km
Height gain: 820ft/250m
   (Note: 1300ft/400m descent)
Time: 1½ hours

Ridge route doesn't begin to describe this entertaining but arduous route of ups and downs. Descend the cairned path winding down the stony north-west flanks that over-look Llyn Du's corrie and Bwlch Tyddiad. Turn right down the gully, descending north-east to the shores of Llyn Du. Round the tarn to the north-east corner and follow a narrow path through the heather, to join the Roman Steps path in Bwlch Tyddiad. Head left along the path.

Near the top of the pass climb right on another narrow path on to a rocky tor where Llyn Morwynion comes into view to the left. The route now works its way between the crags, up and down ravines that cut across the ridge. The ridge eventually changes direction, from NNE to NW, and the path now descends to an area of thick heather before climbing to the next rocky tor and its cairn. Llyn Pryfed comes into view, then a wall ris-ing from its shores joins the ridge-top, almost at the cairn on Craig Wion's summit.

Opposite: Rhinog Fawr from Rhinog Fach.

Rhinog Fach

Distance: 2 miles/3.2km

Height gain: 1150ft/350m

   (Note: 1150ft/350m descent)

Time: 1½ hours

Descend on a winding path heading generally westwards on a short grassy ridge. Take the left fork on nearing the summit rim. This becomes a narrow winding path and descends the rocky east flanks before coming to a flattish craggy arm leading the route SSW towards Rhinog Fach – a few cairns mark this section.

Many walkers go right to the end of this arm, then scramble down very steep slopes of boulder and tangled heather. Instead of doing this, look out for a cairn on the left edge just before the end and descend on the easier slopes above the conifers of Coed y Brenin. On reaching a flattish shelf turn right and descend towards Bwlch Drws Ardudwy. Near the bottom follow a wall on the right to a wall junction where you should go though a gap.

Now a narrow grooved path climbs the very steep north slopes of Rhinog Fach. It levels out and cuts across grassy slopes with crags rising on the right but soon swings right and steepens again as it climbs grassy flanks to gain the ridge by the north summit cairn. Now follow the ridge southwards to the craggier main summit.

RHINOG FACH

The 'little' Rhinog is perhaps even more striking in its form than its bigger neighbour, Rhinog Fawr, from which it is divided by the deep chasm of Bwlch Drws Ardudwy. Seen from the south, it appears as a crag-topped cone with giant scree slopes tumbling into the boulder-fringed shores of Llyn Hywel. Hardly a blade of grass takes root on these hostile flanks. Seen from the east or west, Rhinog Fach has a distinctive, saddle-shaped, Blencathra-like summit.

Four small lakes lie close to the slopes of Rhinog Fach. I've mentioned Llyn Hywel, a magical place, but there's also Llyn Cwmhosan, a tiny lake where bouldered shores are surrounded by pale marsh grasses and heather, dwarfed by the steep boulder slopes of the mountain's west flank. In a seldom-visited basin of heather and grass on the east side there's Llyn y Bi, whose outflow drains into the endless marshy moorland east of the main Rhinogydd ridge. The fourth lake is unnamed and lies forlornly in those same anonymous moors.

Opposite: Rhinog Fach seen from a partially ice-clad Llyn Perfeddau.

Route R22
Nantcol and Llyn Cwmhosan

The finest route in the range

Start: Cwm Nantcol (GR: SH 641270)
Distance: 2¼ miles/4.4km
Height gain: 1705ft/530m
Time: 1½–2 hours

From the road-end at Maes-y-garnedd, a partially flagged path climbs gently into the defile of Bwlch Drws Ardudwy between Rhinogs Fawr and Fach. In places it can become waterlogged, but in most parts it is a delightful ancient highway undulating though dramatic mountainscapes. Y Llethr's slopes on the right are particularly impressive from hereabouts. The mountainsides close in,

then suddenly the defile widens and you come to a marshy hollow beneath Rhinog Fawr's angular slabs.

After traversing the marsh, turn right to cross the second of two ladder stiles in the high wall straddling the pass (this can be difficult in wet weather, when a stream runs at the stile's base). Climb through heather to pass Llyn Cwmhosan. The delightful peat and stone path cuts beneath the bouldery slopes of Rhinog Fach before coming to Llyn Hywel. Trace the bouldery northern shoreline and climb to the ridge wall above Y Llethr Slabs. Here turn left to climb by the wall towards the summit massif. Over a stile in a wall near the top, the path veers left by that wall to reach the highest south summit.

Opposite: Descending Rhinog Fach to Llyn Hywel.

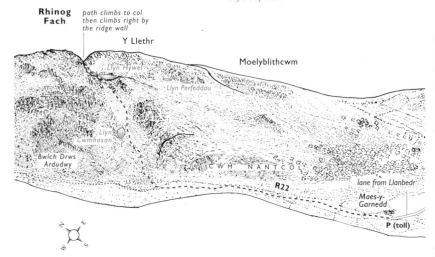

Route R23

Coed y Brenin and the Direct Ascent

A gruelling climb from the pass

Start: Coed y Brenin (GR: SH 685302) car
    park at entrance to forest

Distance: 3 miles/4.8.km

Height gain: 1540ft/470m

Time: 2 hours

Take the right fork track from the car park
before turning left along the flinted track
heading southwards past Graigddu-isaf farm.
Stay with this track all the way to a bridge
over the Afon Gau. Turn right following the
stream's north bank on a forest ride.

After passing through a gate at the plantation's edge, a good path rakes half left
towards the gap between Rhinog Fach and
Rhinog Fawr. As you approach the summit of

the pass, Bwlch Drws Ardudwy, watch out for
a gap in a drystone wall below left. This
marks the start of the direct path up Rhinog
Fach. The narrow path of peat cuts a deep
groove as it winds though heather and rock.

It is extremely steep but very rewarding in
ascent, highlighted by magnificent views
back to Rhinog Fawr's mighty ramparts. A
little grass mixes with the heather as height is
gained and suddenly the path levels out and
traverses a grassy hollow to the east of the
main summit ridge. It soon swings right and
steepens again as it climbs right to gain the
ridge by the north summit cairn. Now follow
the ridge to the craggier main summit and
take in the magnificent views. Make sure you
don't take the left-hand fork path, which
bypasses the summit on the left before dropping down to Llyn Hywel.

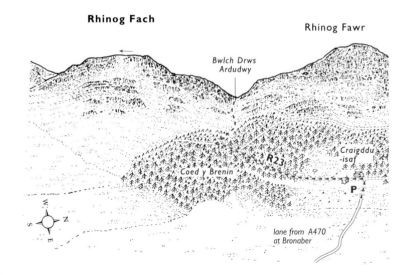

Rhinog Fach

Rhinog Fawr

Other route options

There is a direct route up the west flanks from the back of Llyn Cwmhosan and one that begins higher up on the Llyn Hywel route, using a narrow path threading between the screes of the west flanks to a hollow beneath the north peak of the mountain (see 'Days out', pages 340–41). Routes from Coed y Brenin via Llyn y Bi involve crossing the rather rough and marshy moorland of Cefn Cam.

Below: Rhinog Fach, Llyn Hywel and the Y Llethr slabs.

RIDGE ROUTES

Rhinog Fawr

Distance: 2 miles/3.2km
Height gain: 1210ft/370m
Time: 1½ hours

To call the direct route a ridge walk would be stretching a point, and I couldn't recommend it. The lower slopes to Bwlch Drws Ardudwy are just too steep and unstable to be used safely in descent. The best way is to descend down the south slopes to Llyn Hywel, then take the narrow path down to Ardudwy, passing Llyn Cwmhosan en route.

Climb right to the top of the pass and take the little path angling left to a cross-wall. Squeeze through the hole in the wall. Beyond this the path disappears for a while – you can see by the screes above that some walkers (and many more wild goats) have made a direct ascent of the slopes, but this isn't the best way. Instead, maintain your direction on to a shelf above and below prominent crags and angle up left on easier crags and heather to reach the first of several cairns, which should appear on the horizon.

The steepness of the slopes has now relented and ahead of you lies a flat section of marsh with the domed summit massif of Rhinog Fawr ahead. Follow the ribbed rocks to the right of the marshes. The path keeps north here then zigzags up the rocks and heather of the eastern flanks. Soon it arrives at a large cairn lying on the eastern side of the summit ridge. A bold path heads west to the trig point.

Y Llethr

Distance: 1 mile/1.6km
Height gain: 690ft/210m
Time: ¼ hour

Head east on a path descending alongside a wall, then go right over a ladder stile near the junction with the ridge wall. Keeping the ridge wall to the left, a steep rocky route descends to the col where the Y Llethr slabs plummet into Llyn Hywel. Stay with the wall as it traverses the crest of the slabs and starts the ascent of Y Llethr. The obvious path slants right, away from the wall. It soon becomes loose and eroded as it gains height. The view back across Llyn Hywel to the crag-crested scree peak of Rhinog Fach and the immense south face of Rhinog Fawr is stunning. Soon the path returns to the wall and arrives at the grassy summit plateau, where it's an easy stride to the little summit cairn.

Opposite: Llyn Hywel is cradled by Rhinog Fach (left) and Y Llethr (right), while Llyn Cwmhosan below collects what little light the impending storm allows.

The rugged terraced rocks of the northern Rhinogydd make one defiant last stand on the north face of Y Llethr (which means the slope). This highest peak of the range displays more greenery than those northern neighbours, but ribbed with huge diagonal rock strata and with gigantic, highly tilted slabs plunging spectacularly into Llyn Hywel, it retains all their drama.

Climb to the top of those steep slopes, however, and the drama is gone, replaced by an amiable grass ridge, a tidy ridge wall and a small cairn. The heather has disappeared, as have those loose progress-slowing boulders. You've only just got here, you've wondered at the fine views of the twin Rhinog peaks and the wide seascapes of the western horizon, but already your legs want to stride out over those easy ridges, which could take you all the way to Barmouth should time allow.

But let's halt awhile and check out Y Llethr, for it's a fine peak and those northern crags are perpetuated on the eastern side, where the slopes descend to Llyn y Bi. There's typical Rhinog heather-and-rock scenery on devilishly harsh slopes surrounding Llyn Perfeddau. Just below this tarn and at the head of Cwm Nantcol, the remains of old mines include grassed-over causeways, inclines and the odd shaft. Further south another ridge links the craggy dome of Moelfre, which guards the exit to both the Nantcol and Ysgethin valleys. That leaves only the wild heathery cwm of Llyn y Bi. Although routes from Cwm y Dwaulo involve some bog trotting, paths from the Y Llethr slabs crest can take you down to the seldom-visited lake shore – it's an ideal place for a picnic as long as the evening shadows haven't made it an inviting spot for the midges too!

Opposite: Y Llethr in the calm last light, seen here from the unnamed lake at Cefn Cam to the east.
Right: Y Llethr from the lower slopes of Rhinog Fawr at the head of Cwm Nantcol.

Route R24
Nantcol and Bwlch Drws Ardudwy

The finest way to the top
Start: Maes-y-Garnedd Farm
  (GR: SH 642269)
Distance: 3 miles/5km
Height gain: 1890ft/ 575m
Time: 2 hours

A well-defined, partially slabbed path climbs steadily east towards Bwlch Drws Ardudwy, a heathery defile squeezed between Rhinogs Fawr and Fach. The mountains close in as height is gained but the path briefly descends to a wide marshy bowl beneath Rhinog Fawr's south face. Once across the rushes of the bowl, turn right to cross a ladder stile, the second of two. On the other side a steep, narrow path climbs through the heather past Llyn Cwmhosan, then beneath the bouldery west slopes of Rhinog Fach. Eventually it reaches the shores of Llyn Hywel.

Traverse the boulders on the north shore of Hywel to reach the top of some huge gritstone slabs at the col beneath Y Llethr. Tackle the mountain's steep craggy slopes on a path alongside a drystone wall. A rough, eroded path then climbs above a grassy chute before arcing left to reach the equally grassy summit ridge.

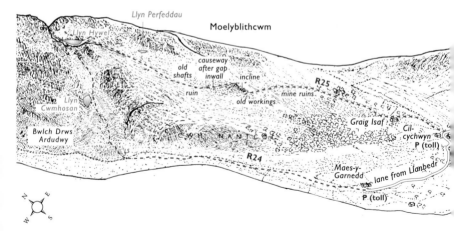

Route R25
Nantcol and Llyn Perfeddau

A fine route with complexities in the middle stages

Start: Cil-cychwyn Farm (GR: SH 633259)
Distance: 2½ miles/4km
Height gain: 1890ft/ 575m
Time: 1½ hours

Follow the rough stony lane past Graig Isaf Farm and the ruins of Graig Uchaf, above the woods, to enter Nantcol's landscape of woodland and pasture. Hereabouts remnants of old mines are slowly crumbling into the bracken and foxgloves. The track, now with a grassy surface, swings to the left, passing more mines. Watch out for the pulley house at the bottom of an incline. Here, turn right off the track and climb the incline. From the top pulley house, a miners' track continues through a broken-down wall and across heather and marshland.

The track has now entered a cwm high above Ardudwy and beneath the wilderness of Rhinog Fach's flanks. It's confusing territory and the paths are not always where the OS shows them to be. The track, now less distinct, passes more mining ruins and cause-

Below: Climbing Y Llethr's upper slopes with the two Rhinog peaks and Llyn Hywel behind.

ways. It ends by a low heather knoll not far beyond a ruined stone building. Here you climb right on a tiny sheep-track of a path weaving its way through shady hollows and past mine shafts. Beyond the shafts the path gains confidence and continues its winding course amid heather knolls and rock outcrops. It would be easy to miss Llyn Perfeddau, as it's hidden behind one of these knolls. When you're just past the little lake, another small path joins in from the right. Double back along this to get a closer look before returning to this same spot.

The narrow path continues through the heather to a larger lake, Llyn Hywel, which lies beneath the huge screes of Rhinog Fach. Follow the path above the south shore before turning right on a steep eroded path up the final slopes of Y Llethr to the grassy summit dome.

Route R26
Moelfre Mines and the Ysgethin Valley
A long and wild approach

Start: Car park beneath Moelfre mines
 (GR: SH 615258)
Distance: 5 miles/ 8km
Height gain: 1970ft/ 600m
Time: 2½–3 hours

From the roadside car park beneath the old Moelfre mines follow the high-gated lane southwards to reach a footpath sign pointing left across the low hillside pastures beneath the grassy dome of Moelfre. The winding grass track comes to a gate in a field corner, beyond which the route turns right to climb by some grassed-over mine spoil heaps. A wall on the right acts as a guide to the route. After a mile the path joins the old Harlech coach road, which has traversed the rough pastureland on the right. The track now

Y Llethr

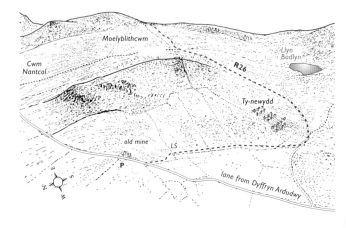

Above: The bare, grassy Moelyblithcwm Ridge seen here links Moelfre and Y Llethr (left).

traverses Moelfre's gorse-scattered southern slopes.

Beyond another junction the now stony left-fork track heads east to pass beneath some pines and the crumbling ruins of Tynewydd, a former coaching inn. Ignore the first sheep track of a path on the left (it will climb to the high pass between the Ysgethin and Nantcol valleys), but take the next at GR 640243. This faint path, shown on the Explorer map as thin black dashes, climbs north across grass hillside before veering right on the approach to the Moelyblithcwm ridge.

It follows the ridge wall at first but veers slightly right away from it before returning just short of the main Rhinog ridge. Go over the ladder stile on the left and climb the steep but well-defined path to Y Llethr's summit.

Other route options

It is easy enough to approach Y Llethr by going down the length of the Ysgethin valley, past Llyn Bodlyn and Llyn Dulyn before climbing left on grassy flanks to the ridge and joining Route R26 at the ladder stile south of the summit.

Above: Y Llethr slabs.

RIDGE ROUTES

Rhinog Fach

Distance: 1 mile/1.6km
Height gain: 490ft/150m
Time: ¾ hour

Descend north by the wall at first, then on an eroded path winding down a grassy chute. The path arcs right, back to the wall beneath some crags, then follows the path down to the col above the Y Llethr slabs, which plummet into Llyn Hywel below. Stay with the wall and climb the rocky slopes of Rhinog Fach. Beyond a ladder stile in a wall the path swings left to follow the wall to the south summit.

Diffwys

Distance: 1¾ miles/2.8km
Height gain: 575ft/175m
Time: 1 hour

Descend the southern grass slopes and go over the ladder stile in a cross-wall at the bottom. The ridge wall acts as an infallible guide as the path undulates over the more rocky ground of Crib-y-rhiw whose uniformly straight east flanks are studded with rock, a contrast to the stark grassy moorland that lies to the east. After passing a couple of pools on the ridge, the path descends to a shallow col at the head of the wild Ysgethin valley, where you can see the lakes of Dulyn, Bodlyn and Erddyn.

Now you begin the ascent of Diffwys, with rocky slopes to the east now tumbling to the afforested Cwm Mynach. There's a short-cut path curving right, slightly below the ridge, but by staying with the crest better views are maintained. The ridge soon kinks to the right to reveal Diffwys's impressively sculpted east face. Not far beyond the path comes to the stone-built summit trig point, which lies precariously close to that face.

Moelfre

Distance: 2¼ miles/4.3km
Height gain: 540ft/165m
Time: 1½ hours

Descend the grassy south slopes and cross the ladder stile at the bottom. Here a faint track veers right along the wide grassy Moelyblithcwm ridge. The track veers left to the south slopes for a while then returns to the crest to follow the wall back to the col. Continue by the wall. Soon the Moelfre ridge becomes bouldery and many walkers may prefer to keep to the left to avoid the most uncomfortable terrain. The boulders relent and the route comes to a ladder stile in the ridge wall. Over it you come to the large cairn marked on the map. The highest and true summit, though not as good a place, lies further west.

MOELFRE

This dome-shaped hill is prominent from the west, where it acts as sentry to the Rhinogydd's inner world and as a dominant peak on the ridge dividing the valleys of Ysgethin and Nantcol. While the southern and western flanks are largely grassy, crags do break through in a north-eastern corrie above Nantcol.

The web of tall stone walls ensnaring Moelfre meant in the past that it wasn't often climbed, but a couple of stiles have been erected since the CROW Act and now the walker has a little more freedom to wander without scaling those walls. The summit is one of rock-scattered, windswept moor grasses with a wind shelter on the western edge, a hollowed-out ancient cairn on the summit and, in the east, a strange fort-like knoll emphasised by a stone wall circle. The views are excellent, with the crags of Nantcol and the twin Rhinog peaks on one side and the wilder but simpler moorland ridges of Ysgethin on the other.

Moelfre also overlooks many of Ardudwy's ancient highways, including the Harlech–London mail coach road and the drovers' roads weaving through Bwlch Drws Ardudwy

Opposite: Moelfre above Nantcol.

and Bwlch y Rhiwgr. Beneath its southern flanks in the valley of Ysgethin, a gaunt stand of conifers guards the innocuous-looking ruins of Tynewydd. The lichenous pile of rubble is all that remains of an old coaching inn, where bandits once robbed a party of London gentlefolk who had halted at the inn on their way to attend a society wedding at Harlech.

At the foot of the mountain, hidden among some hawthorn bushes near the great mansion of Cors y Gedol, lies Coetan Arthur. In real life it's a burial chamber with a capstone, but legend has it that this capstone was flung down from the summit of Moelfre by none other than King Arthur. The legend continues that the imprints found in the rock are the fingerprints of the king.

Route R27
Cwm Nantcol

The best route, taking in the beauty of Nantcol and Moelfre's crags

Start: Cil-cychwyn Farm, parking (toll) (GR: SH 634259)
Distance: 2 miles/3.1km
Height gain: 1310ft/ 400m
Time: 1–1½ hours

From Cil-cychwyn Farm walk back along the road to a footpath signpost on the left, which points uphill across rough, grassy slopes beneath Moelfre's dark craggy north-eastern cwm. The path continues over a ladder stile, then through a gate to the col between Moelyblithcwm and Moelfre. Now you look down on the wide but desolate valley of Ysgethin, where the Bodlyn Reservoir lies in the shadow of Diffwys and its stark crags.

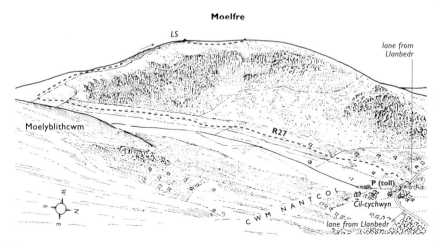

From the moorland col, the route climbs right by the ridge wall. Soon the ridge steepens and is enlivened by a great boulder-field. Near the top you'll notice a strange wall-ringed rocky knoll on the other side of the ridge wall. There's a ladder stile in the ridge-wall at GR 626246. Once over it you're standing very close to the huge summit cairn.

Route R28
Moelfre Mines and the North-west Flanks
A dull but quick route
Start: Car park beneath Moelfre mines
   (GR: SH 615258)
Distance: 1¼ miles/ 2km
Height gain: 1115ft/ 340 m
Time: 1 hour

A grassy vehicle track to the left of the quarry gets the route started as it climbs south. It soon ends but note the position of the ladder stile at the top left corner of pasture (GR 618253). Follow sheep tracks around a grassy depression on the left, then climb left across stony slopes to scale the ladder stile.

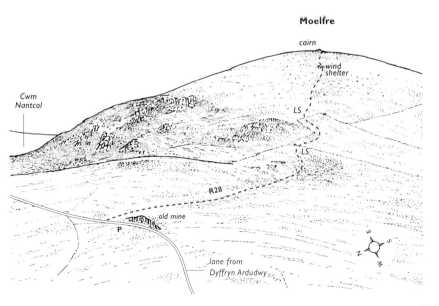

Climb by a wall on the left at first to reach a wall corner, then climb south-eastwards across slopes of boulder and grass to a second stile at GR 621248. A faint path sets the direction (east) up steep slopes but fades into the grass. By maintaining direction you will reach a cairn and wind shelter on the west edge of the hill and now a clear path continues eastwards to the huge summit cairn and shelter.

Other route options

You could start at Tal-y-Bont, climb to Pont Fadog and Cors y Gedol, then follow the old road to Tynewydd (the ruins of an old drovers' inn) before climbing the south slopes to the stile due south of the eastern summit cairn.

Below: Moelfre's summit cairn with Llawlech in background.

Below: The rocky tor east of Moelfre's summit.

RIDGE ROUTE

Y Llethr

Distance: 2¾ miles/4.3km
Height gain: 1115ft/340m
Time: 1½ hours

Go over the stile by the summit cairn and follow the wall (now on your left) down to the col between the two peaks. (Those who don't like boulder hopping can take a course below and to the right of the rocks before rejoining the crest at their far end.) The continuing path, a visible quad bike track, becomes obvious as you descend. Follow it as it climbs the Moelyblithcwm ridge towards Y Llethr. The track veers right in the middle stages but returns to the crest to reach a ladder stile at the foot of Y Llethr's summit. Turn left on steep grass slopes to reach the summit cairn.

Above: Diffwys seen from Crib-y-rhiw at the head of Cwm Ysgethin.

DIFFWYS (SOUTHERN RHINOGYDD)

The most southerly of the Rhinogydd's 2000-footers, Diffwys lies on the elbow of an L-shaped ridge. To the north lies Y Llethr and the main Rhinogydd ridge; to the west lies a long grassy ridge declining to Barmouth.

If that sounds dull, it isn't, for Diffwys shows a defiant craggy face to the Mawddach valley and an unrelentingly steep and almost as rough east face, which towers above the lake and the conifers of Cwm Mynach. In Cwm Mynach, the monks' valley, tramways and crumbling stone-built ruins are relics from an old mining industry and offer perhaps the most interesting Diffwys ascent.

Excitingly, there's gold in these hills. The old Clogau mines, which lie to the south, were until recently mined to supply the gold for the wedding rings of the royal family.

Diffwys looks out to the west along the wild Ysgethin valley, where its sombre slopes of tussocky grass, crag and boulder drop into the enlarged reservoir lake of Bodlyn. The scene here is one of remote desolation but it is not without beauty. High above Bodlyn on the side of the rocky Crib-y-rhiw lies another small lake, Llyn Dulyn, this time a natural one, but still possessing that windswept wilderness appeal.

The summit of Diffwys is divided by a tall drystone wall and has a fine stone trig point overlooking the precipices of the east face. Although it's several miles from the seaside at Barmouth, the feeling is that this mountain belongs to the coast. Salty breezes waft in from Cardigan Bay and the Mawddach estuary to emphasise this impression. The view of the Cadair Idris cliff faces and the Mawddach estuary is truly spellbinding, but this is complemented to perfection by the graceful arced bay of Tremadog to the north-west and the well-remembered peaks of central Snowdonia beyond. Alas, the feet get itchy and it's time to continue along those wonderfully easy-paced ridges either to Barmouth (for a well-deserved portion of fish and chips) or to Y Llethr.

Route R29
Pont Scethin and the Old Harlech Road

A walk through history

Start: Car park beneath Moelfre mines
  (GR: SH 615258)
Distance: 5½ miles/ 8.8km
Height gain: 2035ft/ 620m
Time: 3 hours

From the car park follow the lane southwards to a footpath sign pointing left across the lower hillside pastures of Moelfre. The winding grass track comes to a gate in a field corner, beyond which the route turns right to climb by some grassed-over mine spoil heaps. Now follow the wall on the right across high fields. After a mile the path joins the old Harlech coach road, which has climbed from the coastal plains on the right. This now traverses Moelfre's gorse-scattered southern slopes.

Take the less distinct grassy right fork track by some pines. This traverses the rush-ridden valley-bottom to reach Pont Scethin, an old packhorse bridge. From here a waymarked path soon re-establishes itself as a green road zigzagging up the hillside towards the ridge. A little way up the hill lies Janet Haigh's Memorial Stone, which was erected by her son Melvyn, Bishop of Winchester, after her death in 1953. It reads: 'To the enduring memory of Janet Haigh, who even as late as her eighty-fourth year despite dim sight and stiffened joints still loved to walk this way from Tal-y-Bont to Penmaenpool . . . Courage, traveller.'

On reaching the ridge top turn left alongside the wall. Paths over tufted grass on either side of the ridge wall lead over a subsidiary top on to Diffwys, where a left turn leads to the summit trig point.

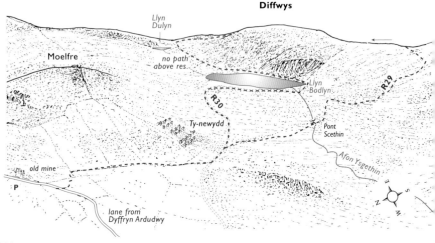

Route R30
Ysgethin Valley and the Bodlyn Reservoir

A seldom-used route on the quiet side of the mountain

Start: Car park beneath Moelfre mines
  (GR: SH 615258)
Distance: 6 miles/ 9.4km
Height gain: 2360ft/720m
Time: 3–3½ hours

As in Route R29 follow the high-gated lane southwards to reach a footpath sign pointing left across the lower hillside pastures of Moelfre. The winding grass track comes to a gate in a field corner, beyond which the route turns right to climb by the old mine spoil heaps. A wall on the right acts as a guide to the route. After a mile the path joins the old Harlech coach road and traverses Moelfre's gorse-scattered southern slopes.

Take the more prominent left fork track heading up the valley of the Ysgethin with the wild, windswept grassy slopes of Y Llethr and Moelfre closing out the rest of the world. The crags of Diffwys are a promise of things to come. Follow the track as it bends right by the shores of Bodlyn then, after crossing the little bridge below the dam, strike out along its bouldery southern shores beneath those previously mentioned cliffs – take care as the boulders can be a little slippery.

There's little in the way of a path from here but the boulder-scattered grassy terrain provides no real problem if you climb the head of the valley to the south of the stream. Suddenly another lake, the smaller Dulyn, comes into view beneath the high bouldery sides of Crib-y-rhiw. Not long afterwards you reach a path skirting the west side of the mountain just below the ridge. Turn right along this. The path rejoins the ridge before climbing beside the ridge wall to Diffwys's summit trig point.

Below: Llyn Dulyn with Moelfre in background.

Route R31
Bontddu and the Old Mail Coach Road

A straightforward if dull route on grass ridges for much of the way

Start: Car park on the minor road north of Bontddu (GR: SH 667197)

Distance: 3½ miles/5.7km

Height gain: 2000ft/ 610m

Time: 2–2½ hours

Follow the metalled lane from the car park to its terminus. Here take the right of two tracks. This is the course of the London–Harlech mail coach road and climbs the grassy spur known simply as Braich. Where the old road passes through the wall on the left before swinging left around the head of Dwynant's hollow, leave it and climb by the wall to the ridge ahead. Once there, climb right by the ridge wall, over a minor top and on towards the craggy top of Diffwys. The dull route is enlivened by splendid views across the Mawddach Estuary towards Cadair Idris. It gains more drama as the path swings left and soon you find yourself looking down precipitous craggy flanks into Cwm-llechwen from the summit trig point.

Opposite: Diffwys from the Cwm Mynach miners' track.

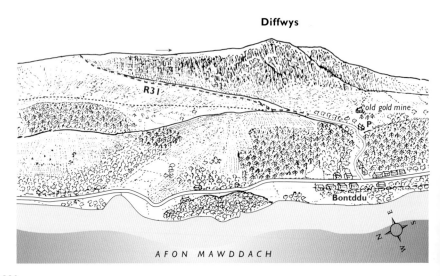

Route R32
Cwm Mynach

A long approach with an exhilarating final climb to the ridge

Start: Lay-by just west of Tycynhaeaf village and the Penmaenpool toll bridge turn-off (GR: SH 684190)

Distance: 5 miles/ 8km

Height gain: 2525ft/770m

Time: 2¼–3 hours

This long route starts on a metalled road up Cwm Mynach, through the charming tree-shaded village of Tycynhaeaf. Beyond Garth-gell Farm it enters conifer plantations. At the end of the tarmac, take the left fork, a flinted forestry road, and follow it towards Llyn Cwm-mynach. About 300m south of the lake at GR 680233 go through a gap in the dry-stone wall on the left to follow a track through the trees. This becomes a rough, bouldered miners' track climbing gradually across the heather slopes with the rugged rock slopes of Diffwys directly ahead. The track ends by old mine workings, but the faint winding route marked on the OS maps with black dashes scrambles to the ridge north-east of Diffwys. Turn left and follow the ridge wall and the precipices to the left to reach the summit trig point.

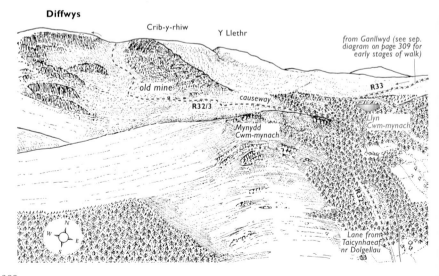

Route R33
Ganllwyd and Rhaeadr Du

A devious walk taking in waterfalls, forest,
*   wild moorland and a lake*
Start: Ganllwyd village car park
    (GR: SH 727244)
Distance: 6 miles/ 10km
Height gain: 2760ft/ 840m
Time: 3½ hours

A tarred lane leaving the A470 road to the left of the village hall leads the route westwards uphill, then into the forest. To the left the Afon Gamlan bounds through the trees on its rocky bed. At a sharp bend in the road, detour left over a footbridge to see the impressive Rhaeadr Du (the black waterfall) before returning to the same spot. The road soon doubles back left. Watch out for a track on the left. Through a gate this climbs parallel to the river and below the house, Tyddyn-y-bwlch. The pleasant walled track joins a forest road, which in turn leads to a riverside crossroads.

Turn left over the concrete bridge and follow the road south-westwards, then westwards though the conifers. The track leaves the forest to traverse moorland with the crags of Diffwys and Y Llethr promising much ahead. It then enters another forestry planta-

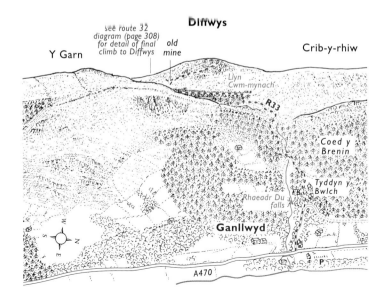

tion in Cwm Mynach. Take the first left fork, then the right fork to round Llyn Cwm-mynach on the west side. About 300m south of the lake at GR680233 watch out for a track on the right, which doubles back through a gap in the drystone wall and continues through the trees. It soon becomes a rough miners' track traversing heather slopes beneath Diffwys. The track ends by old mine workings, but a faint route winds up to the ridge north-east of Diffwys. Turn left along the ridge wall to reach the summit trig point.

Other route options

It is possible to park by the old Bont-ddu gold mine roadside car park and follow paths and tracks into Cwm Llechen before climbing north west on to Craig Aderyn and the rocky south spur of Diffwys. There are no paths on the rough upper slopes, but the views of Diffwys's south-west face are superb.

RIDGE ROUTES

Y Llethr

Distance: 1¾ miles/2.8km
Height gain: 690ft/210m
Time: 1 hour

Follow the ridge wall as it curves right to round the upper recesses of Cwm Llechen before heading northwards, with precipitous drops to the forest and lake of Cwm Mynach. An alternative path leaves the wall to take a shortcut on the left down to some small pools. The high corrie lake of Llyn Dulyn comes into view before a brief climb to the rocky Crib-y-rhiw. Beyond this there's another drop before the route tackles the short but steep grass slopes leading to Y Llethr's summit

Llawlech

Distance: 2½ miles/4.2km
Height gain: 295ft/90m
Time: 1 hour

After the early excitement of Diffwys's precipitous east face the ridge path turns its attentions to the west and follows rough grassland, over a subsidiary but irrelevant grass peak to an unnamed pass at the foot of Llawlech. Here the route is crossed by the old coach road that has climbed from Pont Scethin, which is just visible among the valley-bottom rushes to the north. A gradual climb on grass takes the route to the summit of Llawlech.

Opposite: Rhaeadr Du.

Very few climb Llawlech for its own sake. It plays second fiddle to Diffwys, and is little more than a grassy whaleback, a hump in the Barmouth ridge. Either side of the summit are ancient highways straddling that ridge – to the east, the old London–Harlech road; to the wes,t an old drovers' route through the narrow pass of Bwlch y Rhiwgr. The latter was once a notorious spot, the haunt of highwaymen and bandits who would lie in wait for their victims, perhaps some unsuspecting traveller or a drover carrying clients' money back from the cattle markets of England. No one was safe in this part of Ardudwy.

Llawlech has a smattering of crags and boulders on either side of the ridge. To the north, sheltering on a high shelf above the windswept valley of the Afon Ysgethin lies Llyn Erddyn, the priests' lake – a reference to druids who frequented the area. Nearby are the ancient packhorse bridge of Pont Scethin and the rocky hill of Craig y Dinas, which has a huge pre-Roman fort. This would have been used by local chieftains until the 13th century, so powerful is its strategic position overlooking the coast and guarding the mouth of the Ysgethin.

On the other side of the ridge, the southern slopes decline to the cultivated pastures of Sylfaen and the wooded low hills that overlook the wide, tidal Mawddach Estuary

Opposite: Llawlech seen across a flower meadow above Sylfaen Farm.
Below: Llawlech and Llyn Irddyn.

Route R34
Tal-y-bont and Pont Fadog

Start: Car park, Tal-y-bont (GR: SH 590218)
Distance: 4 miles/ 6.5km
Height gain: 1840ft/ 560m
Time: 2½ hours

From the back of the car park head east along the lane past Y Bedol Inn before taking the path into the woods that cloak this part of the Ysgethin valley. Stay with the main path nearest the stream rather than taking the ones climbing left. Eventually the main path climbs out to a tarred lane next to a stone cottage, Llety-lloegr (the boarding house of the English), which was an old shoeing station and rest stop for drovers.

Turn right along the lane, crossing the fine one-arched bridge, Pont Fadog, before continuing alongside the far banks of the Ysgethin. The lane ends, replaced by two tracks. Take the right fork and follow the clear track over rough pastures towards the nick in the ridge ahead – this is Bwlch y Rhiwgr.

On reaching the top of the narrow pass, climb left alongside the ridge wall to reach Llawlech's windswept summit.

Route R35
Bontddu and the Harlech Coach Road

Start: Car park on the minor road north of
    Bontddu (GR: SH 667197)
Distance: 3¾ miles/6km
Height gain: 1690ft/ 515m
Time: 2–2½ hours

Follow the tarred lane to its terminus and take the right of two tracks, which is the course of the London–Harlech coach road. This soon becomes a walled track climbing Braich, a grassy spur separating the hollows of Hirgwm and the Afon Dwynant. The walls end and the rutted track continues up the spur, soon to join another wall which will act as a guide for about a mile. As it approaches the unnamed peak on the main Barmouth–Diffwys ridge, the old highway arcs left before reaching the ridge wall. The road will descend through a gate into the wild empty valley of the Ysgethin, but the route used here leaves it to turn left by the wall and climb to the grassy summit of Llawlech.

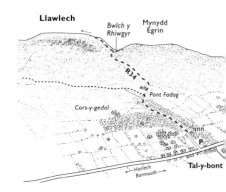

Other route options

It is feasible to use the old Pont Fadog road from above Bont Ddu as far as the pass of Bwlch y Rhiwgr before climbing north-east to the summit. This would offer a good circular when combined with Route R35.

RIDGE ROUTES

Diffwys

Distance: 2½ miles/4.2km
Height gain: 755ft/230m
Time: 1¼ hours

Just follow the ridge wall eastwards to cross the old coach road, then climb more grass slopes to the trig point on the summit of Diffwys. The latter stages will be dominated by the huge craggy drops to the Mawddach estuary and into Cwm Mynach.

Above: Pont Fadog.

Mynydd Egryn

Distance: 1¼ miles/2km
Height gain: 230ft/70m
Time: ½ hour

Again just follow the ridge wall, this time westwards to cross Bwlch y Rhiwgr. A steepish climb on a stony path leads to the huge cairn on Egryn's summit.

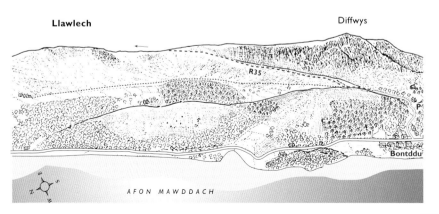

Llawlech · Diffwys · R35 · Bontddu · AFON MAWDDACH

Mynydd Egryn, the last real hill in the Barmouth ridge, is rather like Llawlech, a grassy hump with bouldery sides. It has two summits, the higher eastern one being topped by a huge hollowed-out cairn belonging to the Neolithic era, and is divided by two passes, Bwlch y Rhiwgr, where an old drovers' highway crosses the ridge, and the narrow rocky declivity of Bwlch Cwmmaria.

The hill takes its name from Egryn Abbey near the coast road below. The abbey is now a private dwelling, but was once an important Cistercian grange attached to the Cymmer Abbey near Dolgellau.

Mynydd Egryn is surrounded by fascinating relics from the past. Old sandstone quarries supplied some of the material for the building of Harlech Castle and both Cymmer and

Egryn Abbeys. Running much of the length of the hill are the manganese mines of Egryn and Hafotty. Close inspection will reveal long earthwork remains, shafts and remnants of an aerial ropeway, which would have carried ore down to Egryn Abbey for distribution to Welsh steelworks. In the high fields bordering Ceunant Egryn, the brook that flows down from Bwlch y Rhiwgr, are the twin cairned burial mounds of Carneddau Hengwm. The southern mound is around 150ft/46m long, has three standing stones, a capstone and an intact burial chamber.

For the less serious historian, Mynydd Egryn, like nearby Moelfre, has tenuous connections with King Arthur, including the old stone circle of Cerrig Arthur near Sylfaen Farm to the south of the hill, and Cerrig y Cledd (the sword stone), a split glacial erratic set in woodland near the same farm. An impression of a sword in the latter gives rise to several mystical tales.

Opposite: Mynydd Egryn from the south.
Below: The old fort of Castell y Bermo.

Route R36
Llanaber and Bwlch y Llan

A seldom-used route for those who like their
*   hills quiet*

Start: Llanaber (GR: SH 599181)

Distance: 3 miles/ 4.8km

Height gain: 1770ft/ 540m

Time: 1¼ hours

Note: Car parking on lay-by south of
Llanaber church (GR 605173) – keep
to the side opposite the houses

From the church follow the lane signed to Bryn Bach. Where the lane bends left towards a cottage leave it for a narrow track staggered to the right. This climbs hillside pastures with improving views back to the coast. The track joins one from the left. Here you turn right over a ladder stile. Now a clear track climbs south-west past a small mound marked 'homestead' on the map and enters the access area at a ladder stile, beyond which the route is met by a path from the left. Turn right over another ladder stile then climb half-left on a grassy causeway. After passing beneath an old fort and above another miners' causeway the route heads for the main Barmouth ridge to arrive at Bwlch y Llan. Now you find yourself looking at the wide expanse of the Mawddach Estuary and Cadair Idris.

Turn left on a fairly level path by the ridge wall to the next ladder stile. Don't cross it but follow a rather steep path that climbs north-west up a grassy spur, then north along the Barmouth ridge. There are now ladder stiles in all the cross-walls to make progress easier. The path stays on the east side of the ridge wall as it passes the 461m trig point and descends to the narrow rocky pass of Bwlch Cwmmaria. It climbs steeply out over more stony slopes and over a subsidiary summit before reaching the huge hollowed-out ancient cairn crowning Mynydd Egryn's summit.

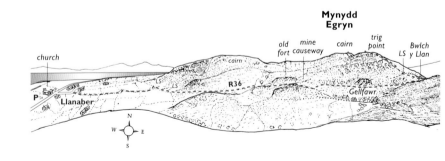

Above: The ancient homestead seen from the Bwlch y Llan track. Right: St John's Church, Llanaber.

Route R37
Goetre-uchaf and Bwlch y Rhiwgr
Another quiet, seldom-used route
Start: Road-end near Goetre-uchaf
   (GR: SH 641192)
Distance: 1¼ miles/ 2.9km
Height gain: 1015ft/ 310m
Time: 1–1½ hours

---

*Note: The lane to the walk is narrow –
please park responsibly*

From the road-end follow the track at the foot of an afforested hill (right) and pastureland (left). The track comes to a T-junction where you should turn left on a track crossing a stream. After going through a gateway it comes to another junction. Turn right here, then left on a path heading for the ridge. After passing beneath stony hillsides it reaches the main Barmouth ridge at the pass of Bwlch y Rhiwgr.

Don't go through the gate at the pass but turn left to climb alongside the ridge wall to reach Mynydd Egryn's summit cairn.

Other route options
There are many obvious routes via Bwlch y Rhiwgr or Bwlch y Llan.

RIDGE ROUTE

Llawlech
Distance: 1¼ miles/2km
Height gain: 460ft/140m
Time: ½ hour

The path lies to the east of the ridge wall and descends on grass and stone with a particularly steep section preceding the last drop to the narrow pass of Bwlch y Rhiwgr, where an old drove road between Harlech and Bont Ddu crosses the range. A straightforward path climbs on the right side of the ridge wall to Llawlech's summit pillar.

Opposite: Diffwys seen from the pastures of Sylfaen.

The first real top on the ridge above Barmouth, Garn, which loosely translated means cairn, is rugged with gritstone crags and huge boulders. The main feature is a climbers' area known as the Slabs (or, more correctly, Creigiau Garn). This is popular with beginners and you can often see groups under supervision tackling the rocks.

The summit is quite a wide and complex area and would be difficult to negotiate in mist or sea fog. Several tors vie for top spot, but the real one lies to the north-west overlooking the verdant pastures surrounding the isolated farm of Gellfawr and the stony slopes descending to Llanaber, north of Barmouth.

Dinas Oleu (the fortress of light), the great rock that rises above the rooftops of southern Barmouth, is an outlier of Garn, and is the Rhinogydd's last stand before tumbling to the waves of Cardigan Bay. On 29 March 1895, Dinas Oleu became the first property donated to the National Trust. The benefactor, Mrs Fanny Talbot, was a friend of John Ruskin and two of the Trust's founder members, Octavia Hill and Canon Rawnsley.

On the shoulder of Dinas Oleu lies the Frenchman's Grave, a walled garden which was the resting place of Auguste Guyard, a 19th-century French philosopher and social reformer. He settled in one of Mrs Talbot's cottages in Barmouth after fleeing from the Siege of Paris. A keen horticulturalist, he cultivated rare herbs and trees on the poor soils of the hill slopes. This site can also be accessed using the hundred steps climbing out from the craggy hill slopes above the harbour.

Opposite: On the path across Dinas Oleu beneath the rugged slopes of Garn.
Below: A young climber on the Barmouth Slabs.

Route R38
Barmouth and Dinas Oleu

A splendid short route with fine views and a
little scrambling
Start: Town car park, Barmouth Promenade
(GR: SH 612158)
Distance: 1¼ miles/2km
Height gain: 920ft/ 280m
Time: 1 hour

From the promenade make your way towards the railway station, going across the level crossing and continuing to the High Street. Here turn right then first left up Dinas Oleu Street. After being joined by Water Street go straight on up Tan y Graig. A Dinas Oleu waymarker points you up the next narrow street, which rakes up the hillside. Take the left fork and at the next two-way footpath sign take the right one, which means maintaining your direction. This takes the route to a patch of open green next to a viewing platform where you can look down on the rooftops of the town and across the Mawddach Estuary and out to sea – the Pembrokeshire coastline may even be visible if it's clear.

Turn left now on a well-used path and take the first right, a winding path that goes through a gate in a drystone wall. You could make a detour (right) to the Frenchman's Grave, but otherwise continue eastwards, with the rugged crags of the Barmouth ridge rising up to the left and the peaks of Cadair Idris soaring high above the sandbars of the Mawddach Estuary to the right.

Ignore paths branching right and stay with the path you're on through the next gate. This veers left towards the foot of the craggy ridge, then right again. Beyond two more gates the path tucks under the climbing crags known as

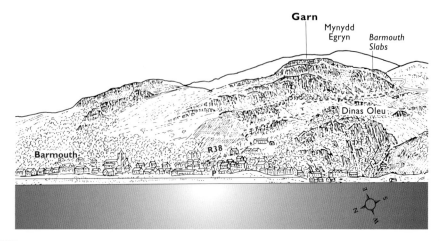

the Slabs, then comes out on to a narrow tarred lane. Stay off the main 'bolted' climbing crags but double back left here on a clear path that climbs among the rocks (ignore any signs about needing permits – this is now part of an access area). Once above the main crags the path disappears and it is just a matter of crag hopping to the summit of Garn, which lies across a small grassy gap beyond the subsidiary summit you will first encounter.

Other route options

The route could be shortened by driving up to the Panorama Walk car park (GR 625166), taking the narrow lane towards Gellfawr Farm and leaving it at the Slabs.

Below: The rocky slopes of Dinas Oleu rising from the sands of Barmouth.

If you've made your way across the damp moors to the south-east en route to Rhinog Fawr you may well have spied a squat but rugged peak rising from the watershed between the rivers Gamlan and Crawcwellt. Craig Aberserw, as it's known, is rough with heather and ribbed with slabs of gritstone in glorious Rhinogydd tradition. Unfortunately, the peak's western sides are submerged by thick plantations of spruce which, along with tall stone cross-walls, don't really allow an approach from this direction.

The area from the summit southwards is part of the National Trust's Derlwyn Estate and it provides a stile in the fence along the north-west edge. A glance at the map reveals that there's a tarn, Llyn y Fran, on top and it's a rather nice one, set in a hollow of pale moor grass between Craig Aberserw's summit and Craig Derlwyn.

There are no paths to the summit but the going is not hard, for corridors of moor grass and rocky slabs make Craig Aberserw a delightful place to be. It's also very colourful when the August sunshine lights up the grasses to a lovely gold and turns the berries of the mountain ash to a fiery red: all of this is complemented by carpets of blooming heather. The views westward take in the whole of the Rhinog range – from Diffwys in the south to Diffwys in the north – while in the east the little-known volcanic crests of Rhobell Fawr and Dduallt peep over the forests of Coed y Brenin.

Opposite: The southern slopes of Craig Aberserw across the upper valley of the Afon Gam.
Below: Looking west from Craig Aberserw to Y Llethr and Rhinog Fach.

Route R39
Coed y Brenin

A splendid, seldom-trod route with surprisingly good views

Start: Coed Maesgwm – parking near the entrance to the Forestry Signs complex (GR: SH 716276)

Distance: 4 miles/ 6.4km

Height gain: 1180ft/ 360m

Time: 1¾–2 hours

A narrow tarred lane heads northwards from the A470 past the Forestry Signs complex and ends at a turning circle and ford across the Afon Serw. After going across the footbridge head straight across the field on the line of the bridleway, ignoring the footpath arrow to the left. Beyond a wooden gate cross the little stream and continue NNE on a faint path through scrub woodland. The route crosses a fence on the left using a step stile then soon afterwards recrosses it using another stile. The bridleway now continues north on the left side of a rather wet meadow to reach a tarred road. Turn left along this.

On nearing the farmhouse of Ffridd-bryn-coch take the right fork track tucking under trees to traverse moorland with the bell-like Rhinog Fawr directly ahead. The fine grass and stone track threads though gorse to ford a stream beneath a small stand of larches. Beyond this it is joined by a track from the large spruce plantation to the north. The track now climbs steadily south-westwards, with the magnificent Rhinogydd mountains soaring above wild moorland to the right. It is soon guided by a fence on the right and a water leat on the left and climbs beneath the rugged slopes of Craig Aberserw. Beyond a gate it fades into the grass. Stay with the fence here until the moorland tops out. Here you'll see a primitive step stile and a National Trust 'Derlwyn' sign (GR 693264).

There are no paths from here on: the secret is to find the grassy rides between the crags and heather. The going is initially rough

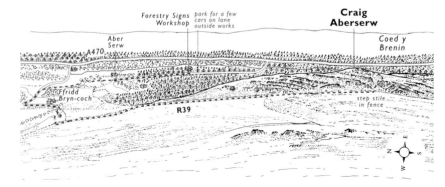

across the unavoidable short heather near to the fence, but by heading very slightly right of straight ahead, you should reach the first of those grassy rides. This angles half-left among tilted typical Rhinog slabs of Cambrian grit. Soon you'll reach the first and best 'summit' at GR 695264. It has an angular rocky crest and a view of Llyn y Fran, which is partially hidden by folds in the pale grassy summit complex. The highest summit, the 445m spot height (OS Explorer map), lies to the north beyond several faults in the rock strata. Just north of this is a small cairn.

Other route options

It is possible to walk from Ganllwyd through the Coed y Brenin forest to the moor at GR 697245, then head north past the ruins of Cefn-carn Farm to the step stile mentioned on Route R38 but the terrain around the farm is confusing and somewhat marshy in places.

RIDGE ROUTE

Y Garn

Distance: 3 miles/5km
Height gain: 1250ft/380m
Time: 2 hours

If you could call this a ridge route, then it would be a rotten, ill-advised one with rough and confusing marshy territory – a forest with no direct tracks and the odd wall to cross for good measure. If you must do it, follow the course of the bridleway to the west of the hill down to the ruins of Cefn-carn Farm. Here the going gets tough as you descend marshy country to cross the Afon Gamlan before climbing to cross the forest road. Beyond that there's a wall to cross before following the forestry perimeter wall to its crest. Now it's a simple matter of climbing right to Y Garn's summit.

Below: A splendid cart track skirting the west side of Craig Aberserw, with Rhinog Fawr ahead.

Y Garn is a real Rhinog but it seems to have been ousted from its rightful position on the main ridge. It lies in isolation to the east, above the afforested Cwm Mynach and the Gamlan valley. The summit is the culmination of a long southern ridge declining to the little peak of Foel Ispri, which overlooks the Mawddach Valley.

Y Garn's northern slopes are chaotic, with no defined ridge, just outcrops of rock set amid deep heather, bracken and the most difficult tussocky grasses. There's a subsidiary peak, Garn Fach, to the west. Here, a rough cwm with a minute lake promises a way down to Cwm Mynach, but what it delivers is a very rough trek.

Opposite: Y Garn from Coed y Brenin.

Tall walls with no gates or stiles and thick heather with few paths have often marred the way to Y Garn, but access agreements and a few stiles have now made life easier. Views from the top make all the effort worthwhile, for here is one of the best views of the Rhinog ridge and the wild country in between. To the north beyond the conifers of Coed y Brenin lies the equally rugged Craig Aberserw. Among the conifers down there the Afon Gamlan has cut through rocky precipices to form a fine cascade, Rhaeadr Du, the black waterfall. This is one of the more popular approaches to the mountain as is the south ridge route, which also takes in the fascinating Foel Ispri area.

Below: Y Garn and the Gam Valley seen from Diffwys.

Route R40
Foel Yspri and the South Ridge

A pleasing route up a well-defined ridge

Start: Roadside lay-by west of Taicynhaeaf
  (GR: SH 685190)

Distance: 4¼ miles/ 6.7km

Height gain: 2200ft/ 670m

Time: 2½ hours

The walk starts high on the hillsides above the Mawddach valley and beneath Foel Yspri (sometimes known as Foel Isbri). This is also the starting point for the New Precipice Walk. Although it is possible to park the odd car above the junction of the Cwm Mynach and the Cesailgwm-mawr roads it is not an easy journey and it is better to walk though Taicynhaeaf, a village off the Dolgellau–Barmouth road opposite the Penmaenpool toll bridge.

The lively Afon Cwm-mynach comes tumbling down through the trees as you climb on the narrow lane past the houses. Just beyond a converted chapel (GR 689200) fork right along a tarred lane signed 'the New Precipice Walk'. Turn right at the next junction on a track that crosses a bridge spanning a stream and follow this to Foel Ispri-uchaf. Just before the house turn left through a metal gate. Over a stile in the next wall the route joins a winding grass track which has climbed from the farm. This comes to a ladder stile in a cross-wall to the left of a ruined stone building.

Maintain direction on a faint path through bracken to reach another grass track on the shoulder of Foel Ispri. Legend has it that the hill was home to the giant Ispri and his attendant group of fairies – it was once known as the hill of spirits. The surrounding area is scat-

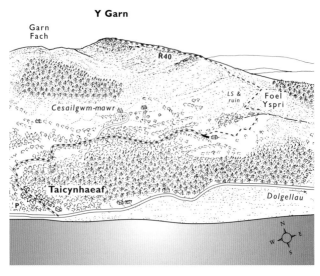

tered with old mines: gold, copper and lead have been excavated since Roman times, although the activities are a long way in the past now.

After passing through two gateways in stone cross-walls turn left to scale a ladder stile and continue past the north shores of a shallow lake. Go over a stile in the wall at the foot of Y Garn's south ridge – a nearby ruin marks the spot. Climb alongside the ridge wall where conveniently placed gates and stiles will allow you to negotiate all the cross-walls. Halfway up the ridge becomes craggy and gets the name Foel Ddu. After going over the stile at a wall intersection where the ridge wall ends – just beyond the little pool of Nannau – head north-westwards on trackless grassy slopes to the summit.

Route R41
Ganllwyd and Rhaeadr Du
A fine waterfall brightens up the forest gloom
Start: Car park, Ganllwyd (GR: SH 763244)
Distance: 3½ miles/ 5.3km
Height gain: 2000ft/ 610m
Time: 2 hours

A tarred lane leaving the A470 road to the left of the village hall climbs into the pretty broadleaved forest surrounding the lively Afon Gamlan. At a footbridge it's worth detouring left to see the impressive Rhaeadr Du, the black waterfall, before returning to the lane, which soon doubles back. Watch out for a track on the left. Through a gate this climbs parallel to the river and below the house Tyddyn-y-bwlch.

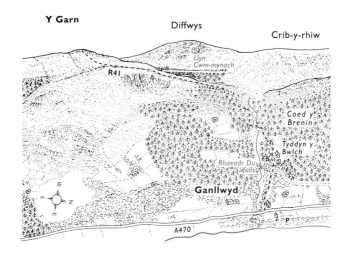

333

The pleasant walled track joins a forest road, which in turn leads through the conifers to a riverside crossroads. Turn left over the concrete bridge and follow the road south-westwards, then westwards though more conifers. Just beyond a right-hand bend a footpath signpost marks the continuing route through the trees. There's no trace of a path for the first 50m, but follow a crumbling wall on the right and one soon appears. Marshy in places, it leads to a gate on the forest's edge. You are now confronted with tussocky grass, crag and thick heather with little path evident. Don't try to find the ridge hereabouts. Be content to follow the wall uphill and to the right where a thin path does develop. As the slopes top out, turn right over grass to reach the summit.

Other route options

I've read about routes leading from the farm of Cesailgwm-mawr in the south over Garn Fach but this would mean crossing non-access land around the farm. I have climbed from Cwm Mynach keeping to the east edge of the hollow between Craig y Merched and Garn Fach but the terrain was horribly rough.

Right: Looking across Cwm Mynach to Y Garn.

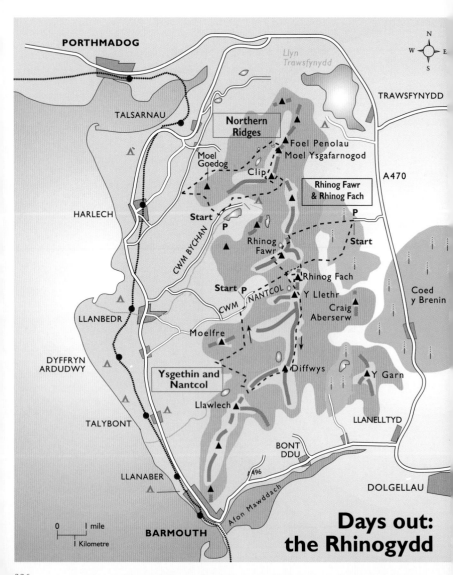

PORTHMADOG

Llyn Trawsfynydd

TRAWSFYNYDD

TALSARNAU

Northern Ridges

Moel Goedog

Foel Penolau
Moel Ysgafarnogod

Clip

A470

Rhinog Fawr & Rhinog Fach

HARLECH

Start

P

CWM BYCHAN

Rhinog Fawr

P

Start

Start P
NANTCOL

Rhinog Fach

Y Llethr

Craig Aberserw

Coed y Brenin

CWM NANTCOL

LLANBEDR

Moelfre

DYFFRYN ARDUDWY

Ysgethin and Nantcol

Diffwys

Y Garn

Llawlech

LLANELLTYD

TALYBONT

BONT DDU

B4496

DOLGELLAU

LLANABER

0   1 mile
1 Kilometre

BARMOUTH

Afon Mawddach

Days out: the Rhinogydd

Days out: the Rhinogydd

The Northern Ridges

A fine route visiting craggy tors, secret tarns
*   and old mines*
Start: Cwm Bychan car park (toll)
    (GR: SH 646315)
Distance: 10 miles/16km
Height gain: 2430ft/740m
Time: 5 hours

Cwm Bychan, with its lake, its magnificent terraced crags, lush green pastures and oak woods, is such an idyllic place it seems wrong somehow to leave it in haste, but before you lies a journey that will occupy most of the day and places that will inspire you to return to the Rhinogydd time and time again.

A signpost 'to Clip' points the way north from the barn up steep slopes. The vague path, not marked on the OS maps, meets the marked right of way from Llyn Cwm Bychan by a waymarking post. Now the route rakes across heather slopes to Bwlch Gwylim, a craggy nick in the skyline between Clip and

Below: Climbing south from Llyn Du (Ysgafarnogod).

Craig Wion. Looking up, the bouldery hollow on the left seems unpromising and rough, but a path eventually develops through it and climbs north-westwards to the rocky ridge at GR 658329. It's well worth detouring south-west to the slabbed summit of Clip for commanding views across Cwm Bychan to Rhinog Fawr. If you do this, retrace your steps to the top of the gully to continue the walk.

From the top of the pass head NNE along the northern Rhinog ridge to a subsidiary summit above Craig Ddrwg, which is decked with huge slabs and littered with boulders. There's not as much heather at this end of the Rhinogydd but, although the going is much easier than Craig Wion, for instance, there are no wide highway-like paths either.

Once you adjust to this it's rather pleasant to pioneer your own way – there's no right or wrong way. Sheep tracks – or more likely goat tracks – do exist and provide good ways around the intervening rocky tors. Sometimes you will use them; sometimes you may want to clamber to the tops for a view.

The first of the fine small lakes you'll come to is Llyn Corn-ystwc, which should be traversed on the east side, as should the rocky knolls beyond. A narrow path comes to a rock ledge, then rakes left on a grassy ramp down low cliffs to reach a second lake, Llyn Du. Turn right on a miners' track on the far side to its terminus then head across a rock-slabbed plateau towards the domed 2000ft peak of Moel Ysgafarnogod.

After descending to a grassy depression studded with rock outcrops, tackle Moel Ysgafarnogod by the grassy slopes on its south-western side rather than trying to negotiate the southern precipices. The main summit is topped by a cairn and stone trig point. If you're looking for a lunch spot, head for the western subsidiary peak, where there's a grassy perch overlooking the horseshoe-shaped lake of Llyn Dywarchen. The seaward view across Tremadog Bay, the Llyn Peninsula and the Isle of Anglesey is enhanced by the distant castle of Harlech and the peaks of Snowdon.

When it's time to leave the western summit, descend NNW to avoid the steep rocky ground dropping to Llyn Dywarchen, then head down a grassy hollow, making a left turn beyond a sheep pen to locate a grass track leading to the northern end of the lake. An old quarry road now takes the route easily south-westwards beneath the mountain crags, with the lakes of Llyn Eiddew-bach and Eiddew-mawr in view ahead. The track passes the dam of the former and should be followed for a further mile to a sharp bend at GR 631338. Leave the track here and go through a gate on the left where a fainter track continues south across rough grass to a stile. Beyond the stile make a right turn on a grassy, grooved track and enter a greener landscape overlooking the coastal plains of Harlech.

Ahead lies the rounded hill of Moel Goedog. The route circumvents its western flanks, passing an ancient stone circle, a couple of large cairns and a standing stone – and it's possible to make a there-and-back detour to see the earthwork rings of an ancient hill-top fort.

Abandon the track for an old quarry road on the left, just before the junction with a country lane. Take the next left fork and follow the track, tracing the southern slopes of Moel Goedog. Leave this track at GR 622322 (the second stile on the right). A meandering path then traverses rough pastures on a generally eastbound course, with Cwm Bychan's heathered crags beckoning directly ahead. You finally descend to the isolated cottage of Cwm-mawr.

The path shown on the map beyond the house necessitates two river crossings, which can be difficult. A better option is to follow the farm's drive down to the Cwm Bychan road, where you should turn left. Another signposted path on the crown of the next bend in the road skirts the northern slopes of an unnamed craggy knoll before re-entering Cwm Bychan. Now there are lovely views of the lake and the dark terraced crags of Carreg-y-saeth and Clip. The path descends to the road by a copse of broadleaved trees just to the west of the car park.

Opposite: Llyn Eiddew-bach and Moel Ysgafarnogod.

Rhinog Fawr and Rhinog Fach
A strenuous rocky day out
Start: Coed y Brenin (GR: SH 685302)
    car park at entrance to forest
Distance: 7½ miles/12km
Height gain: 3020ft/920m
Time: 5 hours

Note: This rough route is for experienced
walkers and scramblers only and would be
unsuitable for all in inclement weather

The two dome-like rocky Rhinog mountains fill the skyline above the sulky green feathered outline of Coed y Brenin's spruce forest, calling like Odysseus's Sirens to walkers setting off from the car park at the edge of the plantation. The only doubt in the mind is which mountain to take first. On this occasion we'll go for Rhinog Fach.

After taking the right fork forest road a left turn takes the route past Graigddu-isaf, a neat farm with a few velvety green fields keeping the spruce trees at bay. It continues southwards eventually to reach a bridge over the Afon Gau. Leave the flinted road here for a path on the right, which follows the stream's north bank on a grassy forest ride. After going through a gate at the plantation's edge, a splendid path climbs steadily over rough grassland towards Bwlch Drws Ardudwy, the gap between Rhinog Fach and Rhinog Fawr.

As you approach the cairn marking the summit of the pass, the terrain becomes more heathery. Watch out for a gap in a drystone wall below left. This marks the start of the direct path up Rhinog Fach. The narrow path of peat cuts a deep groove as it winds though heather and rock. It is extremely steep but very rewarding in ascent, highlighted by magnificent views back to Rhinog Fawr's imposing rock walls. A little grass mixes with the heather as height is gained and suddenly the path levels out and traverses a grassy hollow to the east of the main summit ridge. It soon swings right and steepens again as it climbs to gain the ridge near the north summit cairn.

Turn left along a clear path that goes along the crest of the ridge to the craggier main summit. The view is now dominated by Y Llethr, whose rugged northern face is tempered by two wonderful mountain tarns, Llyn Hywel immediately below it, and Llyn Perfeddau which shelters beneath the mountain's heathery western arm.

It is feasible to descend to Llyn Hywel before continuing down to Bwlch Drws Ardudwy but there's another less-used way. Head back towards the cairn on the northern summit, using the left of two ridge paths when it presents itself. Just before the cairn turn left on a narrow path descending a shallow grassy hollow before threading between large patches of scree. Turn right on a slightly wider path that tucks under the rock and scree of Rhinog Fach's west flanks.

After winding through a heathery hollow the path passes to the left of Llyn Cwmhosan, which forms the ideal foreground to Rhinog Fawr – this is the most magnificent view you can get of the mountain, fashioned by an ocean of heather, golden straw-coloured grasses and steely grey ribs of rock angled in perfect symmetry from pass to summit. The path tries to lose itself in the heather but comes to a ladder stile at the western end of Bwlch Drws Ardudwy.

Turn left on a path across an extremely waterlogged grassy basin to reach *terra firma*, then pick your way to the north side of the basin. Now climb half-left along the second from the left of the diagonal hollows running between the crags of Rhinog Fawr's south face. It's a very rough passage but leads to the easy western arm of the mountain, where a good path leads to the summit. Distant views are similar to Rhinog Fach, but slightly superior due to unrestricted views northwards to the central Snowdonian peaks.

For the onward route follow a cairned path heading west from the trig point. This soon

arcs gently right to reach the top of a boulder gully leading NNE down to the shores of Llyn Du. Circumvent the lake on the east side and follow a narrow path over heather as it traverses the right side of the ridge's crest. To your right the forests of Coed y Brenin appear beyond a grassy basin. The path reaches a larger path which has climbed the Roman Steps and threaded through Bwlch Tyddiad.

Turn right along this to enter the forest. A rather damp forestry break leads to a flinted road. Cross this, following the path past Pistyll Gwyn, which means the white, spout-like waterfall. Eventually the path joins a track, which in turn meets a forestry road at GR 680299 south of the farm at Graigddu-isaf. Turn left to pass the farmhouse, then next right to return to the car park on the edge of the plantation.

Below: The faint path running through the centre of the picture is the way off Rhinog Fach.

Ysgethin and Nantcol

The Southern Rhinogydd – Y Llethr and
*   Diffwys*

Start: Cil-cychwyn Farm (GR: SH 635260)

Distance: 11¼ miles/18km

Height gain: 3250ft/990m

Time: 5 hours

Cwm Nantcol and Cwm Ysgethin are neighbouring valleys, separated only by the Y Llethr–Moelfre ridge, yet they are so different in character. The former has been cultivated and its verdant fields and oak woods contrast with the distinctive dark craggy skyline, while the latter is wide, unkempt and moorland in character. This route will not only explore the best of both valleys, but take in the two highest peaks of the range, Y Llethr and Diffwys.

After following the narrow tarred lane to its end near Maes-y-garnedd Farm, a pleasing stony path winds though the wild upper valley of Nantcol. The angled gritstone slabs of Rhinog Fawr and the bouldered heather slopes of Rhinog Fach soon enclose the path as a tall drystone wall leads into the dramatic shadows of Bwlch Drws Ardudwy, the pass of the door to Ardudwy.

The path leaves the main route at the marshy basin squeezed between the two peaks. Beyond a ladder stile in the wall, a narrow path now climbs through heather, passing Llyn Cwmhosan, a delightful small tarn coloured by straw-tinted moor grass, shimmering green rushes and dark heather. The path continues through a heathery channel to the shoreline of Llyn Hywel, where the gigantic Y Llethr slabs slant diagonally from their crest at the col between Y Llethr and Rhinog Fach to the waters of the tarn.

Turn left to follow the bouldery north shore of the lake before climbing to the col, then right along the crest of the slabs. The path veers right, away from the ridge wall, to avoid the first of Y Llethr's crags. It soon becomes an eroded stony path winding up a steep grassy rake. The gradient eases and the path swings left to the grassy ridge north of Y Llethr's summit, where a small pile of stones top a featureless grassy dome.

Here is one of the classic views of Wales. Beyond Llyn Hywel, Rhinog Fach is truly glorious, with precipitous scree slopes capped and ribbed by faulted rock outcrops. Behind it, Rhinog Fawr looks equally imposing with its diagonal strata of gritstone separated by channels of grass, boulder and heather.

A superb ridge walk is now before you. Continue southwards alongside the wall, first down to a small pool, then over the rocks of Crib-y-rhiw. The strangely uniform craggy western side of the ridge drops down to the wild and empty upland shelf of Cefn Cam. In the distance the dark conifers of Cwm Mynach snuggle around a small lake like an overgrown bird's nest.

As progress is made towards Diffwys, the craggy slopes on the left edge get steeper and higher, while those of the other side decline gently into the wide-open grasslands of the Ysgethin valley. More shallow pools are passed before the path swings right to climb to the stone trig point on the summit of

Diffwys. Now you see clearly across the sandbars of the Mawddach Estuary to the fine cliffs of the Cadair Idris range.

From Diffwys, the ridge arcs westwards. There's a path either side of the ridge wall, but keeping to the left of the wall allows the best views of the Mawddach valley. After straddling a subsidiary peak the paths descend to an unnamed pass, where the old London–Harlech mail coach road crosses. Here turn right through the gate and descend with the winding green track, passing the memorial tablet to Janet Haigh. The tablet tells how this lady, in her 84th year, would pass here on her walk from Tal-y-bont to Penmaenpool.

The path fades a little on reaching the rushy marshes of the valley bottom. The Ysgethin is crossed using the little packhorse bridge, Pont Scethin. Although the map shows a bridleway heading north, directly for the col between Y Llethr and Moelfre, in reality there is nothing but marsh and more rushes. For a better route, follow the prominent track north-westwards to the Bodlyn Reservoir supply road. Turn right along this to pass beneath the ruins of the once infamous inn of Tynewydd, where murderous highwaymen mingled with drovers.

Right: On a wintry ridge with the climb southwards to Diffwys looming ahead. Overleaf: A wintry Rhinogydd scene with the cold screes of Rhinog Fach plummeting into the waters of Llyn Hywel.

The route now needs to reach the col between Moelfre and Y Llethr and a sheep track of a path soon climbs left to pass a ruined stone farmstead before veering right. It soon climbs left again to reach the col. A better path develops beyond a gate in the top wall and descends in the shadow of Moelfre's dark crags to meet the Nantcol Road just a few hundred yards west of the start at Cil-cychwyn Farm.

343

MAPS

Ordnance Survey Explorer (1:25 000)
  OL 17 Snowdonia: Snowdon
  OL 18 Snowdonia: Harlech,
  Porthmadog/Bala
  Explorer 254 Lleyn Peninsula is the best
  for the Eifionydd, which spread over both
  the Outdoor Leisure maps
Harveys Superwalker (1:25 000)
  Snowdonia: Snowdon & Moelwynion
  Snowdonia: the Glyderau & the
  Carneddau
BMC British Mountain Maps (1:40 000)
  Eryri/Snowdonia
Ordnance Survey Landranger (1:50 000)
  Sheet 115 Snowdon
  Sheet 124 Porthmadog & Dolgellau

TRANSPORT

Buses

Sherpa Buses, run by Gwynedd Council and
  Conwy County Borough Council with
  support from the Snowdonia National Park
  Authority, offer a comprehensive network
  through the mountain valleys. They allow
  the walker to select some excellent linear
  walks rather than contrived circulars to get
  back to a car. Buses run from Llandudno,
  Betws y Coed, Bangor, Bethesda,
  Caernarfon, Llanberis and Porthmadog
  into the heart of the mountains.
The Nantlle Ridge is served by buses from
  Caernarfon to Penygroes, Talysarn and
  Nantlle (80), while Carmel, Rhosgadfan
  and Rhostryfan (for Mynydd Mawr west
  approaches) are served by number 81.
  The X32 and 1 between Caernarfon
  and Porthmadog are useful for
  Garndolbenmaen (for Mynydd Craig Goch
  and Craig y Garn). For the Rhinogydd
  there's a regular service between
  Barmouth and Maentwrog (38) for
  Talybont, Llanbedr, Harlech and
  Talsarnau. Service 94 links Dolgellau
  and Barmouth, calling at Llanelltyd,
  Taicynhaeaf and Bont Ddu, while the X32,
  32 and 35 run from Dolgellau along the
  A470 to Maentwrog, calling at Ganllwyd,
  Bronaber and Trawsfynydd and
  Porthmadog.
Bus timetables:
  www.gwynedd.gov.uk/bwsgwynedd

Trains

The Cambrian Coast line from Pwllheli
calls at Porthmadog, Talsarnau, Harlech,
Llanbedr, Talybont, Llanaber and
Barmouth (good for the Rhinogydd). The
narrow-gauge Welsh Highland Railway
runs from Caernarfon to Porthmadog
and is useful for Snowdon, Mynydd Mawr
and the Moel Hebog ridges, calling at
Waunfawr, Rhyd Ddu and Beddgelert.
Rail travel timetables (Railtrack):
www.nationalrail.co.uk
For more information: www.traveline-
cymru.org.uk

Tourist Information Centres (year round)

Barmouth
    Tel. 01341 280787
    Email: barmouth.tic@gwynedd.gov.uk
Beddgelert
    Tel. 01766 890615
    Email: tic.beddgelert@eryri-npa.gov.uk
Caernarfon
    Tel. 01286 672232
    Email: caernarfon.tic@gwynedd.gov.uk
Porthmadog
    Tel. 01766 512981
    Email: porthmadog.tic@gwynedd.gov.uk

Websites

Welsh Tourist Board: www.visitwales.com
Snowdonia information:
    www.visitsnowdonia.info
Accommodation: www.4tourism.com

BEST BASES

Barmouth A lively seaside resort with plentiful accommodation, including hotels of all grades, B&Bs and a campsite, Barmouth is very handy for the southern Rhinogydd ridges, from Garn to Diffwys (south peak). There is only one gear shop but otherwise the shopping is good and includes a large supermarket.

Beddgelert Beautifully sited by the confluence of the Colwyn and the Glaslyn and beneath the more verdant and sylvan slopes of Snowdon, Beddgelert, with its twin-arched bridge and pretty stone cottages, makes an ideal base for Moel Hebog, Moel-ddu and the Rhyd Ddu and Nantgwynant routes to Snowdon.

Caernarfon This is a fine place to stay with its castle, town walls and historic streets, There is good accommodation, including hotels, inns, B&Bs and several campsites. The excellent bus services mean that, although distant from the big hills, the walker can plan quite flexible routes including linear ones. There are scores of shops and lots of cafés.

Dolgellau Although it is sited beneath Cadair Idris some way south of the region, Dolgellau is reasonably placed for the south-east Rhinogydd peaks. The charming country town built from stone and slate has plentiful accommodation, including hotels and B&Bs.

Harlech This pretty castle-crowned town has a small amount of accommodation, B&Bs and hotels. There are many smaller villages nearby, including Talsarnau and Llandanwg, with more accommodation including large coastal campsites but only a limited number of shops.

Llanbedr This small village between Harlech and Barmouth is known as a walkers' centre, although the youth hostel is now closed. It can offer a couple of shops, a couple of inns and nearby campsites.

Llanberis Snowdonia's biggest mountain village has hotels from large to small, B&Bs, cafés and varied shops. Pete's Eats has been described as 'the best chippy in the world'. The large and lively village is handily placed for the Llanberis Pass routes up Snowdon. Nant Peris, its smaller neighbour, has two campsites catering mainly for tents. The Vaynol Arms here is a very good pub.

Maentwrog This very pretty village overlooks the verdant Vale of Ffestiniog and has an inn, a hotel and a couple of B&Bs. It is handy for the northern Rhinogydd, as is the nearby hamlet of Gellilydan, which has a caravan club campsite and a good pub.

Nantgwynant This tiny hamlet, which consists of a few cottages, a youth hostel (Bryngwynant) and campsite, is set among the stunning scenery of the Glaslyn valley between the lakes of Dinas and Gwynant. It's a good base for explorations on the east side of Snowdon.

Porthmadog This bustling resort, sited at the mouth of the Glaslyn estuary, has accommodation to suit all tastes, ranging from hotels – there's even a Travelodge – to B&Bs and campsites. There is a supermarket, several cafés and many specialist shops. Nearby Tremadog, a climbers' centre, has a few inns, a fish-and-chip shop and a village store. Well-known climber Eric Jones runs a café, bunkbarn and a campsite for tents just east of Tremadog (tel. 01766 512199).

YOUTH HOSTELS

Bangor
Tan-y-Bryn, Bangor LL57 1PZ
Tel. 0870 770 5686
Email: bangor@yha.org.uk

Llanberis
Llwyn Celyn, Llanberis LL55 4SR
Tel. 0870 770 5928
Email: llanberis@yha.org.uk

Nantgwynant
Bryngwynant, Nantgwynant,
    Caernarfon LL55 4NP
Tel. 0870 770 5732
Email: bryngwynant@yha.org.uk

Pen-y-Pass
Nantgwynant, Caernarfon LL55 4NY
Tel. 0870 770 5990
Email: penypass@yha.org.uk

Rhyd Ddu
Snowdon Ranger
Rhyd Ddu, Caernarfon LL54 7YS
Tel. 0870 770 6038
Email: snowdon@yha.org.uk

YHA National Office
Trevelyan House, Dimple Road, Matlock,
    Derbyshire DE4 3YH
Tel. 0870 770 8868
Website: www.yha.org.uk

THE WELSH LANGUAGE

Some Welsh words

aber	river mouth
afon	river
arddu	black crag
bach/fach	small
bedd	grave
betws	chapel
blaen	head of valley
bont/pont	bridge
bwlch	pass
bws	bus
cae	field
caer	fort
carn/carnedd/garn/garnedd	cairn/cairns
capel	chapel
carreg/garreg	stone
castell	castle
cefn	ridge
cors/gors	bog
clogwyn	cliff
coch/goch	red
coeden/coed	tree/wood
craig/graig	crag
crib	sharp ridge
cwm	coomb
cwn	dog
Cymru/Cymraeg	Wales/Welsh
dinas	hill fort (or town)
diolch	thank you
du/ddu	black
drum/trum	ridge
drws	door
dyffryn	valley
dwr	water
eglwys	church
esgair	ridge
eryri	eagles' abode
fawr/mawr	large
felin/melin	mill
ffordd	road
ffynnon	spring
ffridd	enclosed grazing land
glas/las	blue
gwrydd	green
gwyn	white
gwynt	wind
hafod	high-altitude summer dwelling
hendre	winter dwelling
isaf	lower
llan	church or blessed place
llwybr cyhoeddus	public footpath
llwyd	grey
llyn	lake
maen	stone
maes	field/meadow
melyn	yellow
moch	pig
moel/foel	featureless hill
mynydd	mountain
nant	stream
ogof	cave
pant	clearing, hollow
pen	peak
person	cascade
plas	mansion
pwll	pool
rhaeadr	waterfall
rhyd	ford
saeth(au)	arrow(s)
troed	foot of

twll	hole, fracture, broken
ty	house
uchaf	high, higher
waun	moor
wen	white
wrach	witch
y, yr	the
ynys	island

Pronunciation of consonants

c	always hard, like the English 'k', thus coed = 'koyd'
ch	as in the Scottish 'loch'
dd	a voiced 'th' as in 'booth'
f	like the English 'v' , thus fach = 'vach'
ff	like the English 'f'
ll	a Scots 'ch' followed by an 'l' (blow air out between your tongue and your top teeth when pronouncing)

Pronunciation of vowels

w	can be a consonant or a vowel. When working as a vowel, pronounced like 'oo' as in 'cook' or 'moon'.
y	can be a consonant or a vowel. When working as a vowel, pronounced like 'i' as in pin or 'ee' as in seen. U is exactly the same.

The letters j, k, q, v, x and z are not used in true Welsh words.